Differentiation

in Middle & High School

Kristina J. Doubet

Jessica A. Hockett

Foreword by Carol Ann Tomlinson

Differentiation
in Middle &
High School

Strategies
to Engage
All Learners

ASCD Alexandria, Virginia USA

1703 N. Beauregard St. • Alexandria, VA 22311-1714 USA
Phone: 800-933-2723 or 703-578-9600 • Fax: 703-575-5400
Website: www.ascd.org • E-mail: member@ascd.org
Author guidelines: www.ascd.org/write

Judy Seltz, *Executive Director*; Stefani Roth, *Publisher*; Genny Ostertag, *Director, Content Acquisitions*; Julie Houtz, *Director, Book Editing & Production*; Miriam Goldstein, *Editor*; Georgia Park, *Senior Graphic Designer*; Kyle Steichen, *Senior Production Specialist*; Valerie Younkin, *Production Designer*

PAPERBACK ISBN: 978-1-4166-2018-1   ASCD product #115008   n7/15
PDF E-BOOK ISBN: 978-1-4166-2019-8; see Books in Print for other formats.

Quantity discounts: 10–49, 10%; 50+, 15%; 1,000+, special discounts (e-mail programteam@ascd.org or call 800-933-2723, ext. 5773, or 703-575-5773). For desk copies, go to www.ascd.org/deskcopy.

Library of Congress Cataloging-in-Publication Data
Doubet, Kristina, 1969–
  Differentiation in middle and high school : strategies to engage all learners / Kristina J. Doubet and Jessica A. Hockett.
    pages cm
  Includes bibliographical references and index.
  ISBN 978-1-4166-2018-1 (pbk. : alk. paper) 1. Inclusive education. 2. Ability grouping in education—United States. 3. Inclusive education—United States. 4. Educational tests and measurements—United States. 5. Middle school education—Curricula—United States. 6. Education, Secondary—Curricula—United States. I. Hockett, Jessica A. II. Title.
  LC3061.D68 2015
  371.9'046—dc23
                                                                                          2015007745

23 22 21 20 19 18 17   4 5 6 7 8 9 10 11 12

Soli Deo Gloria

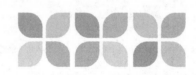

Differentiation
in Middle & High School

Foreword

By Carol Ann Tomlinson

I'd argue that elegant teaching is high on the list of most complex human performances. It calls on teachers to think emotionally, intellectually, logistically, psychologically, strategically, theoretically, practically, and ethically—all at the same time—and to sustain that level of thought hour after hour, day after day, year after year throughout a career. I suspect the intensity tends to cut one of two ways. It causes some teachers to chart and sustain a comfortable course that lessens the demand. It causes others to embrace the challenge and the opportunity it provides to refine and extend a teacher's mind, spirit, and soul. Whether teaching feels like a forge or an anvil, it's not easy—ever. It's possible to make a case that when the students are adolescents, the challenge only expands. By almost any measure, they are likely the most diverse group of students in a K–12 system.

Differing wildly in academic readiness as well as in physical and emotional maturity, executive function, economic status, interests, and motivation, they alternately want to rebel and conform, exert their independence and curl up on the couch next to Mom—or at least the dog. They are brash and afraid, profane and naïve, jazzed and comatose.

Yet within that hash of paradoxes resides their tomorrow. In middle and high school, they—and we—construct their futures.

We have documents aplenty reminding us what it means to teach well in the face of diversity in general—and adolescent diversity in particular. The National Association of Secondary School Principals' guide for reshaping high schools to better meet the needs of diverse adolescents is called *Breaking Ranks*. It proposes the following as key elements in making high school classes work for the broad range of students in those schools: differentiated instruction, personalized learning plans, environments in which students feel safe, and alternatives to tracking and grouping.

The Association for Middle Level Education advises that teaching and learning approaches should accommodate the diverse skills, abilities, and prior knowledge of young adolescents; cultivate multiple intelligences; draw on students' individual learning styles; and utilize digital tools.

The National Board for Professional Teaching Standards reminds us that classes don't learn; individuals do (or don't), and those individuals don't need to learn the same thing at the same moment, or at the same pace.

These guides, standards, and admonitions ask a great deal of us. Indications are, in fact, that many middle and high schools don't exemplify these practices. Yet, based on my experience, at least, most of the teachers at those schools would say they care about and respect their students.

Geneva Gay, author of *Culturally Responsive Teaching*, has challenged and clarified my thinking about what *caring* means. She suggests that there's a profound difference in caring *about* and caring *for* students. Caring about students leads teachers to be sensitive to students, to appreciate them, to form relationships with them—a good thing, to be sure. Caring for students, on the other hand, compels teachers to do whatever is necessary to ensure their welfare, to see to their success—a life-changing thing.

Recently, I read synthesis papers written by my largely undergraduate students at the University of Virginia. In a class on differentiated instruction, they had read, abstracted, and melded key ideas from three books into a coherent framework for thinking about differentiation. As always, I was humbled by how much I learned from them. Three insights from three very different students—all preservice teachers—pushed my thinking in three different ways.

One student investigated Latin root words for *respect*, finding that noun and verb forms mean to look at, to gaze at, to consider, to care for, to provide for, and to look back often at. She said the linguistic roots of *respect* resonated with her because she had long had the sense that respect is inextricably tied to *knowing*. "To look back (or often) at," she wrote, "to *gaze* at: these actions are characteristic of a person actively pursuing the knowledge or understanding of something or someone."

Another student began with a cryptic quote from Arthur Koestler's *The Act of Creation*: "For the anthropomorphic view of the rat, American psychology substituted a rattomorphic view of man." The student went on to say, "Many American educators have settled into acceptance of a 'rattomorphic' view of the American Student as an entity that can be studied and taught interchangeably." He noted that differentiation challenges this rattomorphic view by arguing that "teaching within the constraints of human differences will lead to better learning, better learners, and a more challenging and vibrant teaching experience."

A third student came from quite a different direction, writing a lengthy letter to a teacher she'd had in high school. Full of clear thought about the books she had read, her letter also had a personal tone. Just a semester short of beginning her career as a teacher, the student suddenly realized that she had experienced differentiation once in her own school career. She wasn't sure whether the teacher had known that her approach had a name, but she was able to recount instance after instance in which the teacher had used differentiation to show respect and support for her students. The student concluded, "You knew me as an individual, not just as one blurry face among the hundreds of students who passed through your classroom each week." I think this student would say that this was a class in which she felt respected, cared for—and not at all rattomorphic.

Kristina Doubet and Jessica Hockett are no strangers to middle and high school classrooms. In those settings, they launched their careers. In important ways, those years laid the foundation of the work both of them do now—Kristina in teaching secondary preservice teachers and both of them in working alongside more veteran teachers in middle and high school classrooms. For a time, both of them were my students at the University of Virginia. Since I first met them, they have been my teachers as well. Their clarity, devotion to teachers and students, and creativity in helping teachers at all stages to understand how to abandon rattomorphic pedagogies in favor of ones that respect and care *for* adolescents keep me thinking and hungry for more.

I'm excited for teachers who will learn along with me from this first major publication from the pair of them—and for teachers who will continue both to learn from them and to nurture them over the years.

Carol Ann Tomlinson
Former high school and middle school teacher
William Clay Parrish, Jr. Professor & Chair of Educational Leadership, Foundations, and Policy, Curry School of Education, University of Virginia
Charlottesville, VA

Acknowledgments

This book was born and developed in community with many people we value.

Over the past decades, we have been blessed to learn from and alongside scores of middle and high school teachers and leaders. Their insights, critiques, questions, and dedication inspired and guided this book. We hope the contents honor and strengthen the challenging work they do every day.

Students and faculty in the Department of Middle and Secondary Education at James Madison University provided us with expert content knowledge as well as sound, creative examples. JMU students, in particular, pushed us toward specificity and clarity in our explanations and tools. We are grateful.

We are thankful for the diligence, flexibility, and patience of Genny Ostertag, Acquisitions Editor at ASCD, and for our copy editor Miriam Goldstein, who made sure that we meant what we said and said what we meant. Kori Hockett blessed us by graciously reading and offering helpful feedback on the manuscript in its entirety. We also appreciate the valuable feedback on our proposal and early chapters offered by anonymous reviewers; their comments helped us focus and refine our vision.

We have been fortunate to engage with many talented colleagues in the differentiation effort, including Jennifer Beasley, Catherine Brighton, Marla Read Capper, Eric Carbaugh, Cheryl Dobbertin, Holly Hertberg-Davis, Marcia Imbeau, Jane Jarvis, Tonya Moon, Chad Prather, Judy Rex, Nanci Smith, and Cindy Strickland. Their expertise, examples, and support have inspired us.

We are deeply indebted to our guide and mentor Carol Tomlinson—a wise and selfless human being who has inspired thousands of teachers to love their students and their professions by preaching that which she practices. Her tireless commitment to ensuring that school is an inviting and enriching place for all students changed the way we saw ourselves and our teaching. Her personal investment in each of us individually, as the consummate teacher and advisor, has helped shape us both as people and as professionals. We owe her more than we could ever express or repay.

We are grateful for the unwavering support of our families, both in the process of writing this book and over decades of encouragement. Our parents, Eldon and Susan Doubet and Don and Patti Faber, have modeled hard work and perseverance in pursuit of worthy goals. And they have loved us unconditionally—the greatest gift of all.

Finally, we give our ultimate praise and thanksgiving to our Lord and Savior, Jesus Christ, the Master Teacher who demonstrated that teaching is serving in love and humility.

Introduction:
Is This Even Possible?

The Challenge

Middle and high schools in the United States today are blessed with students from a rich range of racial, ethnic, cultural, linguistic, and socioeconomic backgrounds. This vibrant diversity expands students' understanding of what makes us *us*, and helps equip them to become productive, empathetic, and ethical citizens who can thrive in an ever-changing global society.

Our country's commitment to educating all children well has driven the push for all graduates to be "college and career ready" and globally competitive. In pursuit of that goal, we have increased the rigor of academic standards. A high-quality education is no longer the province of the few or the rich, but the right of every child in every community.

The confluence of these two factors—rising student diversity and increased academic rigor—means that today's middle and high school teachers have greater accountability for a more diverse population of students than ever before. In many schools, appraisal of teachers' performance is based at least in part on their ability to ensure the progress of every student, regardless of background, native language, motivation, or school savvy.

Herein lies the challenge: how do teachers capitalize on the benefits offered by the lavish tapestry of the U.S. secondary classroom while ensuring growth for such a wide range of learners?

Is it even possible?

Attempts to Meet the Challenge

U.S. school systems have historically "handled" student diversity by sorting students into different schools, course levels, or special programs based on test scores or presumed educational destination. Unfortunately, these approaches have tended to widen achievement gaps, exacerbate student status differences, and result in some students receiving a higher-quality education than others.

At the classroom level, middle and high school teachers address student diversity through the kinds of instruction they employ. *Traditional instruction* is the model most familiar to teachers, as it represents the kind of instruction they typically experienced as students. Featuring the teacher as center, this model has all students take in, process, and demonstrate mastery of learning in the same manner during a given time frame. Although instruction may be offered in multiple modes (e.g., audio and visual), all students move at the same pace through those modes. Groupings other than whole-class are atypical in a traditional classroom, although students may occasionally work with self- or teacher-selected partners to complete tasks assigned to the full class.

One attempt to move away from a teacher-centered classroom is *cooperative learning*. In this model, the teacher typically delivers the same content to all students at the same time using the same set of strategies for the whole class. Students process this information collaboratively in small heterogeneous groups, with all groups working on the same task. Although this group work is the norm in this model, the teacher rarely varies grouping configurations or tasks. Students in a cooperative classroom may occasionally receive choices for tasks or assignments, but for the most part, all students complete the same work (albeit in interactive settings).

Unfortunately, both the traditional model and the cooperative model fail to discern the nuances of students' varying learning needs and adjust instruction accordingly.

Differentiation: A Better Solution

One-size-fits-all approaches to teaching and learning will not propel all (or even most) students toward and beyond standards. A more promising and productive way to address student differences is known as *differentiated instruction* (Tomlinson, 2003, 2014a). Differentiation is *not* synonymous with tracking or ability grouping. Rather than describing *where* students learn (i.e., in a classroom with peers who are deemed to be at the same academic level), differentiation articulates *how* the classroom teacher makes important curricular goals accessible to all learners within the same classroom.

Middle and high school classrooms that regularly implement differentiated instruction are characterized by certain hallmarks not typically shared by traditional or cooperative classrooms. In a differentiated classroom, teachers

- Create an atmosphere in which students' unique qualities and needs are as important as the traits they share.
- Uncover students' learning needs through pre-assessments and formative assessment and tailor tasks accordingly.
- Plan experiences and tasks that are bound together by common and important learning goals.
- Present varied approaches and avenues for students to take in, process, and produce knowledge.
- Vary grouping configurations frequently and strategically as a way of granting access to learning goals, providing support and challenge, and building community.

For many teachers, the cultivation of differentiated classrooms is neither natural nor intuitive; such a practice stands in stark contrast to their own experience as students, and traditional and cooperative models feel more familiar and comfortable. But used exclusively, both these models fail to meet students where they are and call them to something higher while offering appropriate levels of support and challenge. This is the goal of the differentiated classroom.

Misconceptions abound as to what "qualifies" as differentiated instruction. In this book, differentiation adheres to the criteria outlined in the bulleted list above as well as to the distinctions laid out in Figure I.1 (Tomlinson, 2003, 2014a).

FIGURE I.1

What Differentiation Is and Is Not

Differentiation *Is*	Differentiation *Is Not*
. . . A philosophy rooted in effective teaching and learning.	. . . A bag of tricks or set of strategies that can be plunked into low-quality curriculum.
. . . Regularly examining evidence of student learning and making thoughtful instructional decisions accordingly.	. . . Either an everyday necessity or a once-in-a-blue-moon "event."
. . . Tailoring instruction in response to patterns in student needs.	. . . Writing individualized lesson plans for every student.
. . . Designing respectful tasks and using flexible grouping.	. . . Sorting or pigeonholing students into static groups or levels.
. . . A way *up* to standards and learning goals.	. . . A way *out* of standards and learning goals.
. . . Critical to improving instruction for *all* students.	. . . More important for certain groups of students (e.g., students with IEPs or English language learners).

To be clear, differentiation is not a "magic bullet." It's not an easy fix, and it can't immediately or neatly solve the complex problems teachers face in their classrooms.

Instead, differentiation is a proactive way of thinking. It's systemic practice. It's hard work. And it offers hope.

What's Ahead

All teachers plan. Differentiation is, in essence, a way of upping the ante in the planning process by calling on teachers to *purposefully* and *proactively* think about how instruction could be more responsive to more kids. As a middle or high school teacher engages in this kind of planning, he or she may wonder,

- How do I set the tone?
- How do I determine what I have to teach?
- How do I know what students already know?
- How do I get students to care?
- How do I help students make sense of it?
- Is my teaching working?
- What if students are in different places?
- Do students get it?
- How do I keep this sane?

These key questions provide practical entry points for thinking about how differentiation influences each phase of lesson design. Their answers form the backbone of this book, which aims to be a comprehensive guide to differentiation in middle and high school classrooms. Here's a brief look at what each chapter addresses:

Chapter 1 presents techniques to promote healthy teacher-student and student-student relationships and foster a growth mindset.

Chapter 2 shows teachers how to prioritize, focus, and "translate" the curriculum into manageable and meaningful learning goals that are fit to be differentiated.

Chapter 3 offers guidelines on how best to gather information about what students already know, understand, and can do prior to beginning a unit or lesson.

Chapter 4 features strategies designed to foster student investment by conceptually linking students to what they are about to read, discuss, see, or listen to.

Chapter 5 explains strategies for actively involving all students in discussions and other kinds of activities aimed at making sense of content.

Chapter 6 provides strategies and prompts for gauging the progress of student learning—both during the course of a lesson and at its completion—with the goal of using that information to inform future instructional decisions.

Chapter 7 focuses on low- and high-prep approaches to adjusting content, process, and product for student readiness, with an emphasis on closely analyzing and planning instruction directly from formative assessment results.

Chapter 8 features strategies that require students to demonstrate command of learning goals while allowing them to choose tasks that appeal to their varied interests and learning profiles.

Chapter 9 offers practical suggestions and tools for navigating potential roadblocks to differentiation in the secondary classroom.

The Conclusion addresses lingering questions about how and where to get started and provides additional resources to help teachers move forward in their quest to create more responsive classrooms.

This book recognizes two fundamental truths: (1) that the real world of middle and high school is characterized by pressure and time constraints that significantly influence what is feasible for teachers in terms of change, and (2) that the most powerful (and efficient) learning often happens by example. Accordingly, Part 2 of each chapter provides a plethora of tools and examples spanning a range of grade levels and subject areas that were developed *by, for,* or *with* real teachers. These can be used to support teacher growth in myriad contexts, including professional learning communities, department or team planning meetings, and instructional coaching relationships. In any of these situations, teachers will benefit from studying examples from both inside and outside their content areas, as different disciplines can learn much from one another. For added utility, select forms and templates from this book can be downloaded at http://www.ascd.org/ASCD/pdf/books/Doubet2015forms.pdf. Use the password "Doubet2015115008" to unlock the PDF.

Used well, this book and its tools have the potential to upgrade what happens in middle and high school classrooms and, ultimately, to improve the learning and the lives of both teachers and their students.

It *is* possible.

1

Building a Healthy Classroom Community

Part 1:

How Do I Set the Tone?

Relationships: A Prerequisite for Learning

"Under construction!" This sign should be flashing above the head of every middle and high school student in our classrooms. As brain experts like Eric Jensen (2005) observe, the degree of change experienced by the adolescent brain is matched only by that of the infant brain. These changes affect many aspects of learning, the most fundamental of which is dealing with emotions. Teenagers struggle to discern their own emotions as well as those of others, which frustrates the two driving goals of adolescence: to *fit in* and to *be known* (Tomlinson & Doubet, 2006).

Adolescents often devote more time and energy to worrying about whether they are safe and accepted than to caring about whether they are learning (Sousa & Tomlinson, 2011). This may be why teacher-student relationships have such a powerful effect on student achievement (Hattie, 2012) and why community-centered classrooms are such an important contributor to academic growth (Bransford, Brown, & Cocking, 2000).

The bottom line is that if teachers ignore the *affective* needs of teenagers, they will be less able to meet students' *cognitive* needs. Navigating the storm of adolescents' competing desires—for independence *and* acceptance, uniqueness *and* conformity—requires time and commitment, but it can produce gains in both socioemotional and intellectual growth.

For teachers who want to create successful differentiated classrooms, cultivating healthy teacher-student and student-student relationships is not a matter of convenience but a necessity. As outlined in the Introduction, to differentiate successfully, middle and high school teachers must

- Create an atmosphere in which students' unique qualities and needs are as important as the traits they share.
- Uncover students' learning needs through pre-assessments and formative assessment and tailor tasks accordingly.
- Plan experiences and tasks that are bound together by common and important learning goals.
- Present varied approaches and avenues for students to take in, process, and produce knowledge.
- Vary grouping configurations frequently and strategically as a way of granting access to learning goals, providing support and challenge, and building community.

Not one of these practices will be successful if students do not feel known, safe, and assured that the teacher has their best interests at heart.

If we ask students to take academic and social risks and to consistently operate outside their comfort zones, we must take deliberate steps to ensure that risk taking will be both supported and rewarded. Clearly establishing class rules and norms (with student input) is important, but it is only the beginning. As is the case with anything worthwhile, relationships take time to grow; they don't magically mature overnight. Teachers can cultivate connections with and among students through both *covert* and *overt* measures.

Developing Relationships Covertly and Overtly

The *covert*, or less visible, means of developing healthy relationships is, at its most basic level, simple adherence to the Golden Rule: it is the commitment to treat students as we would like to be treated, with respect and interest. Greeting students at the door, asking about their weekends, noticing a new haircut or an injury, and connecting students to one another ("Diana, did you know Savannah moved here last year, too?") are small gestures that can play a vital role in weaving the social fabric of the classroom, where relationships among students create the conditions for everyone to do his or her best work.

Covert methods can also be more systematic or strategic. Mr. Myles, a high school English teacher, recognized that the daily time crunch of his many classes could sometimes distract him from being as "human" as he wanted to be with his students, so he began including an extra blank at the top of every paper he collected. After students recorded their names and the date, they responded to a simple but powerful question: "How are you doing today?" As Mr. Myles collected his students' work, he was able to see what was going on in their worlds ("My soccer team is going to the playoffs!" or "My grandma's in the hospital. It doesn't look good."). In time, students started suggesting possible questions. Although they saw these questions as their teacher's way of making sure they wrote their names on their papers, Mr. Myles was subtly strengthening his arsenal for building bonds with and among students. His small proactive step paid off in a greatly increased sense of trust in his classroom.

The typical middle and high school schedule may tempt teachers to forgo more *overt*, or deliberate, relationship-building activities. But the press of time makes such activities even more important, as they yield dividends of increased trust and a better understanding of what it takes to motivate students and move them forward, which *saves* time in the long run. Whether used as a beginning-of-the-year survey or through periodic Exit Slips, questions such as those featured in Figure 1.1 can help teachers gather information for forming student groups according to shared characteristics, preferences, or interests that are relevant to a task. Individual student responses can also heighten teachers' awareness of student sensitivities, experiences, or attitudes that are useful for planning and responding to student needs in general. Even if students are at first hesitant to share certain information, allotting time to intentionally ask students about themselves is a starting point for building classroom community. Without making this investment, assigning and facilitating tasks (differentiated or not), grouping students, and managing the classroom may feel like an uphill battle.

Engaging in such fact-finding about students can help teachers create motivating lessons and manage their classrooms. High school English teachers Ms. Bakum and Mr. Uyeda were able to accomplish these goals through a survey they distributed in their team-taught English class (see Figure 1.2). The teachers used students' responses to (1) present lyrics from students' favorite songs as examples of figurative language; (2) make references to students' favorite shows when discussing character and conflict; (3) create class playlists to play during transitions between activities; (4) create flexible groups (such as "vacation groups" and "restaurant groups"); and (5) gather some preliminary information on students' conception of *theme*. Ms. Bakum and Mr. Uyeda went beyond using their survey as a late-August get-to-know-you exercise by leveraging the information to help them establish routines and reinforce important academic content.

Part 2 of this chapter outlines a number of additional strategies for building strong classroom relationships and uncovering who students are. Teachers need not complete *all* of these activities with every class. Rather, teachers should choose (or adapt or create) *one or two strategies* that suit their personality and teaching style and begin each semester overtly sending the message that each student matters, and that all students must work together for the class to be successful.

FIGURE 1.1

Potential Student Survey Questions

1. Who lives with you?
2. What are your hobbies or extracurricular activities? What do you enjoy spending time on?
3. Describe how you typically spend the time between getting home from school and going to bed.
4. What are you really good at?
5. What do you struggle with? Explain.
6. When people compliment you, it's usually because:
7. If people complain about you, it's probably because:
8. If you were a contestant on a "survival" reality show and were allowed to bring only one item with you to the island, what would you bring and why?
9. If you could invite three people—living or dead—to your house for dinner, whom would you invite and why?
10. What do you often wonder about?
11. When you're feeling great at school, it's probably because:
12. When you want to scratch your eyes out at school, it's probably because:
13. List the last two books you read and tell . . .
    a. If they were assigned or read by choice.
    b. How you felt about each of them and why.
14. How do you like to work (circle your preference in each row)?
    a. independently   with a partner   in a small group
    b. in a quiet environment   with background noise
    c. sitting still and concentrating   I need to move around
15. If you could choose from the following careers, which would you select? Rank your top three, with 1 indicating the career you would most prefer. After you have selected from the list, feel free to add other choices in the space below.
    _____ Actor   _____ Engineer
    _____ Artist   _____ Musician
    _____ Builder   _____ Writer
    _____ Counselor   _____ Environmentalist
16. I learn best by . . . (rank the options, with 1 being the highest)
    _____ Seeing it   _____ Manipulating it (objects)
    _____ Hearing it   _____ Other (explain):
17. Is there anything else you would like me to know about you? If so, please explain.

FIGURE 1.2

Student Survey

Hi! My Name Is_____.   Doodle Box

Fast Facts:

In the section to the right, draw what your doodles look like.

Favorite Food:

Favorite Book: Favorite TV Show to Binge Watch on Netflix:

Pepsi or Coca-Cola: Dream Vacation Destination:

Goals After High School: Least Favorite Weather:

Your Theme Song

Think about the music you enjoy. Choose one song to be your "anthem." Make sure it's representative of you!

Song Title: Lyrics That Most Represent You:

Artist: Explanation:

Source: Lindsay Bakum and Grayson Uyeda. Used with permission.

Mindset: A Necessary Foundation for Differentiation

Complicating the puzzle of teaching adolescents even further is the role *mindset* plays in students' motivation to learn. Carol Dweck's groundbreaking work (2006) has revealed that

1. Students' motivation to learn and achieve is strongly influenced by what they believe about the nature of intelligence.
2. Students who believe their intelligence is malleable (i.e., who have a *growth mindset*) tend to persevere in the face of hardship. Those who believe their intelligence is fixed (i.e., who have a *fixed mindset*) tend to be stymied by challenge (this is true whether students see themselves as high achievers or low achievers).
3. Teachers significantly, and often unconsciously, influence students' perceptions of their own intelligence.

For academic interventions to have their desired effects on student performance, teachers must believe (and communicate the belief) that all students can grow. As is the case with building relationships, fostering the growth mindset in a differentiated classroom is a foundational imperative. None of the hallmarks of differentiated instruction outlined on page 10 will yield fruit without (1) the teacher's unwavering belief in and commitment to student growth and (2) students' belief in their own potential to improve with hard work. More specifically, teachers need to communicate the following truths:

- Mistakes and weaknesses are precursors to growth, not static portraits of ability.
- *All* students have room to grow, no matter where they begin.
- In a classroom of 30 students, there will be a great deal of variety in terms of where students are and what it will take to move each of them forward.
- It would not be "fair" or even realistic to treat everyone as the same person when this variety exists. The teacher's mission is to discover where each student is in his or her learning as well as what he or she will need to grow.
- "Fair" will not mean everyone getting the same thing; it will mean everyone getting what he or she needs to take his or her appropriate next step.
- "Fair" will mean that *all* students will receive learning tasks that cause them to "feel the burn" as they lift appropriately challenging academic weights.

In other words, learning is actually strength training. Every student should expect to receive learning tasks that will make him or her work just as hard and sweat just as much as his or her classmates. When everyone is experiencing exertion in learning, when everyone is making strides in developing personal academic strength and agility—*that* is when the classroom is truly "fair."

Addressing Mindset Covertly and Overtly

Clearly, this vision of *fair* is not the message communicated by the world, or even by school as a historical institution. Students are more likely to have been identified by their strengths and weaknesses than to have been expected to shed such labels as they progress in their learning. Adolescents, in particular, have had ample opportunity to develop the sense that *fair* simply means "the same."

To challenge students' thinking in this area, teachers must send both overt and covert messages about mindset. There are proactive steps teachers can take to help adolescents understand that what is *genuinely* fair is to hold the same expectations of *growth* for every student while varying the *tools and paths* used to help them achieve that growth.

Language is the most powerful tool in a teacher's arsenal for sending growth-mindset messages. Unfortunately, it is also the tool most frequently—and most unwittingly—used to undermine growth. This primarily occurs through the use and misuse of *praise*. In Carol Dweck's (2008) investigations into the link between praise and mindset, she determined that praise focused on students' *intelligence* could shut students down, whereas praise centered on their *effort* could push them forward. Dweck observes that when we consistently tell students they are "smart!" or regularly comment on their "brilliant work," we are communicating a fixed view of intelligence (either you have it or you don't). Such praise can serve as a coveted reward that some students will strive to protect. These students become less likely to take intellectual risks out of fear that their mistakes will detract from their perceived brilliance.

On the other hand, praise that focuses on students' effort or celebrates their learning process can significantly increase their willingness to make mistakes and learn from them. Ms. Ehlers, an 8th grade ELL teacher, makes a point to praise her students' willingness to persevere: "I like the way you tried several strategies on that problem until you finally solved it," and "I appreciate that you are experimenting with new vocabulary words in your writing; this word, in particular, paints a very clear picture in my mind." Dweck's research revealed that students who received this kind of praise were more likely to seek challenge and persist in the face of academic difficulties. For a teacher, changing the nature of praise is a subtle but powerful means of encouraging the growth mindset with adolescent learners, some of whom have already become praise junkies.

It is important to note that students of all backgrounds can come to school with a fixed mindset. Students who have a history of struggling in school may enter our classrooms with the notion that nothing they can do will override their "programmed" tendency to fail. They need to hear that they have a fighting chance and that their brains are like a muscle they can exercise and cause to grow (Jensen, 2005), no matter their academic history. If they don't believe this, they will shut down when a task gets difficult, attributing their failure to a perceived lack of intelligence rather than to a gap in their skills and the need for the right tasks and a lot of effort. Likewise, students with a history of gliding successfully though school without much effort might balk at tasks that actually challenge them.

Because of the reward-seeking nature of many students, it can be helpful to employ overt, deliberate strategies to promote a growth mindset and encourage students to take risks. Part 2 of this chapter outlines a number of such strategies. As is the case with the relationship-building strategies, teachers need not use *all* of them with every class; rather, it is important for teachers to share personal stories of struggle and perseverance and to choose (or adapt or create) *one or two strategies* that match their personality and teaching style. These strategies can help teachers establish the important belief that each student has *room* to grow, that each student *can* grow, and that the teacher will do whatever it takes to ensure that each student *does* grow, regardless of starting point or past experiences.

The Classroom as an Interdependent System

As we move into the tools and strategies for this chapter, it is important to note that simply implementing these techniques at the beginning of the year or semester is insufficient to build a strong classroom community. Teachers must continually cultivate relationships and foster the growth mindset in their curriculum and instruction. Just as many of the instructional techniques presented in forthcoming chapters will rely on the establishment of these bedrock factors, they will also reinforce and develop those factors. To proclaim the importance of community while ignoring it with our teaching is careless at best, hypocritical and destructive at worst. Building classroom community does require work up front, but its ultimate success relies on the caliber of curriculum and instruction we prepare for our students daily.

A Case in Point: Ms. Rissa

In an effort to illustrate what this book's principles and strategies look like in action, Part 1 of each chapter will close by exploring how one of four classroom teachers implemented the strategies featured in the chapter. We will pop into all their classrooms throughout the course of the book.

This school year, English teacher Ms. Rissa and her interdisciplinary team members have agreed to focus on fostering a growth mindset in the students they share. The teachers decided to use content-related examples to ensure that (1) their examples were distinct from one another and (2) their discussions enhanced their respective curricula.

Ms. Rissa decided to weave the discussion of mindset into the Life Soundtrack assignment she uses each year with her students (see pp. 22–23). For this assignment, each student created a four-song soundtrack to tell the story of his or her life, based on the four literary elements of character, setting, theme, and conflict. Not only was the assignment an engaging way to review the literary elements, but it also helped Ms. Rissa get to know a great deal about her students, who relished the opportunity to comb their music collections "for school."

Ms. Rissa realized that she could incorporate the discussion of mindset into students' choices for the "conflict" song: she would ask them to pick a song that summed up how they had faced a major conflict—versus self, others, nature, or society (i.e., one of the four literary types of conflict)—and how facing that conflict had shaped their character. She would have to change her own example to reflect that emphasis, as she always shared her own soundtrack with students to provide an exemplar as well as to present points of appropriate connection with them. Sometimes she and her students shared the same taste in music, but more often, it was a mutual experience, insight, or struggle that provided common ground.

To capitalize on the assignment even further, Ms. Rissa decided to have students share their soundtracks with their classmates as a way to foster student-student connections. By discussing how *conflict leads to progress* in their personal lives, they would also be laying a foundation on which they could build candid discussions about their writing later in the year.

Part 2:

Tools and Strategies

Relationship-Building Activities

What They Are:

Proactive strategies for helping the teacher get to know students, for helping students get to know one another, and for establishing important affective norms in the classroom to facilitate differentiated instruction.

How They Work:

Teachers choose one or two of these activities to use at the beginning of the year to strategically discover the backgrounds and interests of students and to help them find areas of overlap with one another. Strategies can also be used throughout the school year to reignite a sense of connection and shared purpose.

What They're Good For:

- The primary purpose for using these strategies is to help the teacher get to know what makes students "tick" so that he or she can connect with students on a personal, "human" level and ensure they feel seen, known, and cared for.
- Teachers can also use the information gleaned from these activities to target student interests in instructional situations (e.g., interest-based tasks, word problems, writing prompts, student group work).
- By participating in these strategies, students will get to know one another as well. Building these student-student connections not only facilitates student grouping and regrouping but also promotes a trusting atmosphere in which students feel safe to take risks—a necessary underpinning of differentiation.

Tips:

- Although most strategies require a setup, Piecing Together Community (p. 24) is an exception to this principle, as it is an inductive strategy. Don't let students in on the point of this particular exercise until after it is completed.
- Aside from Attendance Questions, all strategies in this section require some debriefing with students following the experience. Do not just assume students got the point of the exercise. A combination of class discussion and individual reflection works best.
- The first five strategies work best when modeled by teachers, so share your own stories and interests first.

Attendance Questions

Directions:
- At the beginning of the class period, pose a prompt (either aloud or on the board).
- Have students announce their attendance in class by stating their name and their answer to the prompt.
- Use a quick question for efficiency (e.g., *Dogs or cats? Pie or cake? Pool or beach? Favorite late-night host? Favorite season? Favorite sports team?*).
- Use a more involved question if it holds the potential to serve as a lesson "hook" (e.g., *Whom do you most admire?* to introduce a discussion of leadership styles; *Favorite video game?* to lead into an examination of cause-and-effect relationships).

Variations:
- **Greeting Graffiti.** While the teacher is in the hall on duty between classes, students enter the classroom to find the Attendance Question posted on the board. They record their answer on the board and sign it. The teacher comments on ideas and patterns before erasing the board and starting class.
- **Good-bye Gabfest.** Students use the awkward time between announcements and dismissal to answer a quick exit question (similar to the quick prompts described above) or a lengthier question dealing with afternoon or weekend plans (e.g., *What are you most looking forward to OR dreading?*).

Pie Charts

Directions:

- Ask students to draw a circle that takes up most of a page of notebook paper or a computer screen (or distribute ready-made circles).
- Tell them this circle represents their interests. They are to turn the circle into a pie chart that represents the things they are most interested in (both in and out of school).
- Each circle must include at least five sections; the dimension of each wedge should reflect the student's level of interest in that topic or hobby (e.g., if the student is most interested in playing soccer, the soccer wedge should be the largest).
- Students should also represent the dimension of each interest as a fraction and a decimal (either in the pie chart itself or below it).

Follow-Up:

- Students share their charts in pairs or groups and discuss similarities and differences. They can also pose questions to one another about the data revealed in their charts.
- The teacher uses the information from these charts throughout the year to form interest-based groups and to create word problems and prompts that will intrigue students.

Who Is It?

Directions:

- Tell students they will be playing a guessing game called "Who Is It?" Ask everyone to stand, and model the activity using your own information. (See following section for how to craft this information.) Tell the class that you will present four statements in succession. Students should stay standing if a statement is true for them, and sit down if it is not. Once they are seated, they stay seated. A teacher example follows:
  "Remain standing if . . .
  — "You were born east of the Mississippi River."
  — "You've been to Disney World."
  — "You did not have a cell phone in middle school."
  — "You saw *Return of the Jedi* in the movie theater in 1983."

- After the last item, you should be the only one standing; at that point, reveal that the four statements describe you.
- Explain that the class will play a few rounds of the game using students' information.
- Ask students to write numbers 1–4 on an index card. Display the following directions:
  — Next to number 1, write something about yourself that you probably have in common with *most* (about 75 percent) of the people in the room.
  — Next to number 2, write something about yourself that you probably have in common with *some* (about 50 percent) of the people in the room.
  — Next to number 3, write something about yourself that you probably have in common with *a few* (no more than 25 percent) of the people in the room.
  — Next to number 4, write something about yourself that is probably *unique to you*.
  — Make sure to write down only things you feel comfortable sharing with the class.

- Collect students' index cards and complete a few rounds using the items on the cards. There is no need to go through all the cards in one class period. Use the cards periodically (e.g., on Fridays) at the beginning or end of class, or during a class period as a way of switching gears, transitioning between activities, or providing a chance to get up and move.

Variation:

Classmates can ask the last student standing questions about his or her items, and the card owner can explain or clarify any of the information from the card.

Life Soundtrack

Directions:

- Each student creates a four-song soundtrack that tells his or her life story in terms of *setting, character, theme,* and central *conflict*. Students should consider the following prompts:
  - *Setting:* Where and how did you grow up? What surroundings have shaped you? You can address this element in a concrete way (e.g., an area of the world or country, your neighborhood, your house), or it can be something more symbolic and metaphorical (e.g., the state of perpetually moving, the "press" of living in a large household or an urban area).
  - *Character:* Who are you? What makes you "tick"? How would people describe you? Would different people describe you differently? Why?
  - *Theme:* Describe your overarching perspective about life and people, and explain why you have this point of view. What would you tell the world if you had the chance?
  - *Conflict:* Describe your central conflict: is it big or small? Momentary or ongoing? Internal or external? Versus yourself, others, society, or nature? Explain how the conflict has caused you to grow or change.

- Each soundtrack should include a soundtrack title, a list of the songs and their artists, and some sort of cover art. Life Soundtracks can be produced in a variety of formats: PowerPoint slides, Prezis, websites, videos, or CD covers with lyric inserts, for example.

- For each literary element, students must include (1) key song lyrics that sum up that element in their lives (if necessary, edit lyrics to make them school-appropriate); and (2) detailed explanations of why they chose these lyrics and how the lyrics reflect their life experiences.

- Each student shares his or her song list and one song (including the key lyrics and explanation of how the lyrics reflect his or her experiences) with the class.

Life Soundtrack

- Criteria for success:
  - Each literary element is represented true to both its meaning in literature and its application in your life.
  - Lyric selections are school-appropriate and clearly communicate the literary element.
  - Your explanations clearly detail how the lyrics reflect both the literary element and your personal experience.
  - The product is of professional quality.

Variations:

- Add the literary elements of *point of view* and *plot* to the soundtrack.
- Rather than reviewing all four literary elements at once, introduce each element separately and have students choose only one song at a time.
- Repeat this assignment with a work of literature later in the year, using the story's literary elements rather than students' personal life experiences. Students can create a soundtrack of a novel, a short story, or a play, following similar prompts and evaluation criteria.
- Include additional academic supports, such as definitions or examples of the literary elements.

Piecing Together Community

Directions:

- Ask students to work in small groups to assemble different portions of a complex jigsaw puzzle. No map or image of the completed puzzle is available for the first five minutes.
- During the second five minutes, allow each team to send a "spy" to gather intelligence by looking at the puzzle box cover and reporting back.
- Circulate and make observations, taking notes on individual student tendencies during group work (e.g., taking over, sitting back, facilitating) as well as group dynamics.
- At the close of the activity, ask students to reflect on what they learned about themselves and their classmates during the activity.
- Share some things you learned through your observations.
- Lead the class in discussing what classroom community should look like and developing collaborative norms and specific guidelines to govern group work.

Strategies for Introducing Mindset

What They Are:

Proactive, concrete, student-involved strategies used to introduce the following ideas:

- Intelligence is malleable.
- Our mistakes serve as stepping-stones for success.
- *Fair* means everyone gets what he or she needs to grow, *not* that everyone gets the same thing.

How They Work:

Teachers choose one or two strategies to use at the beginning of the year to purposely introduce both the expectation and the value of effort. The teacher should debrief or discuss each strategy in terms of the three guiding ideas above. Strategies can also be used throughout the school year to reignite the expectation of hard work and risk taking.

What They're Good For:

- The primary purpose for using mindset-introduction strategies is to instill in students the expectation that they will experience challenge, as it is a necessary precursor to growth.
- Teachers can also use the information gleaned from these activities to reinforce the fact that students *do* have control over their learning. If students believe they can grow, they will.
- These strategies also present the teacher with the opportunity to redefine *fair* and to define *differentiation*. The more proactive we are about sending the message that difference is the norm, the less pushback we experience when different students are assigned different tasks.

Tips:

- Unlike the relationship-building activities, most strategies in this section do not require a setup, as they are inductive strategies. In other words, students should not be let in on the point of each exercise until after it is completed. The first two strategies are exceptions to this principle, as they take a more direct approach.
- All strategies in this section will require teachers to debrief with students following the experience to expose its purpose. Do not automatically assume that students got the point of the exercise. A combination of class discussion and individual reflection works best.
- Each strategy can be used in the context of the following before-or-after readings on mindset and the brain's plasticity:
  — Mindset: http://mindsetonline.com. *Carol Dweck's website, including information, videos, tests, tools, and links to other media.*

— Brain Plasticity: What Is It?: http://faculty.washington.edu/chudler/plast.html. *This site outlines the basics of neuroplasticity and the relationship between brain plasticity and learning.*

— "Students' View of Intelligence Can Help Grades," by Michelle Trudeau (February 15, 2007): www.npr.org/templates/story/story.php?storyId=7406521. *NPR radio broadcast, transcript, and article explore one of Dweck's studies examining the impact of mindset on grades and performance.*

— "Unboxed: If You're Open to Growth, You Tend to Grow," by Janet Rae-Dupree (July 6, 2008): www.nytimes.com/2008/07/06/business/06unbox.html?_r=0. New York Times *article discusses the relationship between mindset and perseverance/resilience.*

Mindset Tracking

Directions:

- Define *mindset* using any of the resources described in the readings on mindset and the brain's plasticity.
- Share three examples of growth and/or fixed mindset in action. You can use personal examples, well-known examples (e.g., athletes or historical figures), or examples from various media (e.g., movies or song lyrics).
- Give students the following prompt for their weekly journals or blogs: *Keep an eye out for indications of mindset—both fixed and growth—in yourself, your friends and family, the news, and other media. For each example you find, record the following:*
  — Which type of mindset is being exemplified, and how do you know?
  — How might having this type of mindset play out in this person's life? Why do you say so?

- Students should keep track of these questions in their journals or blogs and be ready to share their favorite examples with the class.

Variation:

Post student examples on a bulletin board or in another visible area of the room.

Glow and Grow

Directions:
- Give each student an index card.
- On the front side of their index cards, ask students to record (a) their name, (b) the thing in life they do best or enjoy most, and (c) the thing in life they do worst or enjoy least.
- On the back of their cards, have students record or draw a *nonlinguistic representation* (icon or picture) of their answer to question (b) *or* question (c).
- Ask students to circulate through the room with their cards, holding them with the picture side out. They should
  — Try to find someone whose picture is similar or related to their own in some way (e.g., both represent a sport).
  — Meet with that person and share the information on their cards.
  — Ask their partner at least one additional question (e.g., favorite and least favorite foods, music, hobbies, or television shows).
  — Repeat the process with a new partner.

- Following the activity, discuss:
  — "Why should I assume that just because you're in the same class, you share interests, strengths, and weaknesses?"
  — "I won't treat you all like the same person, but I *will* expect you all to move toward expertise, no matter where you start."

Variation:
To find partners more efficiently, students can create icons using technology and display them on the interactive whiteboard.

Redefining *Fair*

Directions:

- Ask students to define *fair* using synonyms; encourage them to go with their gut reactions. Most likely, they will propose the synonyms *same* and *equal*.
- Write their responses on the board and explain that you are going to put these definitions to the test.
- Call up two volunteers—one significantly shorter than the other (do not explain the criteria).
- Stand on a chair and hold a "prize" of some sort (e.g., a dollar bill or a candy bar) just within reach of the taller person but out of reach for the shorter person.
- Explain that you will hold the prize at the same height and enforce the same rules for both of them: no jumping, no running starts, no standing on anything, no using props, no assistance from anyone, no trickery.
- Let the shorter volunteer try first, and then let the taller person finish the trial successfully. Let the taller student keep the prize.
- Ask students if the experience was fair. When they insist it was not, explain that the exercise upheld their definition of *fair*: the prize was held in the *same* place for both students, and the *same* rules were enforced for each attempt.
- Lead a discussion about what would have made the experience fair. Explain that lowering the prize is not an option because the prize represents your high expectations, which you will not lower for anyone. Write other solutions on the board (e.g., giving the shorter person a running start or something to stand on).
- Use the discussion to come up with a new class definition of *fair* (e.g., "*fair* = everyone getting what they need to stretch and succeed"), and post it in a prominent place in the room.
- Because the first round wasn't fair, give the shorter volunteer another chance to get the prize, this time using one of the modifications the class came up with.

Variation:

When students define *fair* as "the same," ask everyone with glasses to take them off because it's "not fair" for some students to have glasses when others don't. Follow the same procedure for discussing and posting a revised classroom definition of *fair*.

The Lineup

Directions:

- Call up a sampling of students (e.g., a range of last names or birthdays) and have them form a line.
- Explain that one end of the line represents "I'm an expert," while the other end represents "I'm a novice" or "I loathe it!"
- Call out a series of diverse performance-based skills (e.g., maintaining a clean locker, playing sports, playing a musical instrument or singing, writing, reading, being patient with younger siblings, or remembering movie lines or song lyrics). You can gather information about students using strategies from this chapter, such as Attendance Questions, Glow and Grow, and Potential Student Survey Questions. This ensures that you pose appropriate criteria that will keep all students moving across the spectrum.
- For each item called, students arrange themselves where they believe they belong on the continuum, using their own personal feelings to judge rather than measuring themselves against others. For example, if the item called is "singing," a student might think, *One of the things I do best is sing, so I will place myself near the expert end. I will not compare myself with celebrities or even friends who sing; I just want to think about my own set of skills.*
- Students do not need to remain in a line but can form "clumps."
- Ask follow-up questions:
  — "Did everyone have a chance to be on the 'expert' side of the line?"
  — "Did everyone have a chance to be on the 'novice' side of the line?"
  — "Did everyone share the same strengths and weaknesses?"

- Finally, share the point of the activity by asking, "Why should I assume that just because you're in the same class, you share the same interests, strengths, and weaknesses?" Then tell students, "I won't treat you all like the same person, but I *will* expect you all to move toward expertise, no matter where you start."

Shoe Race

Directions:

- Call up two students with drastically different-sized shoes (do not call attention to this disparity).
- Tell them they'll be racing against themselves to get their best time.
- The first time, have students walk a defined distance and back *in their own shoes*. Time them, and record their times on the board.
- The second time, have each student *switch shoes with the other* and walk the same distance. This twist should be a surprise; do not announce it ahead of time. Once again, record their times on the board. In most cases, students' times increase.

Follow-Up:

- Compare students' times in the first and second rounds and discuss the benefit of walking in shoes that fit.
- Explain that you'll be ensuring students' learning "fits," too, so that they will perform better and feel more comfortable. Sometimes they will receive work that's different from someone else's; this is because you are giving everyone a task that will ensure his or her growth in both skill and efficiency. Not everyone in the class "wears" the same-size task every day.

Source: Catherine Brighton, Curry School of Education, University of Virginia. Used with permission.

2

Articulating Learning Goals

Part 1:

How Do I Determine What I Have to Teach?

What to Teach

The standards. Chapter 4 of the textbook. Cells. Problem solving. The Great Gatsby. *World War II. The syllabus.* These are all ways of talking about what students will learn and what teachers will teach. Each one *sounds* academic and content-oriented and *seems* like something students should be getting in school. Yet outcomes, topics, resources, texts, and outlines are only snippets of what's truly important for teachers to consider as they craft curricular learning goals that empower students and lay a strong foundation for high-quality instruction.

Middle and high school teachers are increasingly faced with the challenge of addressing an enormous amount of material in a short amount of time. The temptation to teach by "covering" the curriculum is, understandably, strong. But a cycle of racing through content and letting students come up for air only to regurgitate that content on a test covers *the teacher* more than it results in actual learning. Surface-level tours of facts and skills might get everyone through the scope and sequence, but not without a cost. Howard Gardner put it well when he said, "The greatest enemy of understanding is coverage" (Brandt, 1993, p. 7).

Recent discoveries about how people learn confirm Gardner's conclusion and suggest that teaching only for acquisition of knowledge and skills—usually the focus of a coverage approach—is not nearly as efficient as teaching for understanding and transfer (Bransford et al., 2000; Hattie, 2012; Jensen, 2005). Students need opportunities to develop, understand, and apply important ideas and concepts if they are to develop expertise. Careening through topics at breakneck speed works against this outcome. As cognitive science uncovers more about how the brain takes in, stores, processes, and retrieves information, it's becoming clear that students acquire and retain more when they must *analyze* and *restructure* information than when they simply *receive* or *consume* it (Jensen, 2005). The former approach takes more time to plan and implement than the latter does, but it also yields better results.

Planning a Unit, Planning a Trip

Most teachers plan and implement the content of their courses in curricular units that span anywhere from two to six weeks, depending on scope. Simply put, a *unit* includes a set of clearly articulated and closely connected learning goals, formative and summative assessments of those goals, and a sequence of learning experiences delivered through lessons that flow from the goals and equip students for the assessments (Wiggins & McTighe, 2005).

Planning a unit is much like planning a road trip from one city to another. Deciding where to go is an obvious and critical first step, because, as Yogi Berra (2001) put it, "If you don't know where you're going, you might not get there." Wiggins and McTighe (2005) urge teachers to "begin with the end in mind" when designing units to ensure that goals, assessment, and instruction are aligned.

To illustrate this principle, imagine traveling by car from New York City to San Francisco. The destination of San Francisco is analogous to students' intended destination—that is, the knowledge, understanding, and skills a student should "end up" with after a given amount of time. *Assessment* is the means through which teachers gauge student progress toward and arrival at that destination. *Instruction* is the route for getting there. This chapter focuses on how best to determine and articulate the learning goals that constitute the destination. Subsequent chapters will focus on assessment and instruction.

Using Concepts and Big Ideas to Articulate the "Worth" of a Destination

There are many possible and worthy reasons for going to San Francisco: taking a business trip, enjoying a vacation, visiting relatives, attending a conference, studying earthquake-resistant buildings, or sampling the cuisine, to name a few. When a friend asks, "Why are you going to San Francisco?" you wouldn't reply, "To go to San Francisco." Such a response would exasperate the friend and mask your real purpose for going!

Similarly, the reason for teaching something isn't the existence of the thing itself, whether it exists in the standards, in a syllabus, in a binder, or on a list. The contents of such documents are there because they have the potential to equip students with ideas, knowledge, and skills that can be used in and transferred to real-life situations.

Concepts are a valuable and efficient way to articulate the worth and focus of a unit. Concepts are broad, abstract ideas—usually consisting of one to two words—that frame, unite, and organize the seemingly disparate chunks of information that are often presented as curriculum (Bransford et al., 2000; National Association of Secondary School Principals, 2004). They connect topics, content, and skills to the essence of the discipline or subject area that is being studied. Concepts are universal and timeless in their application and provide an integrated lens through which to examine bodies of content (Erickson, 2002). Various curricular topics and texts can fit under the umbrella of a single concept because they share common attributes. For example, social studies students could examine every conflict they study through the uniting lenses of *power* and *perspective*. A geometry teacher could unite his entire curriculum around the concept of *relationships*.

There are two kinds of concepts: general and discipline-specific. General concepts are those that are organizers within and across multiple disciplines, such as *change, perspective, patterns,* or *conflict*. Discipline-specific concepts provide ways of classifying or categorizing topics and knowledge within a particular discipline, such as *linearity* (mathematics), *chronology* (social studies), *experiment* (science), *genre* (English), *composition* (art), or *offense/defense* (physical education). In this chapter, we have included a list of general and discipline-specific concepts for reference (see Figure 2.1).

Carefully selected concepts provide openings through which students can tunnel their way into the core of a subject to discover its deep principles, issues, and controversies. For example, a life science teacher could organize a unit or even the course around the concept of *interdependence* by consistently asking students to explore the ways in which changes to one part of a system (e.g., a cell, an ecosystem, or the food chain) would affect all the other parts of that system. This type of concentration allows for interdisciplinary connections. For example, the science teacher's history teammate could focus on the interdependent nature of cultures (e.g., *geography* determines *products*, which influence *economy*, which is a primary concern of *government*).

It is important to note that concepts don't trump or replace facts; rather, they give students ways to *organize* facts and other knowledge so that they can retrieve them and apply what they learn to new situations as well as to acquiring new information (Bransford et al., 2000; Hattie, 2012). Terez Ivy, a systems architect originally from East St. Louis, Illinois, believes that this approach made a difference in his grasp of science during high school and that it continues to facilitate his growth as a learner:

> I have realized over the years that if you know the concepts and understand them on a fundamental level, you can look up the details to fill in the gaps, but if you only know something as it applies to a singular instance, it is much harder to extrapolate that to the larger context. (Marshall, McGee, McLaren, & Veal, 2011, p. 20)

Both this realization and the use of concepts as an organizational tool make even more sense in light of the ever-expanding body of knowledge in all subjects. Potential history course content, for example, is expanding every hour of every day! Information that decades ago was accessible only in print and only to a privileged

FIGURE 2.1

List of Concepts for Framing Curriculum Units

General
Altruism
Analysis
Approximation
Balance
Behavior
Beliefs
Bias
Bravery
Censorship
Change
Choice
Commitment
Communication
Compromise
Conflict
Continuity
Contribution
Conviction
Cooperation
Criticism
Cycles
Discovery
Diversity
Economy
Environment
Ethics
Evaluation
Evolution
Family
Fear
Habit
Hierarchy
Humanity
Humanness
Ideals
Identity
Independence
Interaction
Interdependence
Justice
Love
Memory
Moderation
Mortality and
  Immortality
Organization
Patterns
Perseverance
Perspective
Philosophy
Power
Progress
Regulation
Relationships
Relativity
Revolution
Rules
Society
Stability
Symbol
System
Theory
Time
Transmutation
Values
Victim

Math
Algorithm
Correlation
Derivative
Efficiency
Elegance
Equation
Factor
Formula
Function
Generalizations
Infinity
Label
Linearity
Measurement
Number
Operation
Permutation
Prediction
Prime/Composite
Probability
Representations
Rules
Scale
Symmetry
Time
Variable

Drama
Audience
Character
Delivery
Interpretation
Memorization
Mood
Performance
Presence
Rehearsal
Set
Stage/Staging

Social Studies
Autonomy
Chronology
Citizenship
Community
Competition
Culture
Democracy
Demographics
Direction
Equality
Exploration
Fact/Fiction
Freedom
Government
Globalization
Investment
Leadership
Location
Needs and Wants
Patriotism
Place
Preservation
Production/
  Consumption
Reform/
  Reformation
Rights and
  Responsibilities
Ritual
Subjugation
Supply/Demand

World Language
Attitude
Code
Comprehension
Conjugation
Context
Conventions
Custom
Delivery
Fluency
Interpretation
Language
Message
Pronunciation
Rules
Semantics
Structure
Translation

Music
Composition
Dissonance
Harmony
Interpretation
Melody
Performance
Repetition
Rhythm
Technique
Tone

Art
Abstraction
Aesthetics
Color
Composition
Creativity
Expression
Form
Materials
Medium
Metaphor
Process
Representation

Science
Adaptation
Conclusion
Conservation
Element
Energy
Equilibrium
Experiment
Force
Habitat
Hypothesis
Matter
Motion
Observation
Population
Principle
Sustainability
Taxonomy

English
Characterization
Composition
Connotation/
  Denotation
Conventions
Fate
Fluency
Genre
Heroism
Irony
Loyalty
Metaphor
Myth
Narrative
Persuasion
Roles
Rules
Story
Style
Symbol
Theme
Voice

Physical Education
Competition
Discipline
Effort
Energy
Exercise
Fitness
Form
Leadership
Movement
Nutrition
Offense/Defense
Position
Space
Strategy
Teamwork

Technology
Access
Algorithm
Efficiency
Hardware/
  Software
Input/Output
Interface
Storage
System
Tool
Universality
Utility

few is now retrievable to billions of people in a matter of seconds. If units and lessons are to help students learn how to wade through and make sense of information, then concepts are key.

Getting from Topics to Concepts

So how can teachers go about efficiently identifying the uniting concepts for their disciplines, courses, units, and lessons? A useful first step in extracting the most powerful ideas is to take the unit, lesson topic, focus, or text and consider what it is a "study" in, like this:

_____, a study in _____.
   (Topic/Focus/Text)   (Concept)

A unit on *cells*, for example, might be viewed as a study in *systems* and *structure and function*. A unit on *the Civil War* could be a study in *unity and disunity*. *Integers* are a study in *relationships*. A series of lessons on *Impressionism* might be a study in *innovation*. A brief look at the work of e. e. cummings could be a study in *style* and *(un) convention*.

In literature, there are usually multiple possible thematic concepts that a text could be used to illuminate. The above exercise helps identify and prioritize concepts that are particularly suitable for different grade levels and curricular purposes. For example, *The Giver* by Lois Lowry could be a study in *society, dystopian fiction (genre), identity,* or *free will versus fate. Lord of the Flies* by William Golding could be a study in *power* or *human nature*. It is also possible to use this prompt even if you have already arrived at a concept or big idea, to identify specific topics or areas of focus. Similarly, the exercise can help teachers connect concepts to one another (e.g., *equations*, a study in *balance and proportion*).

Although there's no special "magic" in this particular prompt—and there are myriad other tools to help teachers consider a unit's purpose (see McTighe & Wiggins, 2004; Wiggins & McTighe, 2011)—it can be invaluable for quickly getting to the heart of what students should be studying.

Learning Goals: Getting Specific About the Destination

Concepts are the *beginning* of unit and lesson design; although they get students headed in a worthwhile general direction, they are not specific enough to constitute *learning goals*. Saying, "I'm teaching about structure and function" is a good start, but we must also develop specific, assessable learning goals for the unit and for individual lessons and tasks.

There are three kinds of learning goals that every lesson and unit must articulate as the destination for students: *understanding goals, knowledge goals,* and *skill goals*

(Tomlinson & McTighe, 2006; Wiggins & McTighe, 2005)—what students will understand, what they will know, and what skills or competencies they will attain. These goals are distinct but interrelated, and they are equally important.

Understanding Goals

Understanding goals (or *understandings*) are the principles, insights, essential truths, or "ahas!" that students should walk away with. They are the "so what?" of a unit. Another way of thinking about understanding goals is as overarching ideas that will last beyond a particular unit. They are written as complete sentences and often unpack and connect concepts. Some examples of understanding goals include

- Living systems at all levels of organization demonstrate the complementary nature of structure and function.
- Independence can be gained and lost through choice, experience, or conflict.
- Reform and regulation can both limit and encourage progress.
- Argument explores and arises from different perspectives.
- Historians use a variety of primary and secondary sources to construct what happened in the past.
- Probability is a mathematical model of what's possible that is based on relationships between outcomes.
- Formulas can be used to describe and predict patterns.
- Conventions are influenced by the writer's purpose, context, tone, and style.

It also can be helpful to think of an understanding as a possible answer to an *essential question* (McTighe & Wiggins, 2013). An essential question is an ongoing, recursive inquiry that drives the study of a discipline, concept, or idea. The relationship between understandings and essential questions can be direct or implied, but when reading them alongside each other, the relationship should be evident:

- Living systems at all levels of organization demonstrate the complementary nature of structure and function. (How do systems "work"?)
- Independence can be gained and lost through choice, experience, or conflict. (How is independence gained and lost?)
- Reform and regulation can both limit and encourage progress. (What impact do reform and regulation have on progress?)
- Argument explores and arises from different perspectives. (What do arguments do? Where do arguments come from?)
- Historians use a variety of primary and secondary sources to construct what happened in the past. (What happened in the past, and how can we know for sure?)
- Probability is a mathematical model of what's possible that is based on relationships between outcomes. (How do I know what's mathematically "possible"?)

- Formulas can be used to describe and predict patterns. (What's a formula good for?)
- Conventions are influenced by the writer's purpose, context, tone, and style. (What choices do writers have with conventions? Who or what decides?)

It is important to note that understandings should be revelations that the *students* have or arrive at through careful, ongoing study. They are not simply statements to be displayed and memorized, and students can't just spit out an understanding to convince the teacher that they "get it." For example, if students truly understand that conventions are influenced by the writer's purpose, context, tone, and style, then they are able to provide examples of how and when this is true, analyze a written work through this lens, use conventions in these ways in their own writing, and explain how and why they have done so. Understanding, then, is meant for the students to "uncover" using knowledge and skills (Wiggins & McTighe, 2005).

Knowledge Goals

Although concepts and understanding should be at the center of learning goals, students unquestionably need to acquire and retain facts as part of developing competency in a discipline. Indeed, a key distinction between experts and novices is that the expert has a deep well of factual knowledge from which he or she can draw (Bransford et al., 2000). But the expert understands those facts within the context of a bigger conceptual framework, not as disparate, disconnected pieces of information (Hattie, 2012).

Knowledge goals include the kind of discrete information that students can memorize or take notes on: facts, terms, dates, events, people, definitions, algorithms, formulas, labels, categories, or rules. Knowledge is easy for students to forget—it is liable to fall out of their brains two minutes after a test—unless it is linked to a concept or related understanding. Knowledge goals can be written as short pieces of listed information, such as the following:

- The first and second laws of thermodynamics.
- Properties of matter.
- Types of inheritable characteristics.
- Shakespeare lived from 1564 to 1616.
- Stylistic devices used by John Steinbeck in *The Grapes of Wrath*.
- Selected comma rules.
- Geographical features of selected French-speaking countries.
- $y = mx + b$.
- Mathematical definitions of *reflection*, *rotation*, and *translation*.
- Graphing calculator commands for creating a scatterplot.
- Events preceding the Civil War.

- Structure of the Constitution—including the preamble, articles, and amendments—and the purposes of those parts.

Knowledge goals can also be conveyed as complete thoughts or sentences. Although this approach is more time-consuming, it is useful when crafting common curricular documents, designing lessons and units with colleagues, or teaching something for the first time. Examples follow:

- Narrative writing conveys experience, either real or imaginary, and uses time as its deep structure (National Governors Association Center for Best Practices [NGA Center] & Council of Chief State School Officers [CCSSO], 2010a).
- A *firsthand account* is a written or oral telling of an event or experience by a person who actually experienced or observed it. A *secondhand account* is a written or oral telling of an event or experience by a person who did *not* actually experience or observe it.
- Specific to early America, *colonialism* is the act of claiming political control over land, occupying it with settlers, and using its resources.
- A *circle* is a closed figure composed of a series of points that are equidistant from a single point.
- An event that is certain to happen will always happen (the *probability* is 1), and an event that is impossible will never happen (the *probability* is 0).
- *Energy* is the ability to work or cause change. Energy can take many forms (e.g., *kinetic, potential, thermal*). Adding thermal energy to or taking thermal energy away from a *substance* can change the *state* it is in.

Phrasing knowledge goals as complete thoughts is also important for designing assessments, making it easier to ensure that prompts and items are aligned to the goals they are intended to assess.

Skill Goals

Skill goals represent the competencies that students will demonstrate as they apply what they know and understand. Examples include thinking skills, habits of mind, organizational skills, skills of a discipline (e.g., literary criticism, chemistry, history, or music), procedural skills, or even attitudes. Skills do not describe or dictate production activities (e.g., filling out a worksheet or completing a Venn diagram); rather, they suggest intellectual avenues (e.g., comparing two texts that speak to the same theme or analyzing primary source documents). Skill goals begin with a powerful present-tense verb that describes what students do with or in their *heads*, not with their *hands.* Some examples follow:

- Explain the author's use of rhetorical strategies and techniques.
- Determine the validity of the sampling method described in a given study.
- Solve linear, quadratic, and exponential equations symbolically.

- Construct grammatically correct sentences in the target language.
- Evaluate one's strengths and weaknesses in delivering a performance.
- Justify a position on a current issue.
- Discern bias among news sources.
- Classify materials as conductors and nonconductors.
- Perform a physical activity of moderate to high intensity for 20–30 minutes.
- Organize coherent arguments and critiques of arguments.
- Write and edit work to conform to style guidelines.
- Represent a pattern algebraically and graphically.
- Analyze relationships between primary and secondary sources of information about the same event.
- Compare causes and effects of conflicts in U.S. history.
- Plan and conduct scientific investigations.
- Assess a director's choices in interpreting a play based on the playwright's intentions for the play.
- Describe the effects of error in measurement.

There are numerous frameworks and schemas for thinking about and categorizing types of skills, some of which are discussed in Chapter 5. Regardless of approach, skill goals that guide instruction and assessment should require students to exercise higher-order thinking and suggest what students will "do" to grapple with the understandings and to apply knowledge.

Where Do Standards Fit?

National and state standards, along with the documents that accompany and explain them, can be useful starting points for developing robust learning goals. Many standards are written as broad or specific skill goals, beginning with a verb and describing what students should be able to do (and what they will be assessed on) by the end of a grade level. Examples from the Common Core standards (NGA Center & CCSSO, 2010a, 2010b) include "Cite the textual evidence that most strongly supports an analysis of what the text says explicitly as well as inferences drawn from the text" (CCSS .ELA-LITERACY.RL.8.1) and "Solve quadratic equations in one variable" (CCSS.MATH .HSA.REI.B.4). These standards are skills and, depending on the focus of a unit or lessons therein, could be identified as skill goals. Like most standards, each includes or suggests knowledge of concepts, terms, or processes (e.g., *textual evidence*, how and when to cite textual evidence, *inference, quadratic equation, variable*). Standards often involve or imply multiple skills and need to be "broken apart" for purposes of targeting instruction and designing assessments that ensure students have mastered the standard by year's end.

Standards do not usually articulate understanding goals—even those standards that use the word *understand*. Take, for example, the Common Core standard

"Understand the concept of a ratio and use ratio language to describe a ratio rela-tionship between two quantities" (CCSS.MATH.6.RP.1). *What* should students understand about the concept of a ratio? *What insight* will students reveal about a ratio relationship between two quantities when they describe it? Since the standard doesn't say, we have to figure it out using what we know or can find out. Possible understandings related to this standard include "A ratio describes a relationship between two quantities" and "Ratios give the relative sizes of the quantities being compared, not necessarily the actual sizes."

Another Common Core standard at the same grade level, however, uses the word *understand* and includes an actual understanding goal: "Understand that a set of data collected to answer a statistical question has a distribution which can be described by its center, spread, and overall shape" (CCSS.MATH.6.SP.2). A good clue that this is an understanding is the word *that:* the text that follows is a full-sentence insight about related concepts (e.g., data and distribution).

In general, we caution against unpacking standards into learning goals by myo-pically focusing on one standard at a time and dissecting it in isolation from knowl-edge, understanding, and skills. A more useful approach is to group related standards together to discern the goals that the standards explicitly state as well as those they imply. Taken together, knowledge, understanding, and skill goals form an interde-pendent relationship rather than a hierarchy of priorities. An insight from Henri Poincaré (1905), the great French mathematician and scientist, offers a useful way of thinking about the connection among knowledge, understanding, and skill goals. He wrote, "Science is built up of facts, as a house is built of stones; but an accumulation of facts is no more a science than a heap of stones is a house" (p. 140). If student learning is a house, then knowledge is the bricks, understanding is the mortar, and skills are the building tools and methods. Just as it takes bricks *and* mortar *and* a pro-cess to build a house, so it takes knowledge *and* understanding *and* skill to construct student learning. Ultimately, we want students to *use* what they *know* and can *do* to show what they *understand*.

The Differentiation Connection: Why Do Learning Goals Matter/Where Do Learning Goals Come In?

We now know how crucial learning goals are. Getting back to our metaphorical trip between New York and San Francisco, we have learned that articulating a worthy des-tination requires a conceptual orientation to the content as well as specificity about the understanding, knowledge, and skills students will attain. This is not a "differen-tiation thing," but requisite for clear and high-quality curriculum, assessment, and instruction in general.

Here's what *is* a differentiation thing: making sure that *all students are working toward the same learning goals.* Different tasks aligned to different learning goals are not differentiated; they are simply different. All differentiated tasks should be centered on *shared* understandings, knowledge, and skills. Teachers are not trying to take students to two or three or four different destinations, and any attempt to do so not only is unmanageable but also creates obstacles to classroom community and student learning.

In subsequent chapters, we will discuss exactly how to assess learning goals and use that assessment evidence to drive the creation of differentiated tasks—in other words, to design different routes to the same destination. This chapter is designed to help us make sure we are first clear about where we are heading. To scaffold that pursuit, Part 2 includes a Checklist for High-Quality Learning Goals (pp. 46–47) and Sets of Learning Goals Across Core Content Areas (pp. 48–56).

A Case in Point: Mr. Mason

Mr. Mason, a biology teacher, decided to structure his upcoming series of lessons on the body's feedback systems in a way that connects well to the other systems his students are going to study. He considered that this unit on *homeostasis*, at its most basic level, is a study in *stability and change*—one of the seven crosscutting concepts outlined by the Next Generation Science Standards (NGSS) (National Research Council, 2012). The NGSS standard he is basing the lesson series on is "Students who demonstrate understanding can plan and conduct an investigation to provide evidence that feedback mechanisms maintain homeostasis" (HS-LS1-3). In essence, this study of "balance" can be related to everything the class has already examined. He articulated his learning goals for the lessons as follows:

Understanding Goals

- All systems strive to maintain balance, or stability.
- As external conditions *change*, the body systematically responds to maintain *stability*.
- *Structure* and *function* enable a *system* to *change* to maintain *stability*.

Knowledge Goals

- Definitions of *homeostasis, stimulus, receptor, regulator,* and *response*.
- The difference between positive and negative feedback regulation loops.
- Structures and functions of the feedback mechanisms involved in maintaining homeostasis (for thermoregulation, pH regulation, and glucose regulation).

Skill Goals

- Explain the role of feedback mechanisms in homeostasis.
- Analyze how organ systems work together to maintain homeostasis.
- Compare and contrast two different organ systems' feedback mechanisms.
- Predict and confirm the result of a disturbance in homeostasis of a body system.

Part 2:

Tools and Strategies

Checklist for High-Quality Learning Goals

What It Is:

A tool to guide the articulation of learning goals for use in planning tasks, lessons, units, and assessments.

How It Works:

Use the checklist on page 47 to guide the creation of learning goals and essential questions.

What It's Good For:

- Assessing the power and efficiency of learning goals and essential questions.
- Ensuring the alignment of learning goals for differentiated tasks.

Classroom Examples:

See Sets of Learning Goals Across Core Content Areas (pp. 48–56) for examples of goals that are aligned with these criteria.

Understanding Goals

☐ Are written as complete sentences and phrased, "Students will understand *that. . . .*"

☐ Focus on a concept or big idea.

☐ Invite inquiry and require "uncoverage" (as opposed to *coverage*).

☐ Hold "transfer" power to self, world, discipline, and other disciplines.

☐ Are capable of being investigated on multiple levels or across lessons and units.

Essential Questions

☐ Are important to real people in the real world.

☐ Raise additional questions.

☐ Are worthy of discussion.

☐ Are provocative and debatable.

☐ Suggest more than one answer.

☐ Relate to or unpack the understanding goals.

Knowledge Goals

☐ Consist of information that can be memorized, such as facts, terms, definitions, formulas, algorithms, categories, and processes.

☐ Focus on *essentials* (as opposed to trivia or things that are "fun" to know).

☐ Are aligned with standards.

☐ Include prerequisite knowledge *if necessary*.

☐ Are related to the skills in which students will engage.

☐ Should be written in complete sentences if used for common planning or for planning assessments (e.g., "*Dynamic characters* grow and change throughout a story," NOT "the definition of *dynamic character*.").

Skill Goals

☐ Focus on student *thinking* (what students do with their heads, not their hands).

☐ Begin with a powerful verb (see Bloom's taxonomy for suggestions).

☐ Incorporate higher-order thinking.

☐ Focus on a measurable verb.

☐ Avoid describing specific activities.

☐ Are aligned with but not limited by standards.

☐ Suggest what students will do to grapple with the essential questions and understanding goals and how they will apply the knowledge goals.

Source: Adapted from *Understanding by Design* (Expanded 2nd ed.), by G. Wiggins & J. McTighe, 2005, Alexandria, VA: ASCD. Copyright 2005 by ASCD.

Sets of Learning Goals Across Core Content Areas

English Language Arts

Literature
(Based on Common Core ELA Standards in Reading: Literature, Grade 7)

Understanding Goals and Essential Questions
- **U1:** Literature can shape and be shaped by *perspective*. (**EQ1:** What is the power of literature/story?)
- **U2:** In literature, the author's perspective is related to but distinct from the characters' perspective, as well as the reader's. (**EQ2:** How are the author's, characters', and reader's perspectives connected?)
- **U3:** Readers read and reread a text to gain a better perspective of the text's "parts" and "whole." (Potential misconception: readers should read something once and just "get it.") (**EQ3:** How do readers get inside the author's and characters' minds?)

Knowledge Goals
- **K1:** Differences among *point of view*, *perspective*, and *narration*.
- **K2:** The *theme* of a literary work is a central topic, idea, or common thread that represents what the story is essentially about. Literary works often convey more than one theme.
- **K3:** When a reader *cites* the text, he or she makes reference to a *detail* from the text to prove a *claim* or an *assertion* about the text.

Skill Goals
- **S1:** Cite multiple pieces of textual evidence to support analysis of what a text says explicitly as well as inferences drawn from the text. (RL.7.1)
- **S2:** Determine a theme or central idea of a text. (RL.7.2)
- **S3:** Analyze the development of theme over the course of a text. (RL.7.2)
- **S4:** Analyze how an author develops and contrasts the points of view of different characters or narrators in a text. (RL.7.6)

Argument
(Based on Common Core ELA Standards in Writing, Grade 8, W.8.1.A-E)

Understanding Goals

EQ: What gives an argument power?

- **U1:** Powerful arguments are fueled by the writer's deep knowledge and understanding of a topic or issue.
- **U2:** Powerful arguments employ reasoning that the audience perceives as warranted. (That is, they use *warrants* to convince the audience that the claims being made are reasonable, given the evidence.)
- **U3:** Powerful arguments effect a change in the audience's beliefs or actions that aligns with the writer's intent. (An argument can be strong and logical, however, without convincing the entire audience.)

Knowledge Goals

- **K1:** An *argument* is an organized way of presenting claims and counterclaims that are rooted in reasons and evidence.
- **K2:** Elements of argument, including their attributes and purpose: *claim, counterclaim/counterargument, reasons/reasoning, evidence, warrant, credible, sound, ethos-pathos-logos.*
- **K3:** Strategies for thinking about, noting, or addressing in writing opposing points of view: *acknowledgment, rebuttal,* and *concession.*

Skill Goals

- **S1:** Discern characteristics of more and less persuasive arguments.
- **S2:** Apply persuasive techniques to constructing arguments.
- **S3:** Organize coherent arguments and critiques of arguments.
- **S4:** Make a claim that supports a position relative to an issue, a question, or a text.
- **S5:** Use sound evidence to support claims.
- **S6:** Distinguish relevant from irrelevant evidence.
- **S7:** Acknowledge and refute counterarguments.

Mathematics

Probability
(Based on Common Core Mathematics Content Standards, High School: Statistics & Probability, Conditional Probability & the Rules of Probability)

Understanding Goals and Essential Questions
- **U1:** Probability can provide a basis for describing what is mathematically possible. (**EQ1:** How do I know what is mathematically possible?)
- **U2:** Probabilities are dependent on what the mathematical elements are, how many there are, and how they are sequenced. (**EQ2:** What makes mathematical possibilities different from one another?)
- **U3:** Probability is a mathematical model that describes a relationship between a specific outcome and all possible outcomes. (**EQ3:** How likely is this [event]? What can we "expect"?)
- **U4:** "Odds" describe the relationship between what you want and what you don't want. (**EQ4:** What are "the odds"?)

Knowledge Goals
- **K1:** Terms and concepts related to probability: *probability, permutations, combinations, Fundamental Counting Principle, "odds," dependent/independent events.*
- **K2:** The Fundamental Counting Principle describes choices that might be made, given many mathematical possibilities.
- **K3:** An event that is certain to happen will always happen (the probability is 1), and an event that is impossible will never happen (the probability is 0).

Skill Goals
- **S1:** Evaluate and apply the Fundamental Counting Principle.
- **S2:** Evaluate and apply permutations and combinations (incorporating technology).
- **S3:** Apply basic probability theory to real-world situations.

Source: Developed with Suzanne Farrand and Tyrone Martinez Black, Evanston/Skokie School District 65, Evanston, IL. Used with permission.

Integers
(Based on Common Core Mathematics Content Standards, Grade 6: The Number System)

Understanding Goals and Essential Questions

- **U1:** A number's sign (positive or negative) tells where the number is relative to 0. (**EQ1:** What's a number's "sign"—and why does it matter?)
- **U2:** Positive and negative numbers are used together to describe quantities having opposite directions or values. (**EQ2:** How are positive and negative numbers related?)
- **U3:** Positive and negative numbers can be used to show change (relative to zero, relative to other values). (**EQ3:** What can positive and negative numbers "do" or show?)

Knowledge Goals

- **K1:** Zero is the midpoint of the number line.
- **K2:** A number is positive (+) when it's greater than 0.
- **K3:** A number is negative (–) when it's less than 0.
- **K4:** An integer is a positive or negative whole number.
- **K5:** Rules for operations with integers.
- **K6:** Terms related to applying positive/negative integers: *withdrawal, deposit, increase, decrease, above sea level, below sea level, profit, loss.*

Skill Goals

- **S1:** Recognize opposite signs of numbers as indicating locations on opposite sides of 0.
- **S2:** Find and position integers on a horizontal or vertical line diagram.
- **S3:** Write, interpret, and explain statements of order for integers in real-world contexts.
- **S4:** Solve integer problems, including addition, subtraction, multiplication, and division.

Science

Force and Motion
(Based on the Next Generation Science Standards [NGSS], MS-PS2)

Understanding Goals and Essential Questions
- **U1:** Objects move and interact in predictable ways. (**EQ1:** How do objects move?)
- **U2:** The ways objects move and interact are governed by laws of force and motion. (**EQ2:** What "controls" how objects move?)
- **U3:** Models can be used to represent systems and their interactions (e.g., how objects move, how forces move objects). (**EQ3:** How can we show/predict how things move?)

Knowledge Goals
- **K1:** Newton's Second Law, Newton's Third Law.
- **K2:** Terms related to force and motion: *speed, acceleration, inertia.*

Skill Goals
- **S1:** Develop a graphical or physical model, based on Newton's Third Law.
- **S2:** Test solutions to a practical problem through trial and error.
- **S3:** Predict the motion of two interacting objects (e.g., cars colliding with cars or stationary objects).
- **S4:** Use simulations to predict outcomes when variables change.
- **S5:** Calculate speed and acceleration.

Earth Systems
(Based on the NGSS, MS-ESS2)

Understanding Goals and Essential Questions

- **U1:** The surface of the Earth changes over time in response to underlying forces (e.g., plate tectonics, heating, pressure, cooling). (**EQ1:** When and how does the Earth's surface change?)
- **U2:** Changes in the surface of the Earth over time can be observed in the Earth's interior systems (e.g., formation of rocks). (**EQ2:** How do we know that the Earth's surface has changed?)

Knowledge Goals

- **K1:** Stages of the rock cycle/types of rocks: *igneous, sedimentary, metamorphic.*
- **K2:** Chemical and physical processes that cycle and recycle Earth materials: *weathering, crystallization, melting, sedimentation, deformation.*
- **K3:** How rocks are formed: solid rocks can be formed by the cooling of molten rock, the accumulation and consolidation of sediments, or the alteration of older rocks by heat, pressure, and fluids.

Skill Goals

- **S1:** Make observations and collect data about rock properties (e.g., hardness, acidity, crystallization).
- **S2:** Generate evidence of rock type (use rock properties to classify them).
- **S3:** Investigate scientific questions about the chemical and physical processes that form rocks and minerals and cycle Earth materials.

History/Social Science

The Civil War
(Emphasis on Cause and Effect)

Understanding Goals and Essential Questions
- **U1:** When compromise is ineffective, conflict can lead to war. (**EQ1:** When can conflict lead to war?)
- **U2:** The goals and motives of Civil War leaders differed according to their regions and changed as the war progressed. (**EQ2:** What motivated Civil War leaders, and how did that change over time?)
- **U3:** *Many* different interests drove the Civil War—economic, social, political, and personal. (**EQ3:** Which and whose interests drove the Civil War?)
- **U4:** The Civil War affected the nation's population, economy, and domestic and foreign policies in both positive and negative ways. (**EQ4:** What was the "price" of the Civil War?)

Knowledge Goals
- **K1:** Terms and concepts related to the Civil War: *abolitionist, secede, compromise, Union, Confederate, emancipation.*
- **K2:** Attempts at compromise: Missouri Compromise, Compromise of 1850/Fugitive Slave Act.
- **K3:** "Strategies" of the Civil War: appeasement of border states, Battle of Fort Sumter, Battle of Bull Run, Battle of Gettysburg, Battle of Fort Wagner, Battle of Antietam, Battle of Appomattox Court House, Emancipation Proclamation, Gettysburg Address.
- **K4:** Civil War leaders: Lincoln, Davis, Sherman, Grant, Lee.

Skill Goals
- **S1:** Explain the reasons behind a political, economic, or social ideology or way of thinking (e.g., slavery).
- **S2:** Evaluate a historical event from contrasting points of view (e.g., Emancipation Proclamation, Battle of Gettysburg).
- **S3:** Critique the actions or decisions of a historical figure (e.g., Lincoln, Lee, Sherman).
- **S4:** Classify sections of proposed compromises according to the degree of tension generated for the opposing interest.
- **S5:** Evaluate the influence of specific events on leadership's goals during the progression of the war.

Historical Inquiry
(Based on Common Core ELA Standards in History/Social Studies, Grades 6–8)

Understanding Goals and Essential Questions

- **U1:** Historians use a variety of primary and secondary sources to construct reasonable interpretations of what happened in the past. (No single source provides "enough" information to construct a complete account of the past.) (**EQ1:** What happened in the past—and how can we know for sure?)
- **U2:** All sources convey a point of view or perspective and have both benefits and limitations. (**EQ2:** What is the worth or value of a source? How should I read it?)

Knowledge Goals

- **K1:** A *primary source* is original material or evidence from or produced during the time or event period being studied (e.g., artifacts, diary entries, interviews, newspaper articles, photographs, speeches, works of art, literature, or music).
- **K2:** A *secondary source* is an interpretation or evaluation of a primary source that was written after the time or event period being studied (e.g., biographies, editorials, textbooks, or website content).

Skill Goals

- **S1:** Cite specific textual evidence to support analysis of primary and secondary sources. (RH.6-8.1)
- **S2:** Determine the central ideas or information of a primary or secondary source. (RH.6-8.2)
- **S3:** Provide an accurate summary of a source distinct from prior knowledge or opinions. (RH.6-8.2)
- **S4:** Distinguish among fact, opinion, and reasoned judgment in a text. (RH.6-8.8)
- **S5:** Analyze the relationship between a primary and secondary source on the same topic. (RH.6-8.9)

World Language: Spanish Geography and Culture

Understanding Goals and Essential Questions:

- **U1:** Effective communication relies on adherence to proper form, structure, and patterns. (**EQ1:** What is the relationship among form, structure, and communication power? **EQ2:** How do patterns reveal information about form and structure?)
- **U2:** The geography of a country affects its culture, history, and development. (**EQ3:** How does geography shape a culture?)

Knowledge Goals:

- **K1:** Key geographical features of Mexico and Central America.
- **K2:** Key historical information regarding Mexico and Central America.
- **K3:** Defining cultural characteristics of Mexico and Central America.
- **K4:** Community-related vocabulary.
- **K5:** Rules for forming commands.
- **K6:** Rules for forming the conditional tense.

Skill Goals:

- **S1:** Locate Mexico and the countries of Central America and their capitals.
- **S2:** Make connections among geography and culture, history, and development (in Spanish).
- **S3:** Compare and contrast different cultures in Spanish-speaking countries.
- **S4:** Use command forms to give instructions/make requests.
- **S5:** Use the conditional tense to speak about preferred travel activities.

Source: Rachel Parrish. Used with permission.

3 Constructing Useful Pre-Assessments

Part 1:

How Do I Know What Students Already Know?

Fortunately for teachers, no student—regardless of background or experience—approaches a concept, topic, or skill "empty" (Jensen, 2005). If students did, they would be vessels to fill rather than people to teach. Our challenge as educators, then, is to discover and leverage what students know, think they know, understand, and misunderstand as a precursor to crafting effective learning experiences. We certainly can't ignore these things; students' misconceptions, in particular, can significantly block learning and are difficult to undo (Bransford et al., 2000). Planning effective instruction, differentiated or not, requires uncovering both what conceptions and misconceptions exist—and why they exist.

How well can students analyze a speaker's argument? What do students think causes the seasons? Where do students' definitions of *revolution* come from? Are students able to interpret and pose questions about data? The teacher's tool for opening up students' brains to find the answers to such questions—to ask, in effect, "What's going on in there?"—is *pre-assessment*.

What Is Pre-Assessment?

Simply put, *pre-assessment* is the process of gathering evidence of students' readiness and interests *prior to* beginning a unit or series of related lessons, and then using that evidence to plan instruction that will better meet learners' needs. At its best, pre-assessment serves as a doorway to student thinking, interests, learning preferences, and experiences, and even the content itself.

Returning to our road trip metaphor from Chapter 2, the pre-assessment gives us up-front information for planning our travel itinerary. We wouldn't dream of traveling from New York to San Francisco without first scouting out potential construction-related detours, "must-see" points of interest, and areas we can skip because our travel companions have already been there. Pre-assessment plays the same role. It lets us know which students aren't yet "in New York," and whether some students are already "en route to San Francisco." Pre-assessment can alert us to "danger zones," where we might need to spend a little more time in the unit, as well as let us know what requires only a brief review. It can also help us determine what might get students excited about taking the journey in the first place.

Unfortunately, pre-assessment has earned a bad reputation, to the point where a middle or high school teacher may see it as a waste of time. It's true that if the exclusive purpose of pre-assessment is to gather results to later compare with post-assessment results, it is little more than a thief of instructional time, a discouraging exercise for students, and a feel-good measure for educators. Hattie (2012) contends that students' innate development and simple exposure to material will naturally cause small jumps in a student's achievement over time, regardless of instructional intervention. So the traditional pre/post model may *reflect* that expected growth, but it does little to actually *effect* change and significantly improve student achievement.

Why Pre-Assess?

At its best, pre-assessment "messes up" the teacher—or at least gives him or her pause. It is all too easy to make assumptions about what students do and don't understand—and which students are high-readiness or low-readiness—based on preconceived notions rather than actual performance relative to upcoming learning goals. Pre-assessment challenges, informs, and illuminates the teacher's preconceptions and beliefs about individual students, about how students learn, and about the content itself.

In contrast to months-old standardized assessment results, pre-assessment results provide current and relevant classroom-level data about student thinking and skills, enabling teachers to make proactive and timely decisions about what learners need to achieve mastery. The most useful pre-assessment is administered shortly before the unit of study or series of lessons is taught so that it provides the most up-to-date information about students' strengths and needs and can tip off the teacher about potential trouble spots. Pre-assessment is a time-saver, too: results can direct a unit's focus more precisely on what's most essential for students to learn or master, given what they do or don't already know.

Another advantage of pre-assessment is that it can provide the teacher with ideas to make the unit more intriguing for students. Including questions that tap into student interests can inspire inviting lesson hooks or reflection prompts. For example, a science teacher preparing her class to study ecosystems may tell students, "Describe an important system at work in your life and how the parts work together interdependently." Students' explanations of video games, their social network, or their family's rotating chore schedule can provide ideas for comparisons and metaphors both to clarify complex ideas and to get students interested in studying the content.

Designing a Pre-Assessment

Pre-assessment design begins by clearly articulating the goals of the unit or series of lessons in terms of what all students should know, understand, and be able to do. Without that compass, pre-assessment design is truly a shot in the dark—as is everything else in the unit! You will most likely not need to pre-assess all the goals in a unit, however, so select goals that you have the least evidence of, especially when it comes to student readiness.

Next, consider any crucial prerequisites. What background knowledge and skills must students already possess to meet the requirements of the unit without great struggle? For example, a pre-assessment for a unit on linear equations would probably include questions that ask students to add and subtract integers.

Then consider ways you might connect the content to students' lives. What's the underlying concept: *interdependence, conflict, synergy, perspective*? How might you invite students to consider the connection between those concepts and their lives outside the classroom?

As you design pre-assessment prompts, make sure the focus is on measuring student understandings in addition to knowledge and skills. Some teachers find it helpful when drafting a pre-assessment to indicate the unit goal to be measured next to each prospective pre-assessment question; in this way, they can see right away the balance they have struck in assessing understandings, knowledge, skills, and prerequisites. Use the Pre-Assessment Planning Template (p. 71) in Part 2 of this chapter to help structure this process.

It is especially important to make sure that at least some items have the capacity to distinguish between students who have solid understanding and students who have truly advanced understanding. Consider what a biology teacher could discern about student understanding from asking the following question on a pre-assessment: "How does a seed turn into a tree? Please be as specific as you can about the *process* and what you think is involved or needed." This question would elicit a range of responses revealing both misconceptions (e.g., thinking water causes growth through expansion) and a strong grasp of the material (e.g., understanding the role of glucose production).

Finally, limit questions on the pre-assessment to those that have predictable instructional implications. Surveying students about narrow bands of dates, names, or definitions, for example, can squander valuable pre-assessment opportunities: such foundational information will most likely be included in the lessons regardless of student answers. Further, students' factual knowledge—or lack thereof—does not provide enough information to guide decisions on how to challenge and support students' processing of the unit's more complex content. It may distinguish who has had the most enriching experiences without identifying who truly understands the content.

A strong pre-assessment taps the well of students' brains to draw out what they might understand, know, or be able to do relative to the upcoming unit. A pre-assessment doesn't need to be long or complicated to achieve this goal. In fact, the best pre-assessments are often short and to the point. More important is that the questions or prompts "wake up" students' minds and prod them to provide the teacher with information that can inform up-front planning.

Pre-Assessment and Differentiation

Because pre-assessment shows where students are starting from, it can help teachers determine when different students may need different things to make progress. As Tomlinson and Moon (2013) point out, "Pre-assessment helps the teacher locate the 'area of the pool' appropriate for each student as a unit of study is about to begin" (p. 28). However, because pre-assessment cannot predict student growth over time, it should not be used as a measure to place students in groupings for the duration of a unit. During the unit itself, teachers must continually check in to see how students' learning is progressing, where students are stuck, what they need to take the next step, and so on. These *formative assessment* checks have the power to reflect what has happened with student learning since the administration of the pre-assessment. Such information not only guides the general course of instruction but also informs *specific* decisions about differentiation. (See Chapters 6 and 7 for more on this.) In other words, pre-assessment is a *starting* point, not a definitive sorting tool.

Part 2 of this chapter contains several tools to help teachers plan pre-assessments. The Pre-Assessment Planning Template (p. 71) guides teachers as they think through what they want to pre-assess and why, and how they'll do it. The list of Sample Pre-Assessment Prompts by Type (pp. 72–73) can be used in tandem with the template to generate questions aligned with desired outcomes. Finally, the Pre-Assessment Examples (pp. 74–80), arranged by content area, can provide both inspiration and clarification during the design process.

Frequently Asked Questions About Pre-Assessment

Because this foray into pre-assessment is often unfamiliar to middle and high school educators, it may be met with much uncertainty and even a little angst. What follow are the most common concerns we hear from the teachers and administrators we work with on designing pre-assessments, along with our responses stemming from both research and practice.

What about using an end-of-chapter test from the textbook as a pre-assessment?

Such tests are usually designed to gauge factual knowledge, not conceptual understanding, so they don't distinguish between students who have solid understanding and students who have truly advanced understanding—which is also why they might not make good summative assessments without substantial revision.

Textbook assessments also tend to rely on question formats that fail to capture students' reasoning or that allow students to answer correctly simply by guessing. In other words, they're not helpful for revealing misconceptions unless students are prompted to explain, defend, or justify their choices.

If I take the time to pre-assess, how will I get through the curriculum?

Wise and selective use of pre-assessment can actually *save* time by informing decisions about content that can be streamlined or skipped altogether. There is no use spending time on what students already know. Although pre-assessment can reveal significant gaps that take time to address, in the end, pre-assessment is still helping you make the best possible use of time.

Remember that you don't need to pre-assess everything. Even if you want to administer a comprehensive pre-assessment, you don't have to give it all at once. If you design a longer pre-assessment, you can administer it in stages or parts (e.g., as exit cards), as you need the information (Tomlinson & Moon, 2013).

It is also possible to use recent *summative* assessment results as pre-assessment results when they relate to the goals for an upcoming unit or set of lessons.

How do I find time to examine pre-assessment results when I teach 100-plus students?

Begin a foray into pre-assessment by selecting *one* class period. It might be the class with the broadest span of readiness levels, or the class with the fewest students. Alternatively, give the pre-assessment to all classes, but take just one class set to do a close analysis and develop a sense of the patterns among students. Then, use those patterns to analyze the results from the other course sections.

I have multiple preps/sections. Do I have to pre-assess in all of them?

Experiment with pre-assessment in one course or section. Consider choosing the subject you're most comfortable with, content-wise, as it's likely to be the one in which you will be able to design the best pre-assessment items and most skillfully analyze responses. Also consider working with colleagues to design pre-assessments that can be shared and used across courses.

How do I keep my students from panicking as they do in a typical test situation?

Often, when students are nervous about pre-assessment (or else don't take it seriously), it's because they believe it is a way of distinguishing "smart kids" from "dumb kids." When pre-assessment is followed by forms of differentiation that create a status hierarchy or static groups, or result in some students engaging in respectful tasks while others work on low-level tasks, that concern is well founded! Designing an invitational pre-assessment with well-worded prompts and item formats can also go a long way toward making pre-assessment "low-stakes."

Dialogue with students about what pre-assessment is and why and how you will use it. Emphasize that it is not graded or scored—it's for your planning and their learning. Students are more likely to believe you and to take the pre-assessment seriously if they experience success through the lessons and tasks you designed from the results. This might require you to explicitly explain throughout the unit how and where you've done so.

If I don't grade, score, or give credit for the pre-assessment, how will I get students to invest?

Experts (e.g., Guskey, 2003; O'Connor, 2010; Stiggins & Chappuis, 2011; Tomlinson & Moon, 2013) agree that grades do not have the extrinsically motivational value we think they do, except perhaps for students who have always earned high grades. If it seems students will engage in or complete tasks only when those tasks are linked to a grade, they have likely learned it from teachers using grades as motivators.

Frequent use of pre-assessment can actually be a good strategy for helping students become more intrinsically motivated. Most students can understand the rationale behind not being graded on something that the teacher hasn't taught yet.

What students *do* want—and need—is to get feedback on their responses. This doesn't mean simply marking answers on the pre-assessment right or wrong and returning it to students. It *can* mean using individual or class responses in lessons (e.g., as hooks or in learning activities) or giving the pre-assessment back to students after certain lessons or at the end of the unit and prompting them to revisit or reflect on their original responses.

What if there is no chance that students know anything about this content?

Generally speaking, no student comes to any topic, skill, or concept completely "empty." That's one of the biggest challenges in teaching: the students already know (or think they know) some stuff! Tapping into students' preconceptions prior to the start of a unit or focus can help you better anticipate roadblocks.

Often, students have experiences with aspects of the content that teachers aren't aware of. An extracurricular activity, special interest, favorite movie, or childhood passion may give some students more knowledge than you're assuming.

Pre-assess the prerequisite ideas and skills that the content assumes students have. Does the novel students are about to read assume familiarity with Greek mythology? Pre-assess that. Or start the unit without pre-assessing, but use formative assessment soon after students have had some exposure to preliminary or foundational concepts and skills.

I gave a pre-assessment, but it didn't tell me anything I couldn't have guessed myself.

The culprit of a pre-assessment that doesn't challenge or inform teacher thinking is more often than not a problem with the pre-assessment items. Ask yourself,

- Is each item truly aligned with unit goals?
- Are there items that gauge *understanding,* or do they all measure knowledge or skill?
- Are there items that have good "discrimination" (i.e., do they have the potential to reveal even the subtlest differences in student readiness)?
- Does the language of a question/item present a barrier to students showing what they know?

I pre-assessed and found out the kids are all over the place. Now I feel like I need 30 different lesson plans!

You don't need 30 different lesson plans! Remember that you are looking for *patterns* in responses. Some of these patterns may suggest the need to create differentiated tasks; others may simply inform the design of whole-class activities. Pre-assessment isn't just a "differentiation thing" or a way of sorting students into groups.

A Case in Point: Ms. Harley

Last year, U.S. History teacher Ms. Harley's attempt to pre-assess her students before a unit on World War II left her frustrated. For efficiency, she had used a multiple-choice format focused on key dates, figures, and events of the conflict. The results were unsurprising: a few students answered all the questions correctly, but most students either did not have or could not readily recall such detailed background knowledge. Ms. Harley was at loss as to how to design instruction that would meet these diverse student needs. She went ahead and taught the unit as usual.

This year, Ms. Harley's professional learning community chose to focus on designing effective assessments, and Ms. Harley decided to give pre-assessment another shot. She realized that last year, her unit goals had focused on discrete knowledge and isolated skills rather than on application and understanding, which in turn had led to pre-assessment items that did the same. Moreover, her multiple-choice format provided few clues about the reasoning behind students' choices.

Working with a colleague, Ms. Harley rearticulated her outcomes in terms of key knowledge, essential skills, *and* conceptual understanding (Wiggins & McTighe, 2005) and designed pre-assessment items that captured the essence of those goals. The following revised pre-assessment yielded far more useful information for Ms. Harley than her previous attempt had done.

Pre-Assessment for a Unit on World War II

1. Describe a situation in which *one* conflict caused *another* conflict to arise. You can use an example from real life, literature, or media.
2. What conflicts fueled World War II?
3. What key people, events, and ideas were central to the war?
4. Who "won," who "lost," and what happened as a result?
5. Examine President Harry Truman's letter to a journalist written almost two decades after his presidency. What can you infer about why Truman wrote this letter? What does the letter reveal about why Truman decided to drop the bomb and how he felt about it? Use evidence from the text to support your answers.

Students' responses to the first question provided examples from movies, books, television shows, and their own lives—references that Ms. Harley could use to hook her students into understanding the relationship between the end of World War I and the beginning of World War II. For example, one student described a time when conflict with his sister led to him being grounded, which in turn caused another conflict with fellow students with whom he needed to meet outside school to complete a group project. Other students cited instances of intertwining conflicts from popular series such as *The Hunger Games, Harry Potter*, and *Twilight*. The first and second questions together offered insight into students' conceptual understanding of the interconnected nature of conflict and gave Ms. Harley some ideas for ways to support and challenge students' thinking about the historical and present-day implications of that interconnection. Student examples from *The Hunger Games*, in particular, supplied numerous analogies for a class discussion on the Treaty of Versailles's contribution to Germany's role in World War II.

The third and fourth questions revealed what students already knew—or thought they knew—about World War II. Ms. Harley discovered multiple misconceptions that she would need to address, as well as a few areas that she could spend less time on than she had originally planned. For instance, many students believed that the United States was involved in the war from its outset. Some students also thought it was the Nazis' heinous acts that motivated the United States to enter the war. Ms. Harley used a short documentary, *Reporting on the Times:* The New York Times *and the Holocaust,* to challenge both of these ideas. She prompted students then and throughout the unit to confront their initial understanding and reflect on how their perspectives had changed in light of historical evidence.

The final question asked students to read a historical document (President Truman's unsent letter to *Chicago Sun-Times* columnist Irv Kupcinet, dated August 5, 1963, available at http://media.nara.gov/media/images/29/4/29-0325a.gif) and to draw and support conclusions from this document. This question provided a way to discern students' readiness to tackle the sources they would digest during the unit. Students' responses showed a range of depth and understanding, which suggested to Ms. Harley that she might need to differentiate through tiered sets of questions for analyzing sources of varying levels of complexity.

Equipped with these pre-assessment results, Ms. Harley felt that she was beginning the unit with her eyes more widely open to the obstacles that she and her students might encounter as well as with a clearer sense of how to surmount them.

Part 2:

Tools and Strategies

Pre-Assessment

What It Is:

The process of gathering evidence of students' readiness, interests, and learning preferences *prior to* beginning a unit or series of related lessons, and then using that evidence to plan instruction that will better meet learners' needs.

How It Works:

Shortly before a unit of study (early enough to provide time to analyze results but close enough to instruction to provide the most recent data), the teacher

1. Articulates the goals of the unit or lessons in terms of what all students should know, understand, and be able to do, along with any crucial prerequisite knowledge and skills.
2. Designs prompts to assess each of these kinds of learning goals (especially understanding) as well as to uncover students' interests.
3. Administers the pre-assessment and analyzes results for overarching patterns.
4. Uses the results to inform general, up-front planning for the unit.

What It's Good For:

- Directing the focus in a unit more precisely on what's most essential for students to learn or master, given what they do or don't already know.
- Alerting the teacher to potential trouble spots (common misconceptions or gaps in understanding) in a unit.
- Revealing which students already know a great deal about the topic—and *what* they know.
- Providing ideas for hooks, prompts, lessons, and activities aligned to student interests.

Tips:

- Include just a few key questions that will provide useful information.
- Align questions with key lesson or unit goals (facts, skills, and understandings), as well as prerequisite knowledge.
- Gauge students' understanding *in addition to* their knowledge and skill.
- Incorporate questions that pique students' interest in what they're about to study.
- Aim to discover what students *do* know, not just to confirm what they *don't* know.
- Include questions that are sensitive to and can reveal even subtle differences in student readiness, especially among higher-readiness students.
- Give students different and multiple ways to show what they know.
- Uncover potential connections between the student and the content.
- Make sure the pre-assessment is accessible to *all* students, not just to those with enriching backgrounds, so that it serves as an invitation, not a barrier, to the learning experience.

Pre-Assessment Planning Template

Use your unit learning goals (or KUDs: what students will *know, understand,* and be able to *do*) as a starting point for pre-assessment prompt ideas. Think through your ideas using this table.

Pre-assessment prompt	K, U, D (or prerequisite) assessed?	What will this prompt help me discover? (Why am I asking this? What am I trying to find out?)	What is the "ideal" or most advanced response to this prompt?	What other kinds of responses am I anticipating or looking for?

Source: From *Professional Development for Differentiating Instruction: An ASCD Action Tool,* by C. A. Strickland, 2009, Alexandria, VA: ASCD. Copyright 2009 by ASCD.

Sample Pre-Assessment Prompts by Type

Pre-Assessing Readiness

- How can someone tell if a website is credible?
- Circle the metaphor in the song/poem excerpt below. Then explain why you think this is a metaphor.
- How is the U.S. president's job different from a U.S. senator or representative's job?
- Create a table for these data that makes them easier to understand.
- Analyze this student's work from a class several years ago. What did he or she do well? What did he or she not do well?
- Use free weights to show your form and optimal weight for 10 reps in the following exercises. . . .
- Why is it important for artists to know which colors are the primary colors?
- Draw and label the parts of a stage.

Pre-Assessing Experience

- What experience do you have with this topic/skill?
- What other classes/activities have you taken or been involved in related to this topic/skill?
- Briefly describe a project, performance, or game you have completed or participated in related to this topic/skill that you are proud of.
- Rate your level of expertise in this topic/skill on the scale below. Please provide evidence or an explanation to support your self-rating.
- In your experience with this topic/skill, what have you found to be the most important or helpful "rules" or principles to remember or practice?
- Where do you use or hear about this topic/skill in your daily life?

Pre-Assessing Interest

- List three goals you hope to achieve in this course/unit. How will you know if you've achieved these goals? How will your teacher know?
- Here are some topics we will study in this course/unit. Which ones sound the most interesting to you? Rank your top three, and provide an explanation for why you chose each one.
- Which interest do you spend the most time on outside school? How might that interest connect to this class/unit topic/skill/concept?

Pre-Assessing Learning Preference

- Describe your approach or process for memorizing things (e.g., lines, vocabulary, facts, formulas, rules).
- So far this year, we've used the discussion strategies listed below. Which one have you liked best, and why?
- Use words and pictures to show what your "ideal" classroom environment would look like, and include an explanation of why it is ideal.
- Use words and pictures to show what your "ideal" practice session and conditions would look like. Be clear about who, what, where, when, and how long. Include an explanation of why this is ideal. Then use words and pictures to compare this with your typical practice session.
- When you're learning about historical people and events, do you prefer to

    _____ Listen to a real person/teacher talk about it.

    _____ Watch a video about it.

    _____ Read about it.

    _____ Other: _____

- When you're learning a new program or tool, do you tend to

    _____ Read a how-to manual or directions before or as you begin.

    _____ Dive right in and learn by doing.

    _____ Neither; I (please complete) _____

Pre-Assessment Examples

English Language Arts

Writing and Reading Arguments
1. Think about a time when someone (e.g., a friend or parent) changed your mind about something. What did that person do or say to make you change your mind? Please describe the circumstance *and* what the person said or did.
2. Name and describe three techniques writers use to persuade others to think a certain way or do a certain thing.
3. Use one or more of the techniques you described in the preceding item to write a paragraph in which you try to convince your teacher not to assign you homework this week. Make sure to underline and label the technique(s) you use.
4. Read the op-ed provided. What do you think are the writer's *most* convincing points? Explain why you find those points convincing. What do you think are the writer's *least* convincing points? Explain why you find those points unconvincing.

ELA/Social Studies Connections

The Research Process			
Research	Question	Methods	Cite
Search	Sources	Process	Attribution
Credibility	Claim	Resources	Audience
Valid	Evidence	Reasoning	

Part 1

1. Review the list of terms above.
2. Write *five* complete sentences that connect *two or more* of the terms *and* that you believe or have found to be true.
3. After each sentence, further explain the idea(s) by using specific examples from your own or others' experiences.

Part 2

1. Choose one of the topics below and write a focused, *complex* research question related to the topic. [Discipline-relevant topics listed here]
2. List five sources that you would consult to try to answer the question above. Be as specific as you can. Then, next to each source, explain *why* you think it would be useful. What would it "do" or provide?
3. Review the stages of the research process below. Explain what you think each one involves. *If you can, provide examples related to the topic/question that you chose in question 1.*
    — Focusing the research.
    — Identifying and assessing sources.
    — Gathering information and evidence.
    — Attributing sources/information.
    — Sharing/reporting findings or results.

Social Studies
The American Revolution

1. What does it mean to "declare independence" from something or someone?
2. Give an example of a time in your life when *you* "declared independence." Explain whom or what you declared independence from, how you declared your independence, and why.
3. Which countries were involved in the American Revolution?
4. In what year did the American Revolution begin? _____. Why did you say this year?
5. How did the American Revolution begin?
6. What were some of the outcomes of the American Revolution? (What happened as a result of the American Revolution?)
7. Check all of the statements in the list below that apply to you.

When we study the American Revolution, I hope we . . .
- — Read documents from the time of the Revolution.
- — Read from our textbook.
- — Watch videos.
- — Do a project. For example: _____
- — Write something creative.

World Geography

Use map A and the data attached to it for questions 1 and 2.
1. Analyze the map (a real but unlabeled country) and data to make and defend hypotheses about how the country's geography will affect its recreation, industry, economy, religion, government, and relationships with neighboring countries.
2. How far is point A from point C? *Approximately* _____.
   a. Describe the terrain between those two points.
   b. How would the terrain affect travel, trade, and access to resources between those two points? List and discuss as many effects as you can think of.

Use maps B, C, and D for questions 3–5.
3. Examine the three maps of the same region of the world. On map B, label any countries, cities, and geographic features you recognize. It's fine to guess.
4. Compare and contrast these three maps' depictions of the same region and explain what you believe is the purpose of each map. If you know the names of the kinds of maps these are, include those names in your explanations.
5. Which map is the most "objective"? Which map is the most "subjective"? Explain.

Science

Simple Machines
1. What makes an object move?
2. Your mom tells you to unload the dishwasher. There are 10 plates of the same size and weight for you to put away. You can either put one plate away at a time *or* put the whole stack away at once. Which would require less "work"? Circle one answer below and explain why you chose it.
a. Putting the plates away one at a time.
b. Putting the whole stack away at once.
c. Both would require the same amount of work.
3. What is *work*? (Give your own definition.)
4. Give *three* examples of work (as you've defined it) that don't involve people or animals.
5. Why do objects have weight?

Source: Developed with Jay Marshall, Antioch Upper Grades School, Antioch, IL. Used with permission.

Life Science: Photosynthesis
1. Plants provide energy for many human activities. List as many human activities as you can think of.
2. How does a seed turn into a tree? Please be as specific as you can about the *process* and what you think is involved or needed.
3. *All life on Earth depends on plants.* Do you agree or disagree with this statement? Why or why not?
4. All living things store and use energy. How is the way that *plants* store and use energy different from the way *animals* store and use energy?
5. What will happen to a plant if it is exposed only to oxygen? Why?
6. What will happen to a plant that is exposed to less light than it needs? Why?

Planning and Carrying Out Scientific Investigations (Based on the NGSS, Practice 3)
1. Imagine that you are designing an experiment to test _____. Write a question that could guide your experiment.
2. Create a chart to show three variables that you could test, how you could test them, and why you would test them.
3. In this experiment you've designed, which variables are independent? Which variables are dependent? How do you know?

Engaging in Argument from Scientific Evidence
(Based on the NGSS, Practice 7)

1. Examine this scientific claim: *Watching* Sesame Street *improves young children's understanding of science.*
   — How could you use science to find out whether this claim is true?
   — What kind of *scientific evidence* would you need to decide whether you agree with this claim?
2. Read the *New York Times* article "The Claim: Eating Carrots Improves Your Eyesight" (O'Connor, 2005; available at www.nytimes.com/2005/05/03/health/03real.html?_r=0#), and then answer the questions that follow.
3. Which statement does the research described in this article support? Check one, or write your own claim.
   _____ Eating carrots helps maintain normal vision.
   _____ Eating carrots can make some people's vision worse.
   _____ Eating carrots has no effect on vision.
   _____ My own claim: _____
4. Explain your choice. (Please use information from the article to show your reasoning!)

Math

Circles

1. What does it mean for something to stay *constant*?
2. Define *circumference* and *diameter*. Label them on the circle pictured.
3. Which of the following is an *irrational number*? Why?
   a. 3.5
   b. $\sqrt{2}$
   c. 34
   d. 3.33333 . . .
4. Give an example of a *relationship* where one thing changes as the result of another (e.g., your weight changes as your height changes).

Source: Developed by Jill Hawkins, Tabb Middle School, Yorktown, VA. Used with permission.

Integers

1. Draw a number line from −5 to 5. Label each whole number on that line. Solve the following problems:
   a. $7 + 10 =$ _____
   b. $7 + -10 =$ _____
   c. $-5 + -6 =$ _____
   d. $-5 + 6 =$ _____
2. Name four numbers greater than −8 and less than −5.
3. Name four numbers less than 2 and greater than −1.
4. What does a number's sign (e.g., +/−) mean or show?
5. Write a brief explanation or "story" for each number model:
   - $8 + (-3) = 5$
   - $-1 - 9 = -10$

Related Arts

Internet Safety

1. What is *privacy*? Give a definition in your own words.
2. How does privacy look (or *not* look) in your daily life? What are some examples or nonexamples?
3. When using the Internet, we are told to be careful with our personal information. Why do you think we are told this?
4. Which of the following are considered personal information? Circle all that apply, and explain why you circled what you did.

   Name

   Passwords

   Street address

   Parents' names

   Phone number

   Plans for the weekend

   E-mail address

   Pictures
5. Our school has posters in each room that describe bullying as *an imbalance of power where aggressive behavior is used to physically or emotionally harm someone.* Based on what you know or have experienced, what does bullying look like when it happens online?
6. What are some ways you can protect yourself online? Try to list three.
7. What would you do if someone from school sent you two text messages threatening to beat you up after school? Why?

Source: Developed with Kathy Strathman, Antioch Upper Grades School, Antioch, IL. Used with permission.

Strength Training

1. Read the following list of claims about strength training. Write *true* or *false* next to each one and explain how and/or why you believe the statement is true or false.
   a. Males and females need different kinds of strength training.
   b. Strength training and weightlifting are the same thing.
   c. Most people shouldn't lift weights every day.
   d. Everyone can benefit from strength training.

2. List any misconceptions you think people have about strength training *or* any questions you have about it. These might be things you have heard and are not sure are true.

3. Give your best explanation of each goal below (i.e., what it means), as well as *how* you think a person could or should achieve that goal through strength training.
   a. Goal 1: Build muscle mass.
   b. Goal 2: Build muscle tone.
   c. Goal 3: Go from being able to bench-press 50 pounds to being able to bench-press 100 pounds.

4. We will be using different equipment for and approaches to building your strength. Consider the types below. (I will show you each one.) Explain what advantages you think each one has. In other words, what can each one "do" or offer?
   — Free weights (dumbbells).
   — Free weights (barbells).
   — Machines.
   — Resistance bands.
   — Body weight/resistance (e.g., push-ups, sit-ups, planks).

5. Performance: I will ask you to do several exercises so that I can observe your approach. I may ask you some questions about what you're doing.

4

Hooking Students into Instruction

Part 1:

How Do I Get Students to Care?

"Please, please, please try to just shake it up sometimes. Give us a variety of work and activities and don't just stick to the same type of lesson every day" (Wiggins, 2014a).

This entreaty from a high school student—a response to a survey question asking kids what would help them learn better—presents a quandary for teachers. The request seems realistic, but it also may feel like a plea for "dessert." After all, with all the curricular "nutrients" students need to ingest, is there really time to ensure that they enjoy their meals, too? It's good for them, whether they know it or not. That should be enough, right?

"The Hook" as a Necessity Rather Than a Convenience

In terms of the way the brain works, it is actually *very* important to make learning a pleasurable experience for students. Presenting content connections in new or surprising ways can stimulate student thinking and prevent "neural fatigue," leading to greater attention and deeper learning (Perry, 2000). Neurologist Judy Willis (2007) asserts that "when students are engaged and motivated and feel minimal stress, information flows freely through the affective filter in the amygdala [the brain's emotional center] and they achieve higher levels of cognition, make connections, and experience 'aha' moments" (para. 3).

This is true of learning in general, but it is even more important for adolescents, who often need to see relevance in what they are studying to invest in it (Willis, 2006). Grant Wiggins's (2014a) survey of high school students elicited a host of responses similar to the student's appeal above. Over and over again, students expressed a desire for something different—for teachers to . . .

- "Actually engage the students in learning."
- "Try something creative when teaching something new."
- "[Try] to not talk the entire time."
- "Make students want to learn by either showing how fascinating subjects can be or show relevance to our lives."

In a standards-based world, these petitions are hard to swallow. With the breadth of the curriculum teachers are responsible for teaching, there is certainly no time for anything "fluffy." The good news is that activating student interest does not require side journeys into unrelated content. Teachers can connect powerful curriculum with what they know about students to "hook" students into learning and hold their attention and understanding throughout the course of study (Wiggins & McTighe, 2005). Such strategies do not strive for entertainment value—they facilitate learning.

Returning to our road trip metaphor, taking time to thoughtfully *plan* the journey (i.e., articulating learning goals) is a necessity. So is discovering information about students' readiness to take that journey and what might motivate them to do so (i.e., administering pre-assessment). Next, before actually embarking on the journey with students, we must convince them to get onto the bus! This is the vital role of the hook: it enables teachers to use what they learned from pre-assessment (and other sources) to get students willing, even excited, to take the journey. And it fosters an investment that keeps students from bailing out when the going gets tough.

What "Hooks" Students into Learning?

So how do teachers foster student investment in the journey while maintaining a focus on important learning goals? Neuroscience and studies on student learning provide some direction:

- Cognitive psychologist Daniel Willingham (2009) maintains that student motivation is not dependent upon an intrinsic interest in the content: "We've all attended a lecture or watched a TV show (perhaps against our will) about a subject we thought we weren't interested in, only to find ourselves fascinated" (p. 7). Willingham contends that regardless of the subject being studied, students are willing to invest effort when they are presented with a *puzzle* or a *challenge* that appears within their reach but which they must stretch to achieve.
- Both brain research (Jensen, 2005; Willis, 2006) and educational research (Bransford et al., 2000) demonstrate that students perform better when they see some *connection* between the content and themselves or the world around them. Middle and high school students, especially, are concerned with seeing the relevance of material to their personal lives. When we find avenues to make such connections, we have a better chance of harnessing student attention and investment.
- Brain research (Perry, 2000; Willis, 2007) also reveals that *novelty* plays an important role in attention and motivation. As Wolfe (2001) explains, "Novelty is

an innate attention-getter. . . . Our brains are programmed to pay attention to the unusual" (p. 82). Introducing or addressing a topic in a unique manner can cause students' minds to "perk up"; as a result, they may attend and retain more than they otherwise would have.

A challenge. A connection. A surprise. These elements draw students into learning, but they are not likely to be found in the standards or in textbooks. As we discussed in Chapter 2, the necessary precursor to crafting *any* meaningful learning experience—including a hook—is to examine and articulate the concepts and principles that lie at the heart of the discipline. Teachers who take the time to thoughtfully consider their content in this manner will be better poised to tap into that content in unusual ways, be it through creating challenges, fostering relevance, or introducing novelty.

Connecting What's Important About the Content with What's Important to the Kids

Chapter 2 presented concepts as important vehicles for planning curriculum. Concepts such as *change, conflict, victim,* and *systems* have the ability to unify large amounts of content and give context to seemingly disparate skills. Concepts also serve as lenses through which students can see their own connection to the content. Let's look again at the "studies" proposed in Chapter 2:

- *Cells,* a study in *structure and function.*
- *Impressionism,* a study in *innovation.*
- *e. e. cummings,* a study in *(un)convention.*
- *Equations,* a study in *balance and proportion.*

Each of these curricular connections can also serve as a link to students' lives. Adolescence is also a study in *balance and proportion,* as middle and high school students struggle to achieve balance among school life, families, friends, jobs, and extracurricular activities. Likewise, the contrast between the *conventional* and the *unconventional* drives the adolescent experience as students seek to fit in while maintaining their individuality. Each of these concepts can serve as an invitation into the content: students can first discuss the concept's relationship to their lives before examining its importance to the discipline. For example, approaching e. e. cummings as a rebel who flips convention on its head to achieve his purpose immediately makes him more familiar and more representative of students' own aspirations.

By examining the concepts central to their disciplines, teachers have already taken the first step to helping adolescent learners see a reason to "lean in" to what they're studying because—in a very real way—adolescents are studying *themselves.*

In Kathleen Cushman's (2005) book *Fires in the Bathroom: Advice for Teachers from High School Students,* a student named Vance reflects on a high school math class experience:

My math teacher kept trying to connect to me using formulas and problems, and to be honest, I don't care enough about math to respond. Maybe it's wrong, but I need something personal to motivate me. If he could connect geometry angles to my interest in art or being an actor, that would work. Just saying, "You need to pass math to get out of high school" isn't enough. Show me how knowing pi is worth something. (p. 105)

Vance is a good example of the kind of student about whom teachers tend to say, "I don't know what to do with this kid. He's just not motivated." This may be a reasonable conclusion based on appearances and attitude alone, but all people have interests, passions, and kinships that motivate them. A more accurate determination, perhaps, is not that the student is *not motivated* but that he or she is not motivated *by the topic or task at hand*.

Although Vance may not be motivated by memorizing formulas, he might be motivated by the idea of a *constant*. In essence, *pi* is the study of a mathematical *constant*. It is a number that mathematicians (and, by extension, students) can rely on and use to calculate, analyze, compare, and predict. To engage Vance in a study of pi, his teacher might begin by displaying the word *constant* and asking students to talk with one another briefly about what it means for something to stay constant and who or what the constants are in their lives. From there, it isn't a far leap to the idea that mathematicians also have constants, and that one of these is a ratio: pi.

Discovering Student Interests

The preceding hook isn't a silver bullet for instantly transforming students who have long been turned off to all things math. It's one small step in what should be an ongoing series of steps toward building students' trust that what they're being asked to learn and do is worth something.

Another small but equally important step is proactively discovering what students care about. Had Vance's teacher inquired, he could have discovered that art and acting captured Vance's imagination and energy. Vance was able to surmise that math must somehow be involved in those disciplines. And he was right! Artists and actors both use angles, albeit in different ways: the former in creating dimension and depth, and the latter through stage design and stage directions. Those connections could have served as powerful motivators for Vance. But his teacher couldn't build those bridges between content and student unless he knew what mattered to Vance.

Pre-assessment is one tool for discovering what is important to students. Although primarily a vehicle for gauging student readiness, pre-assessment can also be a means for discovering the array of interests students bring with them to the classroom. In Chapter 3, we stressed the idea of including pre-assessment items that tap into student interests. We encountered Ms. Harley, who had articulated one of her World War II understandings to be "Conflict leads to conflict." Consequently, she began her pre-assessment with the item "Describe a situation in which *one* conflict caused *another* conflict to arise. You can use an example from real life, literature, or media."

This question tunneled into one of the unit's understanding goals, in terms of how that understanding *related to students*. Student responses enabled Ms. Harley to provide clarifying examples that helped students see the connection between what they knew and cared about and what they were preparing to study.

Student interest surveys serve as another rich source of information about what potentially motivates students. In any beginning-of-the-year survey, it's a good idea to ask at least one question that will uncover what students are interested in outside of school. The list of survey questions in Figure 1.1 (p. 12) includes questions that tap into student interests and provide a starting point for forging connections. In particular, questions 2 ("What do you enjoy spending time on?") and 15 ("If you could choose from the following careers . . .") could unveil Vance's passion for art and acting.

Interest cards (see Figure 4.1, p. 88), a tool designed by Carol Ann Tomlinson (2005), are a streamlined method for more directly gathering information about student interests and for building connections between the subject and what students care about. The four-square format provides an at-a-glance view of each student's interests. The cards can also be cut into fours and easily sorted to create groups based on shared or varying areas of student interest.

Many teachers gather this kind of information as the basis for personal inter-actions with students. But we can also study that information to discover patterns among students' interests, which can help us strategically plan and direct instruction. Whether through formal questionnaires or via pre-assessment prompts, taking such an active step in discovering and studying what is important to our students can give us the power to make school "work" for them.

Strategies for Developing Hooks

Once you've discovered students' interests, how can you use them? Let's return to the suggestions offered by neuroscience: you can (1) present students with an achievable *challenge*, (2) illuminate an important *connection*, or (3) offer *novelty* in your perspective or approach. Below, we present several hook strategies, further explored in Part 2 of this chapter, that can be used to draw students into the content and to "shake it up," as our high school friend suggests at the chapter's opening. Each one provides teachers with a means of "zooming out" and finding important connections that can make a substantial difference in students' learning.

FIGURE 4.1

Interest Cards

Directions: I'll be a better teacher for you if I understand some of your interests. In each box below, record an interest of yours. Write briefly about how you are involved with that interest, and note any ways you can think of in which the interest might connect with this subject.

Name: _____ Interest #1: _____	Name: _____ Interest #2: _____
Experience with it?	Experience with it?
Connection with this subject?	Connection with this subject?
Name: _____ Interest #3: _____	Name: _____ Interest #4: _____
Experience with it?	Experience with it?
Connection with this subject?	Connection with this subject?

1. **Pose a challenge.** *Anticipation Guides* (pp. 97–98) present students with challenging statements to which they must "commit" in agreement or disagreement at the outset of the lesson or unit. Students' general beliefs and interests come into play as they take a stand on debatable ideas with multiple contexts. Students can then revisit and consider changing their assertions at the close of instruction. While usually associated with challenging issues from fiction and history, Anticipation Guides are equally powerful when used to uncover common misconceptions associated with science and math. *Tea Party* (p. 96) is another strategy that requires students to make hypotheses before engaging with content—but it presents students with "pieces" of a text on which to base their theories. Tea Party can be used just as effectively to preview informational texts as to introduce fictional works.

2. **Foster connections.** Perhaps the most versatile of hook strategies, *Concept Invitation* (pp. 92–93) allows teachers to link what is important in their *content* with what is important to their *students* in an active, flexible, and transferable manner. *Entry Points* (pp. 99–100)—a strategy developed by Howard Gardner (2006)—also fosters interest-driven connections to content and uses the avenues of *narration, logic, numbers, philosophy, aesthetics, experience,* and *collaboration*. Both strategies offer teachers a framework for considering conceptual connections rather than topical links, which are often narrow or dry.

3. **Introduce novelty.** *Shake 'n' Share* (pp. 94–95) is a strategy for engaging learners in quick conversation around different aspects of a topic or concept. Its novelty springs from both its structure (students face one another in rotating parallel lines) and its topics (unusual prompts around a concept). *Roundtable's* (pp. 101–102) novelty is also derived from its "rules of engagement." Essentially, it is a structure for fostering productive, interdependent group brainstorming around central concepts.

A Case in Point: Mr. Jacobs

Algebra teacher Mr. Jacobs knew that graphing could be dry for his students. He also knew that it didn't need to be, as graphs, at their most foundational level, are pictures of relationships. Among the learning goals for his upcoming unit, Mr. Jacobs had articulated the following understanding and skill goals:

- Students will *understand* that a graph communicates a relationship.
- Students will *be able to* use graphing to depict relationships among data points in real-world phenomena.

He could see these two learning goals' potential to connect students to content through their interests and preferences. He chose three different graphs and crafted five Entry Points for students to choose from to begin tunneling into the conceptual underpinnings of graphing. He wanted these activities to serve as (1) a review of what students already knew, understood, and were able to do in terms of graphing, and (2) a hook into the beauty of graphs as a reflection of relationships students encountered in their daily lives.

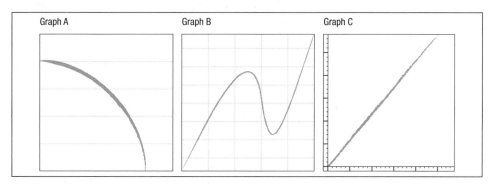

Source: Elisha Hiser, Harrisonburg High School, Harrisonburg, VA. Used with permission.

- *Narrational Entry Point.* Look at Graph B as an illustration of the relationship between time and size. Make up a story or a unique scenario to paint a picture of this change in size over time. Your story can be an imaginative tale of a mythical size-shifting creature, an account of a scientist's experiment with altering the size of people or things, or a more realistic description of an existing time-size relationship.
- *Quantitative Entry Point.* Examine sales-profit relationships for several companies (list provided). Find a company whose earnings over the past five years resemble the relationship portrayed in your choice of graph and explain what the company did to drive this sales-profit relationship.
- *Existential Entry Point.* Think about Graphs A and C as exhibiting relationships between time and wealth. Explain which graph's trajectory you think would lead to the greatest happiness in life (consider "rags-to-riches" stories, "lost-it-all" stories, accounts of how lottery winners' lives changed, and so on).

- *Aesthetic Entry Point.* Imagine yourself participating in your favorite recreational activity (e.g., a day of shopping, going to an amusement park, or attending a NASCAR race). Pick the graph that best represents the relationship between your time spent at the activity and the amount of enjoyment you experience. Explain how and why your enthusiasm waxes and wanes as depicted in the graph.
- *Experiential Entry Point.* Choose either Graph A or Graph B and devise a simulation to re-create the relationship depicted between any two variables. (Clear your choice with Mr. Jacobs.)

Earlier in the year, Mr. Jacobs had used the Pie Chart strategy (p. 20) to discern student interests and learned that some of his students were enthralled with NASCAR and that others were theme-park junkies. Some students made it clear that they loved fiction or were fascinated by science . . . but hated math. Once Mr. Jacobs knew what motivated his students, it wasn't hard to weave those interests into the Entry Point options.

Students selected their preferred Entry Point and then worked to complete the task either alone or with others who had selected the same option. Individuals and groups shared their final products with the full group, and the class discussed how well each product interpreted the relationships depicted in the graphs. Along the way, Mr. Jacobs filled in important learning gaps and discovered connections he could make use of during future instruction. Students were actively involved in the process, and the momentum Mr. Jacobs gained from the activity promised to propel him efficiently through the rest of the unit.

Part 2:

Tools and Strategies

Concept Invitation

What It Is:

A way to foster connections between students and content by introducing a central disciplinary concept via avenues tailored to student interests.

How It Works:

1. The teacher introduces a central disciplinary concept (e.g., *conflict, variable,* or *efficiency*) by asking students to (1) give their own definitions and then (2) compare them with established definitions.
2. The teacher provides several topic-area choices based on interests held by the class (e.g., sports or music) and asks each student to select one topic area.
3. Students work with classmates who chose the same topic area to investigate or discuss how the concept operates in their area of interest.
4. Students present their findings to the rest of the class (through a simulation or demonstration, for example).
5. The whole class revises or expands the original definition.
6. The teacher introduces a "big understanding" containing the central concept for the upcoming unit of study.
7. The class discusses if and how this principle holds true for their interest-based application.

What It's Good For:

- Inviting investigation into a concept that is central to a discipline.
- Building scaffolding in students' brains onto which they can hang future learning.
- Fostering connections among students who share similar interests (and may not know it).

Tips:

- Proactively discover interests via surveys (see Chapter 1) as well as through observation and conversation.
- If you teach multiple sections, use interests that are common to every class, although you may tailor choices to different class periods if you prefer.

Classroom Example:

English teacher Ms. McCaferty began her tiered investigation of the short story (with different groups of students reading stories of varying levels of complexity) with a Concept Invitation lesson on *interdependence*. After the class settled on a working definition of the term ("the parts or members of a group or system having to work together in order for that group or system to 'succeed' or be effective"), Ms. McCaferty offered students a choice of several topic areas to "study" that she drew from a beginning-of-the-year survey of student interests: dance, music, football, NASCAR, and video games. Students divided into interest-based groups and discussed the following questions:

1. How does interdependence play a role in your chosen "system"?
2. What does your system look like when it is efficiently exercising interdependence?
3. What does it look like when one part of the system stops doing its "job"?

Students planned and presented demonstrations addressing these questions. For example, the group that chose music carried out two musical performances: one that was cohesive, and one in which the percussion was thrown off.

Following the presentations, Ms. McCaferty introduced the big understanding for the unit: *A story is a system with interdependent parts, each of which affects the others.* The class examined this principle at work in "The Three Little Pigs" and compared it with the concept of interdependence they uncovered in their areas of interest. This exercise served to scaffold the rest of their investigation: students were able to rely on their understanding to discuss the interdependence of story elements manifested in whichever works they read.

Shake 'n' Share

What It Is:

A strategy for engaging learners in quick conversation around different aspects of a topic or concept.

How It Works:

1. Students stand in two lines facing one another so that each person has a partner.
2. The teacher displays or calls out a discussion prompt or question for each pair to discuss.
3. After a minute or so, the teacher calls time, and one line moves down so that each person has a new partner. (The person at the end walks, skips, or dances down the middle to the other end.)
4. The teacher gives a new prompt for discussion.
5. The process continues for four to eight turns.

What It's Good For:

- Introducing a unit, topic, or concept.
- Review (e.g., before a test or after a challenging lesson).
- Get-to-know-you or community-building time.
- Reinvigorating a topic that has grown tired or exhausted (and, in the process, reenergizing students!).
- Engaging *all* students in discussion and accountable talk.

Tips:

- Use a bell, music, or another loud noise to indicate the end of a turn.
- Have students shake hands with each new partner.
- Tell students who move down the middle to the other end to do something funny or silly as they walk—or to dance!
- When students return to their seats, give them a reflective prompt to think or write about that builds on or connects to what they discussed and heard in the Shake 'n' Share line (e.g., "What's the single most important piece of advice you could give someone about budgeting?").

Classroom Example:

Mr. Roberts and Ms. McIntire co-teach an American Studies class. They use Shake 'n' Share as an introduction to propaganda and its use of logically fallacious techniques by displaying in turn six different political campaign advertisements from different media. Students look at, watch, or listen to each ad and then discuss where they detect a particular technique in the ad:

1. Ad 1: "Do this because you'll feel left out if you don't."
2. Ad 2: "Do this and do it now, because time is running out."
3. Ad 3: "A true American would do this."
4. Ad 4: "If you do this, it will make you better than other people."
5. Ad 5: "Do this because experts say to do this."
6. Ad 6: "Do this or you'll be sorry."

Following the Shake 'n' Share line, the teachers provide the formal name for each technique (*bandwagon, time crunch, flag-waving, snob appeal, appeal to authority, appeal to fear*), as well as a formal definition of *propaganda*. Students work in groups of three to choose the ad from the activity that they believe is the "best worst" example of propaganda. Each group explains the reasoning behind its choice to the class.

Tea Party

What It Is:

A prereading strategy developed by Kylene Beers (2002) that invites students to engage with short excerpts of a text they'll be reading and make predictions about the text.

How It Works:

Each student receives a card with a different teacher-selected excerpt from the text the class will be reading (e.g., an article, a textbook chapter, a novel, or a play). The excerpt can be anything from a single word to a sentence or a paragraph. Students read their cards and imagine what the text might be about. Then they get up and "Tea Party" with other students (i.e., circulate and chat with different classmates, one at a time) for a few minutes, sharing cards and trying to piece together ideas about the subject or theme of the larger text. Students sit down when the teacher calls time and make one to three predictions in small groups or as a class.

What It's Good For:

Tea Party can be used as a prereading strategy with any text, but it is optimal for texts that are challenging or that at least some students might not be interested in reading. Consider using it when you announce the title or subject of a text and hear groans!

Tips:

- It's OK for more than one student to have the same excerpt—say, if there are eight excerpts for 24 students. When a student encounters a classmate with the same excerpt, the duo can still talk about their interpretations and predictions. Alternatively, form three smaller groups and have each group mingle in its own Tea Party.
- Cards can be distributed randomly or intentionally (purposely assigning certain students certain cards).
- Use a bell or other signal to indicate when students should move on to someone else.
- Ask students to hold up their card or a hand as they move around the room to indicate that they are in search of a partner.

Classroom Examples:

- Biology teacher Mr. Kent uses Tea Party with research-based articles from popular science journals and national media sources, especially when he knows the text or content will be challenging or unfamiliar to most students. He tries to give the most intriguing excerpts to students who aren't easily motivated by science topics.
- High school English teacher Ms. Cardella uses Tea Party before beginning the play *Oedipus Rex*. Each student receives a card with lines spoken by a particular character. After the Tea Party, she places students in groups with different characters represented. Each group plans and acts out a brief scene that is based on students' predictions about the play's plot.

Anticipation Guides

What It Is:

Originally developed for use with literary texts, this strategy can help students invest in what they are about to read or discuss by asking them to consider the central ideas as expressed in challenging, puzzling, or controversial statements.

How It Works:

1. Students are given a series of statements presenting either debatable conceptual statements or common misconceptions.
2. Students are instructed to make unqualified decisions about whether they agree or disagree with the statements before being introduced to a new text or new content.
3. The teacher polls the students, tallies results, and asks students to explain the reasoning behind their ratings before the class begins the text or lesson.
4. Students revisit their statements after the reading or the lesson and discuss whether and how their opinions or perceptions have changed.

What It's Good For:

- Discovering preconceptions regarding key concepts or themes behind a text or event.
- Uncovering misconceptions regarding scientific phenomena or mathematical principles.
- Inviting exploration, debate, and discussion.
- Eliciting student questions and fostering critical thinking.

Tips:

- Identify the major concepts, principles, themes, or dilemmas featured in the reading or lesson.
- Consider the beliefs or misconceptions students may have regarding those concepts.
- Craft three to eight debatable statements that challenge students' perceptions about those ideas.
- For humanities topics, phrase statements so that they apply to both content and students' lives.
- Optional: include prompts on the Anticipation Guide that invite students to explain and defend both their initial and their revised thoughts.

Classroom Example:

Miss Grant knew that her middle school science students usually came to her with some major misconceptions regarding lunar phases. This year, she decided to tackle those misconceptions head-on with an Anticipation Guide. Using NASA's presentation of common areas of confusion about the Moon (http://moon.nasa.gov/moonmisconceptions.cfm), she asked students to agree or disagree with six "sticky" questions that were central to her lesson. She made sure to include items that were true yet commonly confused (the first and last items in the table below), as well as items that were false.

Phases of the Moon: Agree or Disagree?		
Before Class		**After Class**
	The Moon is visible during both daytime and nighttime.	
	The Earth's shadow is responsible for the phases of the Moon.	
	Different countries see different phases of the Moon on the same day.	
	The same half of the Moon is in darkness all the time.	
	The Moon goes around the Earth in a single day.	
	The Moon has gravity.	

Entry Points

What It Is:

This strategy developed by Howard Gardner can be used to pique students' interest in a new unit of study or topic at a point of engagement. Gardner (2006) tells us to "think of the topic as a room with at least seven doorways into it" (p. 139) and design tasks accordingly.

How It Works:

The teacher uses the seven points of entry (or as few as two) to create differentiated learning tasks according to interest (Gardner, 2006):

1. *Narrational:* Use story or narrative structure to convey ideas or principles.
2. *Logical:* Use deductive reasoning, argument, or cause-and-effect relationships.
3. *Quantitative:* Provide data; examine numerical relationships and statistics.
4. *Existential:* Pose or think about big questions about life, death, and our place in the world; consider philosophy, meaning, or foundational theory.
5. *Aesthetic:* Emphasize sensory or surface features; activate aesthetic sensitivities.
6. *Experiential:* Use a hands-on approach, dealing directly with materials (physically or virtually), simulations, and personal explanations.
7. *Collaborative:* Use discussions, debates, and role-plays; require students to function as an interdependent team.

Students choose a task to complete (usually within a class period) alone or with a partner and share their work in small groups or with the whole class.

What It's Good For:

- Hooking students into content or topics that typically lack intrinsic appeal for adolescents.
- Offering "tastes" or "previews" of lesson activities that all students will do throughout the unit.
- Designing "Jigsawed" tasks or brief small-group discussion prompts.

Tips:

- Because the primary goal is to motivate students, Entry Point tasks need not all be aligned with the same learning goals. Having students share their work exposes them to a variety of Entry Points and gives them a broad initial perspective of the unit topic(s).
- You can purposefully assign various Entry Points to certain students, have students come up with their own Entry Points, or invite students to choose from limited options.
- Entry Points is also a useful framework for planning learning activities or assessments that will be used throughout the unit, either as differentiated tasks or as tasks that all students will complete.

Classroom Example:

Ms. Howell liked to help her high school consumer science students see the practical applications of their unit on personal finances, so she began the unit by asking students to investigate connections through their chosen Entry Point. Following their collaborative inquiries, groups presented their findings to spark a whole-class discussion.

- *Narrational*: Watch the excerpt from *Broke* (from ESPN's 30 for 30 documentary series), in which professional athletes relate their stories of gaining and then losing large amounts of money. What are the take-away messages for the everyday person? (Alternative: investigate stories of lottery winners.)

- *Quantitative*: Examine tables, charts, and graphs that show a young college student's income and expenses over a period of six months. What patterns do you see? Overall, is this person using money wisely or foolishly? Why do you say so?

- *Existential*: Engage in partner or small-group discussion of "big questions" about money: what is money? What can it do? What can't it do? Is it "the root of all evil"? The key to a long and happy life?

- *Aesthetic:* Walk through demos of the bookmarked online personal finance management tools. Be ready to explain which one you think might be most appealing to adolescents. Consider the ease of use and interface, in addition to other criteria you think are important.

- *Experiential:* Read the scenario provided about a high school student who has just gotten her first paid job and is forming a plan for how to use the money from each paycheck. Consider her goals, situation, and income to give her advice.

Roundtable

What It Is:

Originally designed by Kagan (2008) as a cooperative-learning review strategy, Roundtable can be adapted to use as a conceptual hook to whet students' appetite for what they are about to study.

How It Works:

1. Students work in groups of four, with members of each group facing one another in a square or circle.
2. Each group gets *one* piece of paper, and each group member gets a different-colored pen or pencil to provide individual accountability. Group members write their names at the top of the paper in their unique colors.
3. The teacher provides a concept-based prompt—for example, "List ways in which *balance* allows us to survive and thrive in life, school, work, art, technology, sports, relationships, and so on. Give both concrete and symbolic examples."
4. One group member starts by writing down an idea and then passes the paper clockwise to the next student.
5. This process continues around the circle until the teacher calls time.
6. There is no talking during Roundtable, but group members may point to their notes or gesture or mime to one another.
7. When the teacher calls time, each group first reviews its own answers and then passes its sheet to another group, which will evaluate and "code" the first group's answers:
   — Mark "!" next to new ideas or ideas your group didn't think of.
   — Mark "X" next to ideas your group included on its own sheet.
   — Mark "?" next to ideas your group members don't understand or agree with.
   — Circle the most important example, point, or question included on this sheet.
   — At the bottom, write down the most important idea that seems to be missing.
8. The groups pass the papers back to their owners, and the codes drive a full-class discussion.

What It's Good For:

- Activating prior knowledge before introducing new material, ideas, or concepts.
- Checking the full group's grasp of or questions about the material before moving on to another topic.
- Reviewing factual material before a test or quiz.

Tips:

- When used as a hook, ideal Roundtable prompts include broad concepts (e.g., *change, power, system*) or pairs of concepts (e.g., *structure and function, supply/demand, victim/victor*). Students can write examples of these concepts as they have seen them in life, literature, media, or any other context (see Figure 2.1, p. 36).
- When used as a transition or review, prompts can be cumulative and content-based.

Classroom Example:

To encourage her high school math students to think conceptually, Ms. Monk did a Roundtable exercise in which small groups of students listed *procedures* that people, including themselves, used in their daily or work lives (e.g., unlocking lockers, executing strength-training regimens, conducting surgeries). After the Roundtable was complete, the class discussed the difference between just following steps and knowing the reasons behind the steps—and the importance of the latter.

5

Providing Interactive Learning Experiences

Part 1:

How Do I Help Students Make Sense of It?

You've set the learning destination by establishing clear and robust learning goals. You've determined where students are in relationship to that destination by administering and analyzing a pre-assessment. And you have used insights gleaned from the pre-assessment, students' lives, and the conceptual underpinnings of the content to get students ready—even excited—to take the journey. Now, how do you begin to guide students in their travels?

Surprisingly, the answer is not necessarily "Put them into differentiated groups." In a differentiated classroom, not every moment should be differentiated. Students need common learning experiences and whole-class instruction. They need a healthy balance of times when they come together around shared content and tasks and times when they work individually, with partners, or in groups, using the same processes or different methods to produce similar or unique products or performances. To revisit our road trip metaphor, students can travel together for a while before diverging on different routes—and then meet up again farther down the interstate.

Regardless of whether learning experiences are *differentiated*, they should be *interactive*. In human relationships, the more we interact with people, the more we get to know them. Learning follows the same principle: we can learn only so much through observation. To truly understand content, we must interact both with the content and with one another regarding the content (Hattie, 2012). These interactions should be "visible" enough that the teacher can both evaluate and facilitate student progress (Bransford et al., 2000).

In this chapter, we examine potential obstacles to interactive instruction and offer practical strategies to overcome those obstacles. Detailed directions for each strategy are outlined in Part 2, but we provide applications and adaptations throughout Part 1. Although featured strategies are designed with the primary goal of encouraging academic discourse at the whole-class level, a few can also be used as tools for differentiating instruction to address varying learner needs.

Obstacles to Interactive Learning

Driving each obstacle discussed in the following sections is the ever-present specter of time slipping away. Middle and high school teachers are often haunted by a sense of urgency that leads them to succumb to the temptation to "cover" curriculum in the fastest ways possible—usually by transmitting information to students with the expectation that they will take it in and give it right back. This method may get us through the material by the end of the semester or year—thereby covering *ourselves*—but unless *students* have had enough time to acquire, make sense of, and transfer the material, they won't be able to produce evidence of learning. It is important to note that the strategies proposed in this chapter may initially take more time to implement than would simply covering the content. The good news is that the investment of time is worth it, as students will actually walk away from the learning experiences understanding and retaining the material, allowing the teacher to streamline instruction and spend less time on review (Guskey, 2007/2008).

Obstacle #1: Limited Attention Spans

Anyone who has spent even a few hours with adolescents knows that their attention spans are limited. Handheld devices give students more opportunities to engage their focus elsewhere when their immediate environment has disengaged them, or when social opportunities call (or chat, text, or tweet).

Recent research (Moore, 2008) suggests that attention spans for *all* age groups are shrinking to as low as five minutes or less. Consider the key findings from Bunce, Flens, and Neiles's (2010) study of university students' attention to instruction during lecture courses ranging in duration from 50 to 90 minutes:

- Student engagement alternated between attention and nonattention throughout lectures, with the attention periods ranging between 30 seconds and 10 minutes.
- The alternating pattern of attention and nonattention happened in shorter and shorter cycles as lectures proceeded (i.e., student attention faded in and out more frequently as lectures went on).
- Toward the end of lectures, the average attention span was only two minutes.
- When the instructor used alternative active instructional strategies (e.g., questions, demonstrations, clicker responses), students reported a less drastic decline in attention than they reported during straight lecture.
- Student attention increased during lecture portions that immediately followed the alternative teaching strategies.

These findings confirm the need for teachers to slow down and give students the opportunity to interact with the content and one another. In short, if we ignore the limits of students' attention spans, the students may ignore us!

How to Work Around Short Attention Spans

Narrated Wait Time: Because of the waxing and waning nature of attention, some students may need to "reset" their brains to response mode. Other students may simply need more time to process information and derive a conclusion. Still others need time to reexamine their first assumptions and think more deeply about the content. Teachers can meet all three of these needs by providing students with *wait time*—that is, by not accepting answers immediately and instead giving students time to consider their responses. Doug Lemov (2012, pp. 235–238) suggests that *narrated* wait time can be even more effective in guiding student thinking. This means that during wait time, teachers interject with prompts such as the following:

- *Validating extended thought:* "This is hard stuff. Take your time. No hands for 10 seconds."
- *Suggesting assistive behaviors:* "How can you connect your answer to what we were just discussing?"
- *Encouraging recording of thoughts:* "This is tricky, so questions are good. Jot them down while you're thinking."
- *Encouraging intellectual risk taking:* "Take a chance; we learn by making mistakes," or "I don't expect perfection, but I do expect effort."
- *Encouraging use of evidence in answers:* "Can you prove your answer? How would you defend it?"

By facilitating active thinking during wait time, teachers can encourage students to push beyond their first impressions while giving them an appropriate amount of time to process high-level questions. A logical companion to wait time is Kagan's (2008) Think-Pair-Share strategy: having students form pairs to compare answers, debate findings, or check solutions. Following peer huddles, the teacher should be able to call on any student, regardless of whether his or her hand is raised, with the expectation that the student will have something worthwhile to share. This approach keeps the entire class on its toes, increasing attention and capitalizing on the opportunity for students to hear their peers' perspectives on the questions posed.

Obstacle #2: Dependence on Traditional Lecture

In many ways, traditional forms of lecture are the opposite of interactive (and differentiated) instruction. There are good lectures and bad lectures, of course, but even the best lectures in middle and high school usually involve the teacher standing in front of the classroom, often with a PowerPoint presentation, telling students about a topic or process through narrative, models, facts, or demonstration. There are few, if any, opportunities for formative assessment, differentiation, or discussion.

Time limits, pressure to cover material, and misconceptions about learners' attention spans all likely contribute to teacher dependence on traditional lecture. Another influence is the looming prospect of college instruction, which many teachers experienced as lecture-based courses when they were students. The belief that "lecture works" as a tried-and-true method can prevent some teachers from experimenting with more interactive approaches.

Interestingly enough, results of a recent meta-analysis (Freeman et al., 2014) of student performance in undergraduate STEM classes push back on this assumption. Across classes in 225 studies, students learned more in courses that used such active learning strategies as group work, peer instruction, and student response systems than did students in comparable courses that relied on traditional lecture. Students in traditional lecture-based classes were also one and one-half times more likely to fail the course than were students in the active learning courses.

How to Fortify the Traditional Lecture

In truth, the lecture is well suited for certain situations. Robert Talbert (2012) suggests that the lecture is a reasonable tool for an expert to model thought processes, share cognitive structures, give context, and tell stories. In each of these cases, however, the lecture must be structured in a manner that facilitates learning. Based on what we know about attention span, it is unacceptable to simply talk for extended periods without giving students time to process information, regardless of the lecture's purpose.

The following three strategies can keep teachers from falling prey to what Grant Wiggins (2014b) calls "self-deception and the lecturer." Because a lecturer typically receives little feedback about how well learning is taking root in students' brains, it is easy for him or her to assume that the lecture is working when it's not. By incorporating processing time (and methods to monitor that processing) into their lectures, teachers will be better equipped to determine whether they are connecting with students.

- **Interactive Lecture:** Developed by Silver and Perini (2010), the Interactive Lecture provides a framework for structuring lectures so that students actively process material during content delivery to build memory and deepen comprehension. This strategy, discussed in more detail on pages 116–117, (1) takes short attention spans into account, (2) uses graphic organizers to help students record information in a format that illustrates relationships, and (3) allows time for students to actively process material from the lecture. All three components are consistent with research (Hattie, 2012; Willis,

2006) showing that when we combine words with other media in a way that involves students, students stand a better chance of grasping and retaining that content. The Interactive Lecture can be used in tandem with other multimodal techniques, such as Narrated Wait Time (discussed above) and Logographic Cues (pp. 118–119), a method that incorporates visual symbols or codes to help students process what they read or hear.

- **Interview Model:** Designed to support student thinking, speaking, and listening, this strategy harnesses the power of peer collaboration while providing opportunities for movement and extended thinking. The teacher can use the questions posed on the interview sheet to punctuate the lecture at strategic points to accommodate the adolescent attention span, encourage critical thinking, and provide evidence of student processing to guide the subsequent portions of the lecture.
- **Quartet Quiz:** This technique, outlined in detail on pages 122–123, provides the teacher with a method for checking the understanding of the entire class while generating small- and large-group processing discussions. Implementing the Quartet Quiz at a pivotal point during the lecture (e.g., after the introduction of a complex process) can position the teacher to be able to address misconceptions and to use student-generated questions to drive the remainder of the lecture.

Obstacle #3: Unstructured Whole-Class Discussion

You may say, "But I don't lecture; we *discuss*." Whole-class discussion is indeed a hopeful alternative to the lecture and holds many advantages. Healthy classroom discussions help students become more empathetic and respectful listeners, encourage them to examine ideas critically, and can develop their capacity to create and communicate meaning (Brookfield & Preskill, 1999). Like a successful lecture, however, an effective whole-class discussion requires structure and planning. Without careful preparation, a class discussion can devolve into a small-group conversation between the teacher and a few select students—an experience that is neither interactive nor engaging for the class and may erode rather than foster a sense of community and respect. Further, unstructured class discussions frequently fall victim to "the tangent," leading to more time spent on content that Wiggins and McTighe (2005) describe as "nice to know" than on what is essential. For a class discussion to fulfill its promise, it must

1. Be planned in advance.
2. Incorporate higher-order thinking questions aligned to learning goals.
3. Require active participation from all students—both in the whole group and in smaller-group settings.

4. Provide a community of safety and inquiry in which making mistakes is part of the process.

How to Structure Whole-Class Discussions

Several strategies outlined in Part 2 of this chapter offer structures for planning whole-class discussions that adhere to the criteria above.

- **Analytical Role Cards** (pp. 126–129): This strategy allows students to use material they've encountered in a different context (e.g., a homework assignment or an assigned reading) as fodder for discussion, questioning, and debate.
- **Wagon Wheels** (pp. 130–131): This strategy enables the teacher to plan discussion questions in advance and then place the ownership for their exploration in the hands of the students. Opportunities for students to receive feedback on their thinking are built into the strategy.
- **Debate Team Carousel** (pp. 132–134) and **Structured Academic Controversy** (pp. 135–136): Both of these strategies are designed to help students discuss content through the art of argument. They require students to examine a question from multiple perspectives and draw on pertinent evidence for support.
- **ThinkDots** (pp. 137–140) is a flexible strategy that can be used to process previous learning or to explore new ideas. The teacher designs ThinkDots prompts to guide small-group discussion of homework or a text. ThinkDots prompts can also be used to encourage exploration of a concept, a topic, an idea, or an issue from multiple perspectives.
- **Jigsaw** (pp. 141–144) provides a method to "divide and conquer" the coverage of large amounts of content in a focused, interdependent, and inquiry-driven manner. Each student becomes an expert on one piece of a "puzzle" (e.g., an issue, a question, a method, or a perspective) and shares what he or she learns with other students who studied different puzzle pieces.

By using active discussion strategies like these, teachers can ensure that the entire class engages with the material. No longer can a few students carry the discussion on their own; rather, every student must contribute to make the discourse successful. With the teacher as an expert facilitator on the periphery rather than as the leader in the front of the pack, the locus of learning is with the students. Although teachers must initially work harder to construct these learning experiences ahead of time, they are freed up to engage with students during class, increasing their instructional reach to many more learners.

Obstacle #4: Reliance on Recall Questions

Every strategy discussed thus far relies on the quality of the questions posed within them. By their nature, questions can invite students to interact with content and with one another, both face-to-face and via technology. Although most teachers regularly use questions instructionally, the *quality* of those questions may not foster engagement or elicit high-level thinking. Studies of classroom discourse (e.g., Hattie, 2012; Marzano, Pickering, & Pollock, 2001) reveal that the majority of questions asked in a typical classroom require students simply to recall information, and to do so quickly with little feedback. When recall questions are the focus of any strategy, the potential for that strategy to increase student learning plummets.

How to Design Good Questions

There are numerous methods for organizing and classifying questions, but perhaps the most familiar is Bloom's taxonomy (updated by Anderson and Krathwohl in 2001), which aims to encourage varied levels or types of thinking. Bloom's thinking domains range from remembering to creating:

- Remembering: Recalling or recognizing information. Questions ask students to *define, name, recall, repeat,* or *state.*
- Understanding: Comprehending or grasping prior learning. Questions ask students to *describe, discuss, explain, paraphrase,* or *summarize.*
- Applying: Using information to solve a problem or complete a task. Questions ask students to *demonstrate, illustrate, interpret, solve,* or *use.*
- Analyzing: Breaking down material, examining organizational structure, finding patterns, or relating ideas. Questions ask students to *categorize, compare, contrast, discriminate,* or *distinguish.*
- Evaluating: Appraising or critiquing based on specific standards or criteria. Questions ask students to *appraise, defend, judge, justify,* or *support.*
- Creating: Combining and integrating ideas and information into new schematics, products, plans, patterns, or structures. Questions ask students to *construct, design, develop, formulate,* or *propose.*

It is important to note that Bloom did not intend for the taxonomy to dictate the *order* in which these kinds of thinking should occur (Bransford et al., 2000). Unfortunately, many teachers believe that students must *remember* before they can accomplish anything else and therefore design the majority of instructional questions at the memory and comprehension levels. Some teachers have also been taught that Bloom's taxonomy is a framework for differentiating questions and end up giving some students primarily recall-level questions and other students higher-order questions.

Both of these misapprehensions contradict Bloom's desire to ensure that *all* students wrestle with a *variety* of cognitive demands. He recognized that only in grappling with material would students truly comprehend it and that, as Ritchhart, Church, and Morrison (2011) put it, "Understanding is not a *precursor* to application, analysis, evaluating, and creating but a *result* of it" (p. 7, emphasis added).

Teachers can avoid misusing Bloom's taxonomy—or any of the Questioning Frameworks featured in Part 2 of this chapter—by keeping in mind the following guiding principles:

1. One level of thinking is not a barrier to the next; therefore, questions need not always build from "lowest" to "highest."
2. Use a variety of question types throughout the course of a lesson; avoid over-reliance on any one level.
3. To ensure a variety of questions—especially higher-order questions—plan questions in advance. Without advance planning, lessons will most likely devolve into a battery of recall-level questions, which are the easiest to generate on the fly. The time spent planning questions in advance will increase the level of cognitive discourse in the classroom, involving all students in worthwhile discussion and exploration of content.

There are three Questioning Frameworks presented in Part 2 of this chapter (pp. 145–149):

1. Inferential and Analytical Questions (Dean, Hubbell, Pitler, & Stone, 2012).
2. Depth of Knowledge (DOK) (Webb, Alt, Ely, & Vesperman, 2005).
3. Six Facets of Understanding (Wiggins & McTighe, 2005).

Each is useful for helping teachers plan questions to use in lectures, discussions, investigations, tasks, or assessments. Each one provides a different lens through which to structure questions that ensure students apply, analyze, evaluate, and create throughout the course of a lesson. Teachers may feel more comfortable using one framework over the others, or they may prefer to draw from all three. Regardless of the framework used, good questions should form the heart of classroom instruction.

If we want classroom questioning and discussion to facilitate learning, the presentation of new content must build in time for students to think, discuss, debate, and practice—not just regurgitate what they heard. The teacher must spend as much time *listening* as he or she does *talking* (Hattie, 2012). Such a shift requires thoughtful planning and implementation of classroom questioning and prompting—a practice that can raise the levels of participation and achievement among all students (Marzano et al., 2001).

Using Strategies for Interactivity Versus Differentiation

In our presentation of strategies in this chapter, we have focused on increasing the quality of whole-class learning and teaching. From strengthening the interactivity of a lecture to facilitating a discussion using Structured Academic Controversy to ratcheting up the level of questioning, each has the potential to improve both instruction and student learning.

It is important to note that although these strategies may differ from the normal classroom fare, none is a strategy for differentiation unless the teacher uses it as such. For a task to be differentiated, some aspect of the content, process, or product must be adjusted for specific learner readiness, interest, or learning profile needs. Differentiated tasks aren't just "different"; they are aligned with and lead all students toward the same high-level learning goals.

Several strategies we have discussed lend themselves particularly well to differentiation, including Analytical Role Cards, Debate Team Carousel, Structured Academic Controversy, ThinkDots, and Jigsaw. In the "Tips" sections of the strategy descriptions in Part 2, we give suggestions for how to use these strategies to better meet the wide range of student needs present in most middle and high school classrooms.

A Case in Point: Mr. Mason

As Mr. Mason prepared for his upcoming unit on homeostasis and feedback mechanisms, he reflected on the results of the pre-assessment he had given. Students had confused the concepts associated with "positive" and "negative" feedback. This told Mr. Mason that he would need to (1) spend more time than he had initially planned on these concepts, and (2) construct a particularly interactive lesson to make sure that students had corrected their misconceptions. To achieve this, he devised the following lesson plan:

1. Hook students by introducing them to feedback mechanisms at work in video games and pose the following question: "How would you distinguish between *positive* and *negative* feedback in this situation?" (DOK Level 1).

2. Once students have a rough idea of the difference, ask them to explore it further via the system of their choice: social systems, climate change, or the stock market. Provide websites and video clips for students to consult as they investigate two questions: "How would you compare the feedback systems in video games with those in your chosen system?" (DOK Level 3), and "Using what you've learned, how would you define *positive* and *negative feedback*? Revise your original definition to include basic processes and key distinguishing characteristics from your research" (DOK Level 4). Students record these definitions in a graphic organizer.

3. Ask students to explain those definitions and comparisons throughout an Interactive Lecture using a digital simulation to model the body's feedback response to heat. Throughout the course of this discussion, students engage in Think-Pair-Share huddles to predict each step in the feedback process (DOK Level 2). They also infuse connections to their specialized area of study and record them in their graphic organizers. In addition, students develop Logographic Cues for key terms associated with the lesson's focus (e.g., *homeostasis, receptor/detector, stimulus, integrator,* and *effector*).

4. Following the discussion and demonstration, students get back into their groups of three—now their "home groups"—to extend their learning via a Jigsaw investigation. Each group member chooses one of the following conditions to study in detail: body temperature (in response to extreme cold), glucose, or pH. Working with classmates from other home groups who chose the same condition, these newly formed "expert groups" gather information to complete a cycle diagram demonstrating how the body uses feedback mechanisms to achieve homeostasis. [*Mr. Mason's note to self: during this portion of the lesson, circulate and guide discussions, answer questions, and intervene when misconceptions occur. This guidance will be necessary for students to move on to the next phase.*]

5. Students return to their home groups to share their findings and make sense of the connections among their systems.

6. Each student completes an exit card independently to demonstrate his or her grasp of the lesson's objectives.

Steps 5–6 will provide evidence of what students need in order to be able to move on to the next lesson. The exit cards should reveal students' grasp of the material and whether differentiation will be needed before moving on to the lab.

In this lesson, Mr. Mason was able to meet his goal of serving as a classroom coach dedicated to facilitating the inquiry process and supporting students as they strived to reach their goals—scientific, academic, and personal. His questions, graphic organizers, and interactive grouping configurations proved to be vital tools in this pursuit.

Part 2:

Tools and Strategies

Select forms and templates can be downloaded at http://www.ascd.org/ASCD/pdf/books/Doubet2015forms.pdf. Use the password "Doubet2015115008" to unlock the PDF.

Interactive Lecture

What It Is:

A framework for structuring lectures so that students actively process material during content delivery to build memory and deepen comprehension.

How It Works:

The teacher plans the lecture with four necessary components:

1. Connect students to learning goals with a hook (see Chapter 4 for examples).
2. Present information in manageable "chunks," using graphic organizers for students to record what they are learning. Effective visual organizers require students to think about relationships among aspects of the content rather than simply record verbatim or paraphrased notes. Types of effective graphic organizers include (but are not limited to)
   — *Matrix:* A table with rows and columns. Students record connections, comparisons, or contrasts among items in the rows and columns when those items intersect.
   — *Cause-effect:* Usually a series of boxes with arrows that demonstrate the relationships among the items listed in the boxes; can include chain reactions or more simplistic one-to-one relationships.
   — *Flowchart:* Captures steps in a process or cycle, the steps' connections to one another, and what happens at critical decision or hinge points in the process or cycle (e.g., when there are multiple possible outcomes).
3. Provide opportunities for students to process information during the lecture, giving particular attention to questioning and to multiple modes and representations of content. Refer to Part 1 of this chapter for guidance in developing questions to ask throughout the lecture.
4. Engage students in reflection and application to use what they learned in a new context. Use the strategies outlined in the remainder of this chapter to help students process what they have encountered during the lecture.

What It's Good For:

Increasing student involvement with and retention of material from lectures or videos, whether delivered in a face-to-face or "flipped" fashion.

Tip:

Examples and templates for graphic organizers are included in *The Interactive Lecture* (Silver & Perini, 2010) and in *A Handbook for Classroom Instruction That Works* (Pitler & Stone, 2012).

Classroom Example:

As Mr. Butler prepared his lecture on the Boston Tea Party, he devised a matrix-style graphic organizer to help students understand the conflict from the perspectives of (1) colonists who supported it, (2) colonists who condemned it, and (3) the British by considering political, geographical, and cultural factors. He planned analytical, Webb's DOK Level 3 questions that prompted students to consider the biased portrayal of the Sons of Liberty in primary sources (visual and written), as well as the effect perspective has on distinguishing *revolution* and *rebellion*. For the wrap-up activity, which took the form of Structured Academic Controversy, students debated the following: *The Boston Tea Party was a justified and defensible response.*

Logographic Cues

What It Is:

A strategy developed by Kylene Beers (2002) in which students come up with visual symbols, or *logographs,* to serve as signposts in their reading that alert them to important aspects of the text or narrative.

How It Works:

1. The teacher develops a series of ideas for students to note as they read (e.g., literary elements, literary devices, elements of historical analysis and interpretation).
2. Students devise a visual code or symbol to represent each of these ideas.
3. As they read, students indicate the targeted ideas by jotting down the Logographic Cues in the margin of their text, on sticky notes, using the edit function of a PDF, or in some other way.

What It's Good For:

- Logographs help "cue" student attention during reading.
- Logographs help students reflect on important content after reading.
- Codes can direct students to important text to share during class discussions.
- Although it's best for students to develop their own codes, some codes can be developed by the class and used to flag important content in the teacher's lecture notes or in graphic organizers.

Tips:

- Develop long-term cues to use for concepts that reappear throughout the year or for ideas you want students to be in the habit of exploring. (See Logographic Cue Examples, page 119.)
- Encourage students to record logographs on bookmarks for easy access during coding.
- *For differentiation:* Using varied levels of text but the same cues allows for full-group discussion.

Classroom Example:

Ms. Varsha wanted her 9th grade biology students to examine everything they read—the textbook, informational texts, websites, and so on—through the lens of the seven cross-cutting concepts outlined by the Next Generation Science Standards. During the first nine weeks, students discussed the meaning and implications of those concepts and developed Logographic Cues for each:

- Patterns: ❖
- Cause and effect: √
- Scale, proportion, and quantity: ❬ ❭
- Systems and system models: ↺
- Energy and matter: ✳

- Structure and function: ⊙
- Stability and change: ▲

Ms. Varsha began with a few concepts and associated cues and added more as the class progressed through the quarter. The cues enabled students to (1) quickly note the concepts as they read and (2) readily weave concepts into discussions and investigations. Throughout the quarter, they compiled the Logographic Cues they collectively developed on a poster, but students were also encouraged to develop their own cues and record them in their notebooks.

Logographic Cue Examples

General cues for text interaction include
- ✔ = *I knew that!*
- ★ = *Important information/statistic/quote.*
- ? = *Debatable or questionable idea.*
- ! = *Interesting . . . I want to explore this further.*

Teachers can also allow students to create their own Logographic Cues to indicate all kinds of elements, such as the 4 *C*s, different types of imagery, and standards requirements.

The 4 *C*s:
In their book *Making Thinking Visible*, Ritchhart, Church, and Morrison (2011) suggest the following four *C* prompts to help students interact with "meaty" nonfiction texts:
- ___ = *Connections*: What connections do you draw between the text and your own life or learning?
- ___ = *Challenge*: What ideas, positions, or assumptions from the text do you want to challenge or argue against?
- ___ = *Concepts*: What key concepts or ideas from the text do you think are important and worth holding on to?
- ___ = *Changes*: What changes in attitudes, thinking, or action—either for you or for others—are suggested or reflected by the text?

Imagery:
- ___ = *Sight*: Words that draw pictures in your mind—that help you *see* things.
- ___ = *Sound*: Words that portray things you can *hear.*
- ___ = *Smell*: Words that portray or remind you of *scents.*
- ___ = *Taste*: Words that depict *flavors, textures,* or *temperatures* in your mouth.
- ___ = *Touch*: Words that communicate *textures, temperatures,* or *pressure* on your skin.

Historical Thinking Standard 3 (Historical Analysis and Interpretation) (Crabtree & Nash, 1996):
- ___ = *Values at play!* Similarities and differences of values among individuals or groups.
- ___ = *Perspective alert!* Perspective contributing to motives, beliefs, interests, hopes, or fears.
- ___ = *Unsupported expression of opinion.*
- ___ = *Historical evidence.*
- ___ = *Historical inevitability.* Challenge the assumption that this event was unavoidable.
- ___ = *New* information, voice, or interpretation.
- ___ = Potential *influence of past decision* on present or future (*limitation*).
- ___ = Potential *influence of past decision* on present or future (*possibility*).

Interview Model

What It Is:

Adapted from a cooperative learning strategy designed by Kagan (2008), this model can be restructured to support student thinking, speaking, and listening while fostering peer collaboration. It also provides opportunities for movement and interaction.

How It Works:

1. Students are given a prompt (e.g., a question, an interesting quote, or a thought-provoking work of art) and asked to think, silently recording their responses in the appropriate cell of the graphic organizer (see Classroom Example below).
2. Each student gets up and moves around the room to find a partner. Partners interview each other, and each records his or her partner's new ideas in the second column of the organizer.
3. The teacher leads a brief discussion of ideas developed during the think and interview phases, clearing up misconceptions, introducing new points, and providing clarifying examples.
4. Students individually and silently reflect on the prompt, recording new ideas from the class discussion and their revised thinking on the prompt in the third column of the organizer.
5. Students repeat steps 1–4 in response to new prompts (or questions or visuals), finding a new partner for each prompt until all prompts have been addressed.
6. Students complete the last cell (or two cells) of the graphic organizer as an "exit card."

What It's Good For:

- Focusing student thinking (silence during think phase, movement to find new partners, structured listening during interviews).
- Fostering productive peer conversations about content.
- Guiding classroom discussions while providing the teacher with information about how the class is processing content both during and after instruction.

Tips:

- Be sure to *plan* the whole-group discussion phase that precedes the reflection period. This might include specific or illustrative examples, specific points of clarification, or new questions.
- Students can reflect on each question immediately after an interview round, or after all interview rounds.

Classroom Example:

In Ms. Queen's high school art class, students are studying the self-portraits of famous artists before creating self-portraits of their own. Ms. Queen wants students to notice how subtle detail and techniques affect the overall portrayal of a subject, so she uses the Interview Model to facilitate an active examination and discussion of four of van Gogh's 1887 "straw hat" self-portraits. She leads the class discussion before each *reflect* step to gauge what students have noticed and what she needs to draw attention to.

Prompt (From teacher)	Think (Record your thoughts)	Interview (Record your partner's differing thoughts)	Reflect (Record new/revised ideas or questions)
Note similarities/differences among the hats in each painting.			
Note similarities/differences among the backgrounds in each painting.			
Note similarities/differences among the facial features in each painting.			
Note similarities/differences among the techniques used in each painting.			
Exit Question: The painting that appeals most to me is _____ because:		**Exit Question:** One technique I'll use in my own self-portrait is _____ because:	

Quartet Quiz

What It Is:

A technique developed by Carol Ann Tomlinson to check the understanding of the entire class while generating small- and large-group processing discussions and situating the teacher to address questions and misconceptions.

How It Works:

1. The teacher poses a question about content from a lecture, video, text, or other medium.
2. Students individually prepare their responses to the question.
3. Students meet in quads to check and share their answers ("we know" statements) and develop questions about the content ("we wonder" statements).
4. The "summarizer" from each group reports "we know" and "we wonder" statements.
5. The teacher records student answers for the "we know" responses on the board, document camera, or other display, correcting misconceptions as they arise. The teacher continues rotating from group to group until all "we knows" have been recorded.
6. The teacher records student answers for the "we wonder" statements, placing them next to any "we know" items to which they might relate (if possible; there may be no relationship, and that's OK). The teacher continues rotating from group to group until all "we wonders" have been recorded.
7. The class discusses the "we wonder" statements, and the teacher ensures all questions are answered.
8. The class develops closure/clarification/summary statements.
9. The teacher can follow up with an exit question regarding how students' thinking has progressed since step 2, if desired.

What It's Good For:

- Checking in to see how students are grasping the lecture, video, text, or other content source.
- "Catching" and redirecting misconceptions.
- Picking up from a discussion begun the previous class period.
- Structuring the analysis of complex content.

Tips:

- Be sure to use an open-ended quiz question that is likely to yield multiple responses that can be classified as "we know" statements. *What are the three branches of government?* is not a good Quartet Quiz question, whereas *What are the benefits of having a system of checks and balances?* is.
- As an additional step, quartets can pass their synthesized we know/we wonder chart to another group for feedback. Groups can indicate agreement, pose and answer questions, or make suggestions.

Classroom Example:

Ms. Koh gave her students a Quartet Quiz after a series of lessons on photosynthesis. She posed two questions: (1) *What ideas were clear from the readings on photosynthesis?* and (2) *What questions remain?* Students synthesized their responses in their quartets in the same Google Docs document (see below), which Ms. Koh displayed as groups were working.

Photosynthesis

We Know	We Wonder
1. Uses light energy, CO_2, and H_2O. 2. Produces oxygen and carbohydrates in plants. 3. Occurs only in the leaves of plants (not stems) because of chloroplasts. 4. Steps 1–3 occur in light reactions. 5. Dark reactions need by-products from light reaction but don't need light.	• Are photons and light energy the same? • How does this result in growth in plants? • Are plants/photosynthesis the source of all of our oxygen? • Does ATP play a role in light reactions or dark reactions? • What exactly is a dark reaction?

Face to Face

What It Is:

A strategy for reviewing homework in an interactive and efficient manner.

How It Works:

1. Students arrange their desks so that two students can sit across from each other and have a conversation. In most classrooms, this results in two parallel rows of desks with chairs on either side of both rows.
2. Students sit at their desks facing their partners.
3. The teacher displays discussion prompts or questions that ask students to evaluate answers on their homework, check for misconceptions, find patterns, and so on.
4. After the pairs finish discussing each prompt, the teacher calls time, and one row of students moves down one desk so that each student has a new partner.
5. The teacher posts a new prompt for discussion.
6. The process continues for three to five turns.

What It's Good For:

- Encouraging students to complete their homework.
- Checking problems, questions, or readings completed for homework.
- Engaging *all* students in discussion or accountable talk.

Tips:

- Students must display their homework (or notes on the reading, etc.) to be able to participate. If they don't have this "entry ticket" into the activity, they should sit around the perimeter of the room and complete the assignment individually rather than participating.
- If the class size is an odd number, the teacher can jump in or form one group of three.
- Use a bell, music, or other signal to indicate the end of a turn.
- For each rotation, post a greeting question (like Attendance Questions) and an anchor question (application of content) for students to answer if they finish before time is called.
- Circulate constantly to answer questions and keep students on task.
- End Face to Face by asking students to respond to the prompt "What's clearer than when we started? What's muddier?"

Classroom Example:

Mrs. Brooks uses Face to Face at least once a week to review students' algebra homework. Today, students answer greeting questions such as "Worst cafeteria food?" before discussing the following homework questions (one per round):

1. Check your answers and process for question #___. What was similar or different about your approaches? What other approach might someone have used?
2. Look at question #___. What if the *x* were cubed rather than squared? Show the revised process and answer.
3. Change the endpoint in question #___ to a negative endpoint and graph the result. Summarize the similarities and differences between the two graphs.
4. Which was the most difficult problem to solve in this assignment? Why?

Students who finish early can answer the anchor question "When have you used math in real life this week?"

Analytical Role Cards

What It Is:

A strategy for structuring and differentiating reading and text discussion.

How It Works:

Students are placed in groups by the similar or dissimilar role card (Director, Lawyer, Detective, Philosopher, Psychologist, Architect) that they have chosen or are assigned. Each role card provides a lens or focus for reading and directions for responsibilities during small-group discussion. The teacher provides the focus for each role, which students write in before beginning their reading.

What It's Good For:

Reading and processing any text that students read before or during class.

Tips:

- Introduce and model the role cards to students one at a time with different readings so that they can learn what each role entails.
- You don't need to use every role for a given assignment; choose only those that make sense for that particular reading or discussion.
- Display key discussion questions that link the reading focus for each "role" (versus having students simply share what they read through their particular lens).
- Use the cards in a Jigsaw fashion: students meet and discuss in similar-role groups before returning to their dissimilar-role groups to complete a new task or discuss a new question.
- Laminate the cards for easy use and reuse.
- Differentiate the prompts *within* roles, when necessary (e.g., not all Philosophers need to have the same focusing prompt).

Classroom Example:

Mr. Belmont uses analytical reading and discussion role cards with students' first reading assignment in *A Christmas Carol,* a novel he's framed with the questions "What makes people change?" and "Is anyone beyond redemption?" He chose the four roles that made the most sense for this passage and formed small groups of four students each to divide and conquer. The four roles follow:

- **Philosopher:** Relate Stave 1's events/characters to this saying: "We reap what we sow."
- **Detective:** Search for clues about what other characters think of Scrooge.
- **Lawyer:** Gather evidence that either supports or refutes this claim: "Scrooge was a nicer guy before Jacob Marley died."
- **Director:** Capture the scenes, moments, passages, or dialogue that shed the most light on Scrooge's nature.

Students break from their small groups of four to record key ideas and textual evidence before returning to their groups to present their findings and to discuss the following questions:

1. Who is Ebenezer Scrooge? What is he like? What is his life like? How do you know?
2. Who is Jacob Marley? What is his relationship to Scrooge? Why does it matter?

Analytical Role Card Templates

Philosopher Reading Lens

Background:
- The Philosopher is interested in the "big picture" of the text—its overall purpose, important questions it answers and raises, and how it connects to essential or transcendent "truths."

As You Read/Reread:
- Your job is to connect or relate the people/characters, events, or ideas in this reading to this [concept/essential question/idea]:

Philosopher Discussion Role

During Discussion:
- Make sure all group members contribute to the discussion and feel included.

Sound Bites:
- "What do you think about that, ____?"
- "I agree/disagree with what you said, ____, because . . ."
- "After I make this point, I want to hear what ____ thinks."
- "What was your job, ____?"
- "Wait, ____, I think you might have just interrupted ____."

Detective Reading Lens

Background:
- The Detective is interested in inspecting certain details within the text to arrive at reasonable conclusions based on available evidence in the text.

As You Read/Reread:
- Your job is to search for "clues" about . . .

Detective Discussion Role

During Discussion:
- Make sure the discussion moves at a good pace.
- "Refresh" the discussion when you "detect" it's lagging.

Sound Bites:
- "We've talked a lot about ____. Can we also talk about ____?"
- "We have ____ more minutes, so let's also talk about ____."
- "I'm also wondering about ____."
- "Here's something else to think about . . ."
- "It sounds like we agree/disagree about ____."

Lawyer Reading Lens

Background:
- The Lawyer is interested in proving whether a certain allegation or assertion related to a text is true.

As You Read/Reread:
- Gather "evidence" that either supports or refutes the following claim:

Lawyer Discussion Role

During Discussion:
- Make sure all group members back up their claims, feelings, and observations by citing evidence from the text.

Sound Bites:
- "Can you give an example?"
- "Do you remember where that is in the text? Can you show us?"
- "How is that related to what we read?"
- "That's an interesting insight. How did you figure that out?"
- "What line/section/page is that from?"

Analytical Role Card Templates *(continued)*

Director Reading Lens	Psychologist Reading Lens	Architect Reading Lens
Background: • The Director is interested in identifying key parts of the text that illuminate or bring to life a certain idea or aspect of the narrative or purpose. **As You Read/Reread:** • Your job is to capture the "scenes," moments, passages, or quotes that you think shed the most light on . . .	**Background:** • The Psychologist is interested in getting inside the mind of the author or key figures/characters in a text to discern motive or purpose. **As You Read/Reread:** • Analyze the text for evidence of how/what [the author/character/person] is . . .	**Background:** • The Architect is interested in how the text is designed—the structure, word choice, syntax —and how those elements influence one another and work together to convey ideas. **As You Read/Reread:** • Evaluate ____ in the text to determine . . .
Director Discussion Role	**Psychologist Discussion Role**	**Architect Discussion Role**
During Discussion: • *Begin* the discussion. Use the question(s) that the teacher has posted as a starting point. • Make sure the discussion doesn't get off topic. • Bring the discussion to a close when time is called. **Sound Bites:** • "Let's start by . . ." • "Can we get back to . . . ?" • "What about . . . ?" • "Let's end by . . ."	**During Discussion:** • Your job is to be aware of and monitor people's feelings during the discussion. You redirect individuals and/or the course of the conversation when it seems like emotions are getting in the way of productive discussion. **Sound Bites:** • "What do you think, ____?" • "Can we hit the pause button for a second?" • "OK, everyone, breathe . . ." • "It sounds like we're pretty passionate about this issue/point." • "How do we all feel about . . . ?"	**Before and During Discussion:** • Your job is to plan the discussion using the directions, questions, or protocols that are provided to you. During discussion, you'll monitor the group's progress with the plan, redirecting when necessary. **Sound Bites:** • "Our next task/question/focus is . . ." • "According to the directions/discussion plan, we should be . . ." • "That's sort of a tangent. Can we save it for later?"

Wagon Wheels

What It Is:

A technique for fostering active small-group discussions that enables students to receive feedback along the way.

How It Works:

1. Each student receives a card with a question on the front and the answer on the back.
2. Students stand in two facing concentric circles so that each student has a partner in the other circle.
3. The student in the outside circle asks the question on his or her card. The student in the inside circle answers, and the first student gives the correct answer and feedback.
4. The student in the inside circle asks the question on his or her card. The student in the outside circle answers, and the first student gives the correct answer and feedback.
5. Time is called (via a signal of some sort), and partners switch cards.
6. Students in the outside circle rotate one space clockwise.
7. Students repeat steps 3 and 4 with new questions and partners.
8. The process continues for several turns or until students reach their original partners.
9. If students return to their original partners, they can review the questions they encountered since parting and jot down any concluding thoughts or lingering questions.

What It's Good For:

- Checking for understanding.
- Reviewing and reinforcing concepts and skills.
- Best with more discrete tasks rather than complex discussion topics.

Tips:

- Make sure the answers don't show through the front of the note card (choose ink and cards carefully).
- In addition to the answer, record some examples or reasons why the answer is correct to help students provide their partners with feedback.
- Students can make Wagon Wheel cards on class topics as a "Side Work" task (see Chapter 9).
- Questions from Wagon Wheel cards can be used on tests or quizzes.

Classroom Example:

Ms. Roy wanted her Spanish I students to practice distinguishing between *ser* and *estar*, both verbs meaning "to be." She made 22 cards (one for each student) featuring sentences depicting both permanent or lasting attributes (*ser*) and temporary states or locations (*estar*) but missing the verb. On the back, she recorded the proper verb choice as well as an explanation (e.g., *ser*—lasting attribute—occupation; *estar*—temporary attribute—location). She put students into two concentric circles of 11 students and gave every student a card. They rotated through the Wagon Wheels activity, supplying verbs and receiving feedback, until Ms. Roy was sure every student had seen every card.

When they finished, she polled the class to determine students' readiness to use *ser* and *estar* appropriately. Those who needed more practice worked with Ms. Roy to create a decision tree (Burke, 2002) for determining proper usage, while those who felt ready to move on composed a new set of *ser/estar* Wagon Wheel cards featuring examples and situations that were more difficult to discern (e.g., characteristic [*ser*] versus condition [*estar*]).

Debate Team Carousel

What It Is:

A strategy for conducting structured debate or discussion through writing.

How It Works:

Sitting in groups of four, each student receives either a template or a blank piece of paper (which students fold to create four squares). The teacher poses a dilemma (e.g., "Did the main character really have a choice in this situation?"); an essential question (e.g., "Is a person's health primarily determined by genetics?"); or a challenging issue (e.g., "Agree or disagree: voting should be mandatory."), and the carousel begins:

1. In box 1, students respond to the question with a claim or belief and provide their reasoning or evidence. They then pass their paper to a group member.

2. In box 2 of the paper they receive from their fellow group member, students write something to strengthen the argument in box 1, regardless of whether they agree with what was said, using reasoning or evidence. They then pass the paper to another group member.

3. Students read what was written in boxes 1 and 2 of the paper they receive from the second group member and make a counterclaim in box 3 with supporting reasoning or evidence. They then pass the paper to the last group member.

4. Students read what was written in boxes 1–3 and add their two cents in box 4.

5. Students return the papers to their original owners and read their classmates' responses to their own ideas.

What It's Good For:

- Introducing, exploring, synthesizing, or wrapping up an issue, concept, or topic.
- Pre-assessing students' thinking and argument-writing skills or understanding of a concept.
- Brainstorming or organizing ideas for argument-based writing.
- Analyzing a piece of writing (e.g., best argument made, place where voice most emerges).
- Warming up the class for Structured Academic Controversy.
- For math: working through homework problems that students got wrong, reviewing for a test, or strengthening mathematical reasoning skills.

Tips:

- Follow the carousel with whole-class, small-group, or partner discussion (e.g., offering opposing viewpoints, evaluating how one's thinking changed).
- Vary the prompts for each box to suit different needs or purposes (see Debate Team Carousel Examples, p. 134).
- Post guiding questions or clarifying prompts for each box while students are working.
- Have students initial each box they write in so that they (and you) know who wrote what.
- *For differentiation*: Assign different groups prompts of varying complexity. Although the topics up for debate may differ to stretch or support student thinking, the analytical skills exercised in the activity are the same for all students.

Debate Team Carousel Examples

General Debate Team Carousel

1. Make a claim and explain your rationale. Say what you think, and why.	**2. Add supporting evidence for the claim.** Read your peer's claim. In this box, add something that would support that claim or make it stronger.
3. Make a counterclaim or provide evidence that challenges the claim. In this box, make a claim or provide evidence that argues against what is written in boxes 1 and 2.	**4. Add your two cents.** Read what is written in boxes 1, 2, and 3. Add your opinion and your reasoning in this box.

Math Debate Team Carousel

1. Solve the problem and show how you solved it.	**2. Check the solution.** Review the process and solution in box 1. Give two reasons you think it is correct or incorrect.
3. Provide another way of solving the problem. Solve this problem in a way that is different from the process used in box 1.	**4. Detect errors and misconceptions.** Note any errors or misconceptions you see in box 1, 2, or 3. If you don't see any, explain why you agree with what is written.

Peer Review Debate Team Carousel

1. What do you believe is the strongest point in your essay? Why?	**2. Add on!** What would make this point even stronger?
3. Counter! Identify and explain why this is not the strongest point.	**4. Chime in!** Read what is written in boxes 1, 2, and 3. Make suggestions for revision that take all of this feedback into account.

Text Analysis Debate Team Carousel

1. What do you believe is the most powerful word, phrase, or line in this text, and why?	**2. Give additional reasons** why the word, phrase, or line in box 1 is the most powerful.
3. Push back against what is written in boxes 1 and 2. Explain why this is *not* the most powerful word, phrase, or line by pointing out weaknesses in the selection.	**4. Suggest and explain** another word, phrase, or line that is just as powerful as or more powerful than the one suggested in box 1.

Source (Debate Team Carousel strategy and General Debate Team Carousel example): From *Total Participation Techniques: Making Every Student an Active Learner*, by P. Himmele & W. Himmele, 2011, Alexandria, VA: ASCD. Copyright 2011 by ASCD.

Structured Academic Controversy

What It Is:

A method developed by David and Roger Johnson (n.d.) for exploring, discussing, and coming to consensus on complex issues that emphasizes perspective, collaboration, and problem solving.

How It Works:

1. Select an issue or a question for discussion that fits with content or process goals.
2. Place students in groups of four, and pair them up within that group.
3. Have the groups flip a coin to decide which partners will argue the affirmative side of the issue first.
4. Groups split into pairs of students both working on the same side to create a set of points to present for their side. They can research their position using available materials (teacher-provided or student-sought), or simply use what they already know from experience and what they've been learning.
5. The foursome reconvenes after a set amount of time. Side A presents arguments as Side B listens. Then Side B presents while Side A listens. After both sides have presented their arguments, foursomes use the remaining time for open discussion and questions.
6. Each partnership then switches positions to create a set of points different from those presented in the first round. So, Side A partners now argue for Side B, and vice versa.
7. Repeat Step 5.
8. The foursome collaborates to write and present a consensus statement based on the strongest arguments made on both sides.

What It's Good For:

- Introducing controversial topics, concepts, or issues.
- Providing a context or "use" for primary or secondary sources, data, or research.
- As a pre- or post-writing activity that emphasizes argument skills.
- Compelling students to revisit a challenging text.

Tips:

- Have students practice the mechanics of the strategy first, using a silly or easy topic.
- Frame the controversy in stark, dichotomous terms so that students arrive at consensus.
- To gauge individual learning, have students write a brief post-activity reflection.
- Assign differentiated readings (e.g., by level, complexity, or language) for seminar preparation.
- Visit http://teachinghistory.org/teaching-materials/teaching-guides/21731 for more guidance and ideas.

Classroom Examples:

- Mr. Tate uses Structured Academic Controversy with document-based questions (DBQs) in his U.S. History class so that students can use primary and secondary source analysis the way real historians do.
- After her students read and act out parts of *Romeo and Juliet*, Ms. Holcomb stages an academic controversy around the question "Were Romeo and Juliet victims of free will, or victims of fate?"

ThinkDots

What It Is:

Conceived by Kay Brimijoin, ThinkDots is a versatile strategy for thinking and talking about a concept, topic, idea, or issue from multiple perspectives.

How It Works:

1. The teacher creates six ThinkDots cards, each with a number corresponding to one of the "dots" from a die on one side and a prompt or a question on the other side.
2. Students work in groups of two to six with one die and set of ThinkDots per group. Each student is responsible for one card's prompt or question.
3. There are three ways to conduct a ThinkDots activity:
   — *Option 1*: Students take turns rolling the die, finding the card with the corresponding number of "dots," and reading aloud and responding to the prompt.
   — *Option 2*: Students roll the die to divide the cards. They silently read and respond to their prompts and then take turns sharing in numerical order.
   — *Option 3*: Jigsaw-style, students form groups with students from other groups who have rolled the same number. Together, they discuss their prompt, jot down answers, and then return to their home groups to share those ideas.
4. For all three options, students should use tracking sheets to take notes on their conversation (see ThinkDots Graphic Organizer, p. 138).
5. All groups of students can work with the same set of ThinkDots or with different sets that have been designed for varying readiness, interest, or learning profile needs. Different sets can be coded with different-colored dots—a form of "stealth" differentiation because students are usually unaware that different versions are being used.

What It's Good For:
- Introducing a unit.
- Processing lesson or reading content.
- Fueling general small-group discussion activities.
- Test or concept review.

Tip:

Use one of the frameworks in the table on page 138 for brainstorming ThinkDots questions or prompts. (*Note:* If using Webb's DOK questions, include a combination of Level 2 and Level 3 questions for each set of six ThinkDots.)

Performance Verbs	Wiggins and McTighe's Six Facets of Understanding	Webb's Depth of Knowledge (DOK)		de Bono's (1999) Six Thinking Hats
		Level 2	Level 3	
• Describe it • Analyze it • Associate it • Compare it • Apply it • Argue for or against it	• Explain • Interpret • Apply • Have perspective on • Empathize with • Self-reflect on	• Categorize • Estimate • If/then • Organize • Predict • Find patterns	• Assess • Critique • Formulate • Hypothesize • Investigate • Revise	• Red Hat (emotions, feelings) • Purple Hat (drawbacks, critical) • Yellow Hat (benefits, positives) • White Hat (objective, data-driven) • Blue Hat (summarize, overview) • Green Hat (creativity, possibilities)

ThinkDots Graphic Organizer			
Side #	Teammate Name	Task/Question Rolled	Ideas/Evidence/Responses
1			
2			
3			
4			
5			
6			

Food Chains

(⚀ 1)	(no dots)	(⚅⚅ 6)
What would happen if the top of this food chain disappeared? What would happen to the rest of the organisms? Diagram and/or write about how removing the top of the food chain affects the equilibrium of the system.	Compare this food chain with another system we've discussed in class (e.g., a band, the human body, a dance team). How is the food chain like this system? How is it different? How do all the parts depend on one another in both systems?	How is this food chain like our own food chain? Think about what you eat on a typical day. What would happen if all those food sources disappeared? What kinds of food would you have to eat to survive? How would this affect your environment?
(⚁ 2)	(⚄ 5)	(⚅⚅ 6)
What do you think is the most important part of this food chain? Why do you think so? Explain your answer using both words and pictures.	What do you think is the most important part of this food chain? Take on the voice of this animal and explain to the rest of the food chain why you are the most important. You can use words and/or pictures.	Find a way to explain to your younger brother, sister, cousin, or neighbor why your food chain is so important. Explain the parts and how they interact. Use both words and pictures in your explanation.

Language Arts—Word Choice

Directions: Each side of your die represents an overused word that needs to be spiced up. After you have rolled your word, use the dictionary and thesaurus (hard copy or electronic) to locate more descriptive synonyms. After you've recorded your ideas, rank the synonyms in order from least to greatest amount of "spice."

Say/Said (⚀)	Go/Went (⚂)	Nice (⚂)
Mean (⚁)	**Happy** (⚄)	**Angry** (⚅)

Equations

- The teacher can write one problem on the board for everyone to use (undifferentiated).
- The teacher can give a differentiated problem to each small group or write different problems on the back side of each card, differentiated for each group (should use formative assessment evidence to decide on different problems).
- Can be used for sense making after the introduction of a new concept or problem type, as a review, or as part of homework check.

(⚂ 3)	(⚄ 5)
What's one question someone should ask him- or herself when he or she first looks at this problem?	What mathematical concepts or terms/vocabulary does this problem show? Be specific!
Create and solve a problem similar to this problem. (⚁ 2)	
Write a step-by-step set of directions that tells someone who was absent today how to solve this problem. (⚅ 6)	
Solve this problem. What was easy about it? Not so easy? (⚀ 1)	
What's a mistake someone might make in trying to solve this problem? Why might he or she make that mistake? (⚃ 4)	

Novel Study

(⚂ 3)	(⚄ 5)
What has the protagonist gained in this chapter? Consider multiple facets, such as material things, relationships, knowledge, insight, motivation, etc. Cite textual evidence as support.	Record at least five important symbols from this chapter. Explain the significance of each symbol as it (1) appears in this chapter and (2) connects to past chapters. Cite textual evidence.
Whom (e.g., other characters, himself or what (e.g., situations, events)) should the protagonist be cautious about? What should he be concerned about? Cite textual evidence. (⚁ 2)	
If you were to end this story now and make it turn out "happily ever after," what would happen? Outline a final chapter that ends with all conflicts resolved; provide textual evidence that proves this is a defensible hypothesis. (⚅ 6)	
How does the protagonist feel about what just happened in this chapter? Are his feelings justified? Explain using textual evidence in your response. (⚀ 1)	
Compile a list of characters whose lives will be affected by the actions of the protagonist in this chapter and briefly explain how, citing textual evidence as support for your suppositions. (⚃ 4)	

Historical Document Analysis (Tier 2)

Origins
Did the author(s)/creator(s) of this source have firsthand or secondhand information about the topic, event, etc.? How do you know? (● — 1 dot)

Purpose
What evidence in this source tells you why and for what audience it was produced? Quote or cite evidence from the source. (● — 1 dot)

Time and Place
What evidence in this source suggests that it is and/or is not representative of the ideals, thinking, controversies, or other aspects of the time and place in which it was created? (●● — 2 dots)

Connections
In what ways could this source help you or someone else better understand other historical events or perspectives? (●● — 2 dots)

Source Appeal
Who might have been interested in this source at the time it was written, and why? (●●●● — 4 dots)

Missing Pieces
What questions about the events or people described/depicted in this source are left unanswered, but might be "answered" in another primary or secondary source? Identify the questions and the sources; defend your thinking. (●●●●●● — 6 dots)

Drama

I'm Excited!
Read this scene as if it's the best news you've ever received. Be very excited—make us feel your joy! (● — 1 dot)

I'm Devastated!
Read this scene as if it's the worst news you've ever received. Be really sad—cry if you want to! (● — 1 dot)

This Is Hilarious!
Read this scene as if it's the funniest thing you've ever heard. It's OK if you have to take a break for a fit of laughter. (● — 1 dot)

I'm Terrified!
Read this scene as if it's the scariest thing you've ever heard. Be sure to look around to make sure no one is after you! (●●●● — 4 dots)

I'm Confused!
Read this scene as if it makes no sense to you at all. Your brow might be wrinkled and your statements may sound more like questions . . . but that's OK, right? (●●●●● — 5 dots)

I'm Angry!
Read this scene as if you're burning with rage. Shout if you want to. Make us want to run and hide from your anger. (●●●●●● — 6 dots)

Historical Document Analysis (Tier 1)

Origins
Who produced this source? When did he/she/they produce it? How do you know? (● — 1 dot)

Purpose
Why or how was this source produced? How do you know? (●● — 2 dots)

Time and Place
Identify and explain two or more things that the source tells you about life in the time and place it was written. (●●● — 3 dots)

Connections
In what ways could this source help you or someone else better understand recent or current events in our city, country, culture, or world? (●● — 2 dots)

Source Appeal
Besides a historian, who might be interested in this source, and why? (●●●●● — 5 dots)

Missing Pieces
Write two questions to the author/creator that are left unanswered by this source. Then offer possibilities for where and how you might find the answers. (●●●●●● — 6 dots)

Music

Describe
Describe this song. Is it fast or slow? Is it smooth or choppy? Is it in a major or a minor key? Explain your choices. (● — 1 dot)

Compare
Which of the other songs we've listened to is this song most like? Explain how they are the same and how they are different. (● — 1 dot)

Feelings About
How do you think the composer was feeling when he wrote this song? How does this song make you feel? Why? (●● — 2 dots)

Parts Of
What instruments do you hear playing in this song? Think about strings, percussion, brass, woodwinds, and so on. (●● — 2 dots)

Use Of
What if you could pick this song to use as a soundtrack for a movie, cartoon, or storybook? Which would you pick? What would it go well with? Why? (●●●● — 4 dots)

Good and Bad Parts
What in particular do you like about this song? What are its best qualities? Explain. What don't you like about this song? Why doesn't this appeal to you? (●●●●●● — 6 dots)

Jigsaw

What It Is:

A cooperative learning strategy originally developed by Aronson (Aronson & Patnoe, 1997) in which each member of a small group becomes an expert on a different aspect of the content and shares his or her expertise with the other group members.

How It Works:

1. Students meet in home groups for task introduction and division of labor. Each home group member selects or is assigned one "piece" of the larger task "puzzle" (e.g., a chapter, a perspective, or a subtopic). These groups are usually heterogeneous.
2. Students reconfigure themselves into expert groups composed of students who share the same "puzzle piece."
3. Expert groups work to compile information on their chapter, perspective, or subtopic. The teacher provides guiding questions, resources, graphic organizers, and any other necessary supports to facilitate the process.
4. Expert groups disband, and members return to their home groups. In the home groups, each member shares his or her respective piece of the puzzle, providing information, examples, and insights. The teacher supplies a graphic organizer to facilitate this sharing process.
5. When all home group members have finished sharing, the class engages in large-group discussion to address questions, seeming contradictions, and interesting observations.
6. The teacher collects evidence of home group understanding (e.g., via a synthesis question on the back of groups' graphic organizers; one member from each group turns it in).
7. The teacher collects evidence of individual understanding (e.g., via an exit card).

What It's Good For:

- Dealing with large amounts of information or varied perspectives.
- Increasing student investment through choice of puzzle piece and/or increased accountability in home groups.
- Designing and managing collaborative tasks.

Tips:

- Find and organize appropriate materials (e.g., readings, illustrations, websites) for each expert group; develop appropriate guiding questions and organizers for both home groups and expert groups.
- Model the process students should follow in each grouping configuration.
- Circulate vigilantly to catch misconceptions during both expert and home group work.
- Set and enforce time limits for each phase.
- Consider implementing Jigsaw in a block period (or two-period phase on a traditional schedule). This will give you a chance to conduct an understanding check (via Exit Slip or other method) of what students learned in their expert groups, so that they don't go to their home groups with misconceptions to pass on.
- Design the Jigsawed task at the outset of the planning process. This task should go beyond reporting to one another for the purpose of completing a graphic organizer. Any information-gathering tool should be a means to the end of completing a home group task that requires students to bring together and transfer what they've learned in their respective groups in a new way.
- *For differentiation:* It is possible to tailor expert group materials and tasks to meet the specific readiness of students (e.g., strategic choices of reading levels, number of facets addressed, complexity of material). If this is the goal, *assign* students to expert groups rather than letting them choose.

Classroom Example
Chaucer Jigsaw

Task Introduction			
We will be talking about narrators, characters, and authors in this Jigsaw. In your home groups, decide who wants to read each tale (see me for summaries/teasers). You will be responsible for individually reading your tale and answering questions while you read (I will supply resources to support your reading). In your expert groups, you will talk about what you learned from the text and then return to your home groups to share.			
Expert Group 1 *The Knight's Tale*	**Expert Group 2** *The Wife of Bath's Tale*	**Expert Group 3** *The Miller's Tale*	**Expert Group 4** *The Pardoner's Tale*

Expert Group Understanding Check

Before speaking with their home groups, students will reflect on their own reading and answer the questions within their section of the Jigsaw graphic organizer. Then they will move to their expert group and discuss their tale in detail, adding to the notes until they feel completely comfortable explaining the tale and its meaning to the home group.

Home Group Synthesis/Sharing Task

Students return to their home groups and explain how their tale, their narrator, and their characters depict society. They will summarize the tale and then answer the questions succinctly to their classmates. Then they will take notes on the appropriate tales that their classmates worked on. When students are finished sharing, they must reflect on what they've learned and answer the following prompts on poster paper: How are the narrators similar? How are they different? To what do you attribute these similarities and differences? What does examining multiple perspectives reveal about the nature of this society? What parallels can you find between this and our own society (school, local, national, or global)?

Whole-Class Discussion/Sharing

We will regroup after sharing and talk about how narrators can convey perspective on a society, as well as how an author (like Chaucer) can convey his opinions by using a narrator. We'll also talk about how specific characterization can affect how society is portrayed.

Home Group Accountability	**Individual Understanding Check**
Students will all turn in their graphic organizers to show what they've learned and processed from their classmates. Their notes and poster will tell me what we need to address further as a class.	*Exit card:* Using an example from each tale, explain Chaucer's perspective on a societal issue of your choice.

Chaucer Jigsaw Graphic Organizer

	Teammate	Task Charge	Ideas/Answers
The Knight's Tale		<ul><li>*How does the knight depict chivalry?*</li><li>*How does the narrator depict society?*</li><li>*What does this story reveal about the narrator?*</li><li>*How does the narrator's perspective compare with the author's perspective?*</li><li>*What tone have you heard within this story? Why?*</li></ul>	
The Wife of Bath's Tale		<ul><li>*How does the narrator depict society?*</li><li>*What does this story reveal about the narrator?*</li><li>*How does the narrator's perspective compare with the author's perspective?*</li><li>*What tone have you heard within this story? Why?*</li><li>*What is the role of women in this story?*</li></ul>	
The Miller's Tale		<ul><li>*How does the narrator depict society?*</li><li>*What does this story reveal about the narrator?*</li><li>*How does the narrator's perspective compare with the author's perspective?*</li><li>*Is this tale ironic? What's the tone?*</li></ul>	
The Pardoner's Tale		<ul><li>*How does the narrator depict society?*</li><li>*What does this story reveal about the narrator?*</li><li>*What is the lesson you've learned from this story? Is it sincere?*</li><li>*What does this story reveal about Chaucer as the author?*</li><li>*Is this an honest story?*</li></ul>	

Source: Katherine Porzel, Deep Creek High School, Chesapeake, VA. Used with permission.

Questioning Frameworks

What They Are:

Three different frameworks for structuring questions that align with the higher levels of Bloom's taxonomy and require students to process, organize, evaluate, and create knowledge rather than regurgitate it.

What They're Good For:

Planning questions for any of the other strategies discussed in this chapter.

1. *Inferential and Analytical Questions* (Dean et al., 2012). This team's research findings stressed the danger of focusing on tangential questions in an effort to make learning "engaging." To ensure *cognitive* engagement, questions should focus on the essence of the upper range of articulated learning goals. By planning inferential and analytical questions centered on predetermined, higher-order learning goals, teachers can help students fill in gaps from a lesson, generate their own questions, and synthesize prior knowledge with new information.

2. *Depth of Knowledge* (Webb et al., 2005). Norman Webb designed the Depth of Knowledge (DOK) framework as a tool for examining the alignment between the cognitive demand of standards and the cognitive demand of assessments measuring those standards. His framework can also be used to examine the match between learning objectives and the questions posed to unpack those objectives. For example, if a teacher's skill goal is written at the evaluation level, he or she would be remiss in asking questions that merely asked students to recall or analyze the content. Webb's framework can help teachers ensure that the depth of their classroom questions—whether posed in discussion or in tasks and activities—is consistent with the depth of their instructional objectives and assessment items.

3. *Six Facets of Understanding* (Wiggins & McTighe, 2005). The Understanding by Design framework operates according to the principle that deep understanding—not just attainment of facts and skills—should be at the center of teaching and learning. Wiggins and McTighe contend that if someone truly understands something, he or she can explain it, apply it, interpret it, have perspective on it, show empathy with it, and reveal self-knowledge about it. These six facets of understanding can be used to design questions and tasks that compel students to autonomously transfer and apply their knowledge and skills to authentic performances and situations.

Tips:

- Inferential and analytical questions and Webb's DOK Level 2 and 3 questions work well in Interactive Lectures, on Wagon Wheel cards, as prompts in the Interview Model, and as questions for ThinkDots and Face to Face discussions.
- Webb's DOK Level 4 questions can serve as Jigsaw prompts for longer-term investigations and as topics for debate in Structured Academic Controversies.
- Use the six facets of understanding as Analytical Role Card prompts, to structure Think-Dots discussions, or to drive a round of Face to Face.

Classroom Examples

1. Inferential and Analytical Questions. In the chart below, we have created sample questions from English, history, math, and science that align with the criteria for inferential and analytical questions developed by Dean and colleagues (2012).

Question Type	Nature of Question Type/Overlap with Bloom's	Sample Questions
Inferential (Regarding things or people, events, actions, states of being)	Students must use prior knowledge to explain or interpret a situation, phenomenon, or set of circumstances. This question type calls for thinking associated with Bloom's Applying.	• Things or people: What is the nature of the relationship between Nick and Gatsby? • Events: Why did this conflict begin at this point in history? • Actions: How is the area of the triangle changed by doubling the length of the hypotenuse? • States of being: Why does an individual sweat when exposed to extreme heat? Explain the body's effort to maintain homeostasis in this situation.
Analytical (Analyzing errors)	Students must find and address errors in reasoning and problem solving. This question type calls for thinking associated with Bloom's Analyzing and Evaluating.	• How would you correct this flawed sentence structure? • Which amendment from the Bill of Rights is improperly represented in this speech? • What are the errors in this solution to the problem? • What misunderstanding is exhibited in this solution? • How could the weaknesses in this experiment's design be improved?
Analytical (Constructing support)	Students must provide data, evidence, and examples to construct or strengthen an argument. This question type calls for thinking associated with Bloom's Analyzing, Evaluating, and Creating.	• What evidence would you add to this argument to make it stronger? • What counterclaims might you introduce to strengthen this argument? • Is there another way we could write the same equation to see if it would still work?
Analytical (Analyzing perspective)	Students must assume a perspective other than their own or the one presented and provide insight into that perspective using data, evidence, and reasoning. This question type calls for thinking associated with Bloom's Analyzing, Evaluating, and Creating.	• Why were some colonists opposed to the tactics of the Sons of Liberty? • Why might people disagree with this amendment, and how would they defend their stance? • What is another way to solve this problem? Why might that method be preferable to some people? • Who might accept or encourage this environmental danger? Why?

2. Depth of Knowledge. In the chart below, we have created sample questions from English, history, math, and science that align with Webb's Depth of Knowledge framework.

Webb's DOK Level	Overlap with Bloom's	Key Verbs	Sample Questions
Level 1: Recall *Who, what, when, where, why*	Remembering/ Understanding	Arrange, calculate, define, identify, list, measure, recall, recognize, repeat, state, use	• How would you explain the difference between internal and external conflict? • Where were the majority of the battles in this war fought? Why? • Find the equation of the straight line that has slope $m = 2$ and passes through the line $(-1, -4)$. • What is meant by "negative" feedback and "positive" feedback with regard to maintaining homeostasis?
Level 2: Skill/Concept *Beyond recall; requires processing*	Applying	Categorize, estimate, identify patterns, consider if/then, organize, predict, separate, summarize	• What ideas show which type of conflict—internal or external—is at work in this passage? • What inference can you make about what was lost on both sides (in addition to soldiers' lives) in these battles? • Examine the three different slopes represented in graphs of three different lines. Predict the order of the lines' slopes from least to greatest. • Summarize the body's negative feedback system in maintaining homeostasis regarding body temperature when exposed to extreme cold.
Level 3: Strategic Thinking *Requires mental processing at a higher level*	Analyzing/ Evaluating	Appraise, assess, compare, critique, formulate, hypothesize, investigate, revise	• Assess this character's response to conflict thus far. How has conflict changed her, and how has she changed in her response to conflict? • How might have the strategy on each side of the battle been adjusted to minimize losses? • Using what you've learned from our exploration of finding slope by examining the relationship between the increase in x and the increase in y, how would you generalize a formula for finding slope? • Compare the positive feedback system that occurs in women's bodies during childbirth with one of the positive feedback systems associated with climate change.
Level 4: Extended Thinking *Requires planning and developing; therefore, extended time is necessary*	Evaluating/ Creating	Apply concepts to, connect, create, critique (more factors), design, prove, synthesize	• Which character from this literary work might you point to as someone for this character to emulate in handling future conflicts, and how should the character follow suit? • Taking multiple, consecutive battles into account, what could have been done to maximize resources and minimize risks? • "Conduct an investigation, from specifying a problem to designing and carrying out an experiment, to analyzing its data and forming conclusions" (Webb et al., 2005, p. 59). • "Plan and conduct an investigation to provide evidence that feedback mechanisms maintain homeostasis" (NGSS-HS-LS1-3).

3. Six Facets of Understanding. In the chart below, we have created sample questions from English, history, math, and science that align with the six facets of understanding developed by Wiggins and McTighe (2005).

Facet	Nature of Question Type/ Overlap with Bloom's	Sample Questions
Explain	Put information, ideas, principles, and processes into own words and explain thinking. This question type calls for thinking associated with Bloom's Understanding (i.e., Comprehending).	• Demonstrate two different ways in which authors show readers what their characters are like. • Describe what you view as the three most powerful factors contributing to the U.S. Civil War. • How would you describe the difference between the *mean* and the *median* of a number set? • Explain what causes the different phases of the Moon.
Interpret	Make sense of ideas, principles, and processes by creating comparisons, analogies, and stories. This question type calls for thinking associated with Bloom's Analyzing and Creating.	• The reader's process of characterization is like what process in science? Math? History? Art? Explain. • Describe President Lincoln's thought process as he debated whether to let the Southern states secede. • How might the mean and the median be compared with (1) siblings in a large family, (2) candy in a Halloween bag, or (3) fish in a pond? Explain your comparison. • How would you describe the appearance of the Moon during each phase of a lunar eclipse using *new* terms (other than *waxing, waning, gibbous, crescent,* etc.)?
Apply	Use information, ideas, principles, and processes in new contexts and situations. This question type calls for thinking that moves beyond Bloom's Applying and into Creating.	• How would you use the techniques Shakespeare did in this scene to characterize a family member or friend? • What issue in the modern-day United States has (or might one day have) the power to divide the U.S. government as in the time of the Civil War? Why? • What patterns do you see in the comparisons of means and medians across these sets of neighborhood housing prices? Which measure better reveals what a buyer should expect to pay? • How would you illustrate the relative positions of the Moon, Earth, and Sun during each of the lunar phases in a way that elementary-level students would understand?

Demonstrate perspective	Recognize and articulate the many possible different viewpoints regarding a situation. This question type calls for thinking that moves beyond Bloom's Analyzing and into Evaluating.	• Describe how three different characters perceive Hamlet. How does Shakespeare communicate these different perceptions? • How would you justify or condemn the issue of slavery from the perspective of four different people with different occupations living in different areas of the United States at the time of the Civil War? • How might different parties (e.g., an ad agency, a concerned parent group, a teenager) view this data set on cell phone usage in terms of the communication power of mean and median? • What other titles have been given to the U.S. "Civil War," and what ideology does each title represent? • What misconceptions might people have about the causes of lunar phases, and why might they hold those misconceptions?
Display empathy	Take on the viewpoint, concerns, or opinions of another and argue from this perspective. This question type calls for thinking associated with Bloom's Evaluating and Creating.	• Is Hamlet a hero or a coward? Choose one character and argue convincingly from his or her perspective. • How would you explain the perspective on the justification or condemnation of the Civil War that you believe is least understood by the U.S. public? • Create an imagined argument in the voices of mean and median discussing how they feel when people do and do not use them appropriately. • How would you explain the differences between the lunar phases and the lunar eclipses to someone who is confused about their causes or believes they are the same?
Self-reflect	Reflect on one's own connection to, use of, and strengths and weaknesses in ideas and processes. This question type draws on Bloom's Analyzing and Evaluating in terms of fusing metacognition with content and skills.	• How are your strengths and weaknesses like Hamlet's? Describe specific examples from the play and your life. • Where in your life do you see your personal perspective limiting your consideration or understanding of others' perspectives? • How might you use mean and median to make decisions in your life? Explain potential contexts, whether you rely more heavily on one measure than the other, and the merits or shortfalls of this tendency. • How have you grown in your grasp of the lunar phases? What was the most complicated aspect for you to fully understand?

6

Checking for Understanding Using Formative Assessment

Part 1:

Is My Teaching Working?

As Ms. Rissa wrapped up the class discussion of John Donne's poem "A Valediction: Forbidding Mourning," she was feeling positive about her lesson. The class had been lively and interactive yet focused. Many students had participated, and a few of their contributions were unusually insightful regarding the poem's central *conceit* (an extended metaphor used as an argument throughout the poem). As students filed out of the room on the way to their next class, however, Ms. Rissa overheard one student remark to another, "You know, I still don't see how the guy in the poem was conceited." Unfortunately, this student (and possibly his classmate) walked out of class with a significant misunderstanding! And his teacher knew this *only* because she happened to overhear his remark! Her impression of the lesson changed as she wondered how many other students had failed to grasp the poem as well as she thought they had.

Although this account is based on a true story from just one classroom, many middle and high school teachers have similar tales to tell. When reflecting on the effectiveness of a lesson, we tend to focus on how it went for us as *the teacher*. That is, we say a lesson was "good" if most students were well behaved or engaged (from our perspective), or if the instructional strategies and tasks flowed smoothly. In reality, such criteria set a low bar for success and fail to reach the heart of what matters most: *whether students are learning.*

The principles and strategies presented in Chapter 5 can help teachers design learning experiences that require students to actively grapple with content to make sense of it. They also provide opportunities to monitor whole-class progress and make on-the-fly adjustments for the larger group. But at the end of such a learning experience, we cannot gauge our success according to our own impressions of how interactive, lively, or focused the lesson was. Instead, we should pointedly ask ourselves, "Is my teaching working?" This inquiry pushes teachers to shift from seeing themselves as managers of students or deliverers of content to seeing themselves as "evaluators of their effects on students" (Hattie, 2012, p. 14). The evaluator-teacher wonders, "What are my learning goals? What am I hoping that students now know, understand, and are able to do better than they did before? Are students reaching those goals? Who is? Who isn't? Why?"

The best method for helping us answer each of those questions is formative assessment.

What Is Formative Assessment?

Formative assessment is the ongoing process of taking regular and varied snapshots of students' learning during or after a lesson or series of lessons to inform next steps in instructional planning. Through formative assessment, teachers gauge where students are relative to learning goals and uncover misconceptions and gaps in students' skills or knowledge, as well as evidence of mastery and advanced insights.

Let us once again consider the road trip analogy: you've planned the learning destination by establishing clear and robust learning goals, you've administered and analyzed a pre-assessment of key goals to determine first steps, and you've planned active strategies for engagement and discussion to help students progress in their journey. In this analogy, formative assessment is the incessant question "Are we there yet?" that asks how far a student is from the learning destination. If we wait until the end of the unit to find out that some students are back in Iowa while others arrived in San Francisco days ago, it's much too late to do anything about it, let alone make adjustments to the route. On a road trip, a GPS device can give the driver information about progress, time remaining, where the next rest area is, and points of interest along the way. This information is most beneficial when it is up-to-the-minute and accurate. For teachers, formative assessment serves the same purpose.

Is This Formative Assessment?

Certain practices are sometimes confused with formative assessment. One is "assessment by sampling" (Hockett, 2010). Say you pose a few questions at the end of a lesson to see if everyone "got it." Two students respond with reasonable answers. You infer that this sample is representative of all students' thinking, or that because all students have heard these responses, everyone now gets it. Although structured whole-group discussion can be a valuable tool (see Chapter 5), it is not a means for tapping into individual minds—and therefore is not assessment.

"Noticing" or monitoring what students do or say is also often mislabeled as formative assessment. All good teachers keep a close eye and ear on students as they work individually or in groups, and respond accordingly when they see students struggling, coasting, or getting off track. The best teachers go a step further and conduct close and careful analysis of student thinking as students make sense of the content. However, unless the teacher is systematically observing individual students' sense-making processes and gathering or recording information about them, the chances that he or she is administering an assessment are slim.

Ms. Rissa's use of questioning was an important part of her whole-class learning experience about John Donne's poem, but if we examine the lesson against the preceding guidelines, we see that it did not qualify as formative assessment. Her use of class discussion did not provide data on individual students' grasp of learning goals. Further, it gave her little information about how to strategically move individual students forward in their learning during the next lesson.

Had Ms. Rissa planned for formative assessment, she may have ended the discussion by asking students to individually answer a few key questions about the material, such as

- What is a *conceit* in literature?
- Explain the conceit John Donne used in "A Valediction: Forbidding Mourning."
- Evaluate Donne's use of the conceit. Was it more effective than making his point more directly would have been? Why or why not? Cite the text in your response.

These exit questions would have allowed Ms. Rissa to discover who failed to grasp the learning goals for the day (e.g., the students she overheard voicing their confusion); who grasped them on a basic level (those who recalled definitions and applications); and who was able to think critically (those who could evaluate the effect of the conceit used in the poem). She could have addressed these patterns proactively the next class period before moving on to new material. This sort of targeted feedback would have the potential to significantly improve her students' learning (Hattie, 2012).

Constructing Useful Formative Assessment Prompts

So how can teachers structure formative assessment prompts to glean information about student learning in a powerful but efficient manner? The process is remarkably similar to the one for designing a pre-assessment, but it is narrower in scope. As with pre-assessment, start by articulating what you want students to understand, know, and be able to do—but do so in terms of your learning goals for a *lesson* or short series of lessons rather than for the entire unit.

Next, design questions or prompts that would require students to demonstrate their grasp of key concepts or goals from the lesson. As is the case with pre-assessment, there's no need to assess every single thing you have taught; rather, ask yourself what the *pivotal* points of the lesson are. In other words, what must students really "get" before they can move forward in the content? What misconceptions could prevent future learning from taking hold? Which processes must students firmly grasp if they are to build on those processes with further steps? By determining these pivotal points, you can target formative assessment questions to reveal this information in an efficient manner.

It is important to remember that powerful formative assessment asks students to do more than simply regurgitate facts. Fact-based formative assessment reveals little evidence of students' expertise with the content and provides teachers with limited instructional implications. Fact-based assessment cannot tell us *why* students don't understand a concept or even *how deeply*. And, owing to its predictability, it can end up feeling like a waste of time for both the teacher and the students. Assessment questions that require students to make connections, to use their knowledge in some way—in essence, to provide evidence that will convict them of learning (Wiggins & McTighe, 2005)—are the questions that give teachers the most bang for their buck. In sum, the most useful formative assessment prompts

- Are aligned with pivotal learning goals (understanding, knowledge, and skill goals).
- Are administered deliberately and intentionally (not off the cuff or as an afterthought).
- Are limited to a few key questions.
- Gauge *individual* student progress and learning needs.
- Invite application, synthesis, and transfer—not just regurgitation.
- Provide evidence to which a teacher can respond in time for that feedback to have an impact on student learning during the instructional unit.

One method teachers can use to arrive at such prompts is to consider, "If I asked students what the big idea or point of the lesson was, what would the ideal response sound like? Now, what would a prompt or question designed to elicit that response sound like?" Student answers to such aligned, targeted thinking questions enable the teacher to discern patterns in how well students grasped the learning goals and what he or she needs to do to move the entire spectrum of learners forward.

In general, it's advisable to use varied questions and strategies over the course of a unit. All learners, adolescents included, appreciate variety. It's also a good idea to walk through the potential range of student responses and consider what you might do or plan as a result. If the students' responses don't matter or if there's only one right answer, the assessment isn't likely to yield useful information—or at least information you couldn't have intuited by observing or listening to the students during class. Save your questions for those things that really matter and avoid giving an assessment just for the sake of it.

Types of Prompts

Thus far, we have looked at formative assessment prompts through the singular lens of gauging student readiness to tackle the next phase of learning. In Part 2 of this chapter, we include multiple examples of *general readiness prompts* (p. 165) and *subject-specific prompts* (pp. 166–167) to assist teachers as they plan and implement investigations into students' grasp of key knowledge, understanding, and skills.

Although student readiness is the main target of formative assessment, gauging other factors that influence readiness is equally important to instructional planning. Therefore, we include examples of *additional prompts* that can help teachers gather other kinds of information pertinent to the learning process:

- *Progress:* where students are with a task or process; work habits, attitudes, or dispositions relative to a task or topic (p. 168).
- *Interest/motivation/preference:* the level or nature of students' interest in what they are learning; how or under what conditions students prefer to learn (p. 168).

Uncovering this varied information about student progress is important because it provides a more complete picture of what students are learning, increases student metacognition and investment in the instructional process (Bransford et al., 2000), and helps mitigate student fatigue and robotic responses that can result from overusing the same kind of prompt.

Strategies for Formative Assessment

Exit and Entry Slips

Exit and Entry Slips (pp. 164–168) are likely the most commonly used methods of formative assessment in middle and high school classrooms today. Teachers appreciate them for their flexible structure, their ease of administration, and their ability to be collected and analyzed efficiently. In general, Exit Slips (administered at the end of class) are a better mechanism for letting students' responses drive instruction than are Entry Slips (administered at the beginning of class). This is mostly because Exit Slips give the teacher time to read and digest the information and plan accordingly, whereas he or she would have to build time into class for analyzing Entry Slips. An exception is teachers using the "flipped" instructional model (Bergmann & Sams, 2012), who may rely more heavily on Entry Slips to discover how well students grasped the information they processed at home. Ideally, students would post these Entry Slip responses to a class blog or discussion board to give the teacher time to examine them before students come to class the next day.

Frayer Model/Diagram

The Frayer diagram (pp. 169–172), based on a model named for Dorothy Frayer, is a four-square organizer that asks students to provide the *definition* of a concept, its *characteristics* or *attributes*, some crystallizing *examples*, and some *non-examples* that may be frequently confused with examples. The categories of the original Frayer model are better suited to some concepts and topics than to others. A good "test" is whether myriad examples and non-examples can "fit" under the concept. For some learning goals, the traditional categories are not the most efficient. In such instances, the categories of the diagram can be tweaked to better capture student thinking.

Using the Frayer diagram as a formative assessment measure has many benefits. It helps students organize their thinking, even as they share what they have learned. It even allows them to sketch or draw their understanding if the prompt is conducive to visual representations. Designing a Frayer also helps the teacher organize content in a clear fashion that may spill over into more organized instruction. Further, the organization of student responses in the diagram can make it easy to spot patterns in the results. Part 2 includes examples of both traditional and modified Frayer diagrams to demonstrate how such an organizational structure can serve as a learning check for students and an instructional tool for teachers.

Is Formative Assessment Really Worth It? and Other Questions and Concerns

In recent years, experts have heralded the power of formative assessment to improve student achievement (see Black & Wiliam, 1998; Guskey, 2003; Hattie, 2009; Stiggins & Chappuis, 2005). Even more recently, however, the focus has turned to what teachers actually do with the information garnered from formative assessment (see Guskey, 2007/2008; Hattie, 2012; Wiliam, 2012). James Popham (2006) asserts that assessment can be considered "formative" only if it is used "during the instructional segment in which the assessment occurred to adjust instruction with the intent of better meeting the needs of the students assessed" (p. 4). So collecting Exit Slips and tossing them in the recycling bin is most likely not worth the time invested, whereas collecting Exit Slips, examining results, and shaping instruction accordingly can yield tremendous dividends.

Buying into the necessity of formative assessment is one thing. Putting it into practice is another. Teaching "up to the bell," the prospect of looking through all those student responses, concerns about how to manage the results, and the general day-to-day challenges of teaching can discourage teachers from adopting formative assessment as a regular practice.

As with all worthy pursuits, the first few steps of the journey are often the most difficult. What follow are snippets of conversations we've had with teachers as they begin to design and implement formative assessment in their classrooms.

How much time should this take?

There's no rule of thumb for how much time formative assessment should take. Much depends on such factors as the kind of evidence being collected, what has led up to the assessment, students' age, and the length of the class period. A general guideline, however, is to dedicate at least 10 percent of class time to administering formative assessment. Doing so helps students solidify their learning and enables the teacher to streamline instruction the following class period. Assessment is a part of teaching—you can't do one without the other (Earl, 2003)—and our lesson plans should reflect that synergy.

If I take the time to formatively assess every day, then I won't have time to teach everything.

Assessing *is* teaching if conducted in an informative manner (Earl, 2003; Stiggins, 2005). Saving a few minutes at the end of a lesson to administer a formative assessment helps students retain what they've learned because they have a chance to reflect on it and to process it in a new way (Jensen, 2005). In addition, regular use of formative assessment increases the efficiency of instruction during class: teachers can address misconceptions as they go rather than build new learning on the shaky foundation of partial or erroneous understanding. It takes more time to "undo" misconceptions at the end than it does to correct them along the way (Bransford et al., 2000).

It's a good idea to reserve a chunk of time at the beginning of each class to address the results of your formative assessments. This may mean answering a few recurring questions, reteaching something everyone struggled with, or spending a short time in small-group work (see Chapter 7). Adjust to the habit of building that time into the lesson plan, and you will naturally restructure the rest of your teaching activities to fit.

Finally, remember that you need not assess every single learning goal. Planning formative assessment as an ongoing process rather than as an "event" allows you to focus on the goals that are most crucial in determining whether students are ready to move forward.

I teach 100-plus students. I barely have enough time to evaluate other assessments, let alone formative assessments!

First, make the assessments short enough to be usable. Focus on a couple of key questions that have a lot of "juice for the squeeze." Experiment with formative assessment in one course or section until you find the proper balance of time and question type.

As with a pre-assessment, you can give the formative assessment to all classes but do a close analysis and develop a sense of the patterns among students with one class set. Then use those patterns to analyze the results from the other course sections.

If I don't give credit, points, or a grade on the formative assessment, then students won't do it.

In general, assessment and grading experts (Guskey, 2003; O'Connor, 2010; Stiggins & Chappuis, 2005; Tomlinson & Moon, 2013) advise teachers to exclude formative assessment results (or at least to de-emphasize them greatly) when calculating a grade.

Have an open conversation with students about what formative assessment is and why and how you will use it. You can liken it to practice before the big game (Tomlinson & Moon, 2013): scores are not recorded for practice drills or even within team scrimmages because they are opportunities for players to learn from their mistakes and improve before it really counts. Emphasize that formative assessment is for your planning and their learning. Make sure they understand that it is just as much an assessment of your teaching as it is of their learning. If students see that you are looking at and using the information, they will be more likely to complete the assessments authentically. If they see you're not attending to their responses, they will know you're not invested, and they won't see the need to invest time in completing them.

Using formative assessment regularly can gradually decrease the amount of homework needed because you're finding out what you need to know in a proactive way. If students understand this connection, frequent ungraded assessment can serve as a motivating factor in and of itself.

What about just giving a quiz? Isn't that formative?

Giving a quiz and marking student responses as correct or incorrect without analyzing and making sense of those responses and what they imply cannot rightfully be characterized as formative assessment. A quiz can be used as a formative assessment if the teacher analyzes results and uses them to drive instruction, but if it is used in this manner (i.e., to check in on student learning), ideally it should not be considered in calculating grades (see previous section).

What do I do with those few students who regularly grasp everything on my formative assessment questions?

Consider the quality of the questions. Are they truly "sticky" questions whose responses will reveal deep thinking? If they're not, revisit "Constructing Useful

Formative Assessment Prompts" (p. 155) and consult Part 2 of this chapter for examples. If they are, see Chapter 7 for ideas to help students go deeper in their thinking once they've mastered the initial learning goals.

What do I do with students who have language barriers or writing disabilities?

Consider presenting the assessment in alternative formats. For example, you might allow students to

- Provide information in a bulleted list rather than writing it out.
- Illustrate ideas rather than explaining them.
- Speak answers aloud to the teacher or a co-teacher.
- Use assistive technology to record responses.

What about data from standardized assessments? Are they formative?

First, it's worth noting what standardized assessments—including state-mandated accountability tests, benchmark assessments, achievement tests, and district-developed common assessments—can do. Interpreted appropriately, they may

- Provide one of many data sources for district and school leaders to use in judging the effectiveness of programs and initiatives, especially over time.
- Reveal general patterns of strengths and weaknesses across a district, within a school, within a grade level, and so on.
- Provide a reference point that enables schools and educators to discern and report general patterns of student growth over time.
- Give individual teachers a sense of their own instructional strengths, tendencies, and areas of growth relative to goals measurable by the test design and item format and content.

On the other hand, standardized tests generally do not

- Allow teachers to see the actual test questions in a timely manner (that is, alongside student results).
- Provide individual student responses.
- Use item formats that would provide insight into a student's thinking (i.e., why the student chose or gave a certain response).
- Align with specific unit or lesson goals that the teacher aims to address in the classroom at a particular time.
- Provide the most recent information about individual student performance relative to learning goals.
- Reveal the instruction that students need in order to progress in their learning.

In other words, data from standardized tests can be used to paint, in broad strokes, an Impressionist's view of the learning landscape. But these data are not useful for the more exacting and immediate task of designing meaningful learning experiences for all students.

A Case in Point: Ms. Rissa

"The beauty of 1st period," Ms. Rissa mused as she watched her students disappear into the hallway, "is that there's 2nd through 8th periods." She knew she would need to do things differently throughout the rest of the day to avoid leaving students with the misconceptions she had discovered in her 1st period students. For the remaining periods, she ended the class discussion 10 minutes earlier than she had in the first block and asked students to respond to three questions aligned to her learning goals:

- What is a conceit in literature? (Knowledge)
- Explain the conceit John Donne used in "A Valediction: Forbidding Mourning." (Skill)
- Evaluate Donne's use of the conceit. Was it more effective than a more direct approach would have been? Why or why not? Cite the text in your response. (Understanding/Skill)

As she pored over student responses at the end of the day, she noticed similar patterns emerging from every class. In each section, there were students who used textual evidence to argue persuasively about Donne's use of conceit. Others were able to repeat what had been discussed in class but could take it no further. Still others seemed to miss several of the learning goals completely. Ms. Rissa knew she'd need to lead a small group in each class the next day to work through misconceptions. She would ask those who had constructed sound arguments on the Exit Slip to preview Act 3, Scene 5 of *Romeo and Juliet* and compare Shakespeare's use of conceit with Donne's to determine who they thought used the technique more effectively.

It was beginning to make sense to Ms. Rissa that her instruction should be driven by recent, relevant information about student learning. It occurred to her that the playwright George Bernard Shaw (1903) had it right when he had a character reflect, "The only man who behaved sensibly was my tailor: he took my measure anew every time he saw me, whilst all the rest went on with their old measurements and expected them to fit me." She realized that without ongoing, classroom-based formative assessment, she was simply using "old measurements" to guide her planning. No wonder she was so often frustrated by finding that the instructional "fit" was not optimal for all students!

Part 2:

Tools and Strategies

Exit and Entry Slips

What It Is:

An efficient and simple method for formatively assessing students during the learning cycle. An Exit Slip is administered at the end of class, while an Entry Slip is administered at the beginning of class.

How It Works:

1. The teacher poses one to three prompts at the beginning or end of a lesson for students to answer on a half-sheet of paper or an index card, or via an online or technology tool.

2. Prompts can be designed as assessments or self-assessments of

   - *Content/skill readiness:* what students understand, know, and can do relative to the learning goals.
   - *Progress:* where students are with a task or process; work habits, attitudes, or dispositions relative to a task or topic.
   - *Interest/motivation/preference:* the level or nature of students' interest in what they are learning; how or under what conditions students prefer to learn.

3. The teacher collects and analyzes individual responses, looking for patterns among students in the class or course.

What It's Good For:

Students' responses on Exit and Entry Slips can inform adjustments to whole-class instruction, guide plans for differentiation, provide ideas for lesson activities, inform grouping decisions, and help refine small-group work or individual conferences.

Tips:

- To avoid student fatigue and robotic responses and to gain a more complete picture of what students are learning, vary the format and type of prompts in Exit and Entry Slips over time.
- Avoid reducing Exit and Entry Slips to an instructional routine (e.g., as a way to begin or end class); instead, use them to gather valuable evidence you might not otherwise get.
- Avoid using an Exit or Entry Slip every day. Intermix with Frayer diagrams (pp. 169–172), and vary the medium (online versus handwritten) to give students a sense of variety.

Classroom Examples:

For clarity and readability, the following examples of Exit and Entry Slips are organized into four categories:

1. *General readiness prompts for all content areas:* Examples of prompts that can be used to gauge student understanding, knowledge, or skill across content areas and topics within a content area.

2. *Subject-specific readiness:* Examples of content-based items related to specific topics, concepts, or skills in math, English language arts, history/social studies, world language, fine arts, and science.

3. *Progress monitoring/reflecting for all content areas:* Examples of student self-assessment of readiness, work habits, attitudes, or dispositions relative to a task, topic, or method of instruction, and individual or group progress toward a goal.

4. *Gauging interest/learning preference:* Examples of prompts for tapping into what students find motivating or intriguing during a unit of study, including the level or nature of students' interest in what they are learning and how or under what conditions students prefer to learn.

General Readiness Prompts for All Content Areas	
Don't Misunderstand Me . . . • One misunderstanding someone might have about [*technology in ancient civilizations*] is . . . • Here's what I might say to that person to help him or her better understand the "truth":	**Concept Connections** • Look at the list of concepts/topics on the board. • Work with a partner to write one to three complete sentences that connect these concepts/topics to one another. • Your sentences should reveal important connections or relationships in what we're studying.
Be Sure To . . . • What should someone "be sure to do" when [*solving the kind of problem we have been working on this week*]? • He or she should be sure to _____ because _____.	**Defend or Destroy** Select two claims from the list: one that you can "defend" and one that you want to "destroy." Use evidence from [*this lab, the text, the sources/documents*] and your reasoning to explain and justify your thinking.
3-2-1 • Three things I learned about [*the topic*] are . . . • Two ways I contributed to class are . . . • One question I have is . . .	**Important Things** • Some important things about [*primary sources, linear equations*] are _____ and _____. • But the *most* important thing about [*primary sources, linear equations*] is _____ because _____.
Debate Follow-Up 1. What was the most convincing evidence you heard today on *both* sides of the issue? 2. How has today's debate changed or strengthened your opinions? 3. What next step would you take to investigate this issue further? What would you hope to find?	**Discussion Take-Aways** 1. What was the central question or issue in this discussion? 2. What did you think or believe relative to this question or issue at the beginning of the discussion? Why? 3. What do you think now? Why? 4. What *new* questions do you have?

Subject-Specific Readiness	
Geometry ▲ What was the *point* of today's lesson? ■ What's all "squared away" for you? ● What from today's lesson can't you quite *wrap your head around* yet? *Source:* Rebecca Yaple, Renaissance Academy, Norfolk, VA. Used with permission.	**How Sure Are You? (Math/Science)** 1. Solve the problem. 2. How sure of your answer are you? *I'm _____ percent sure.* ☐ If you are 100 percent sure, why are you sure? (How do you know your answer is correct?) ☐ If you are less than 100 percent sure, what would make you *more* sure? *Source:* Anna Maria D'Ippolito. Copyright 2013 by ASCD.
Calculus A rocket is launched from a field while a ground-level camera stationed 60 feet away films the launch. If the rocket is rising at a rate of 15 feet/second at the instant when the rocket is 60 feet above the ground, find the rate at which the angle of elevation of the line of sight from the camera to the rocket is changing. (Assume the ground is level and the rocket rises perfectly vertically.) Picture: Equation(s) relating variables: Situational information: Differentiate and solve: *Source:* Scott Leverentz, Lakes Community High School, Lake Villa, IL. Used with permission.	**Algebra** **3:** Provide *three* ways in which we can solve a system of linear equations. **2:** Write *two* questions you have about solving systems of linear equations. **1:** Solve this *one* system of equations using the method of your choice. Then explain why or why not another method would also work. $$x - y = 11$$ $$2x + y = 19$$ *Source:* Jennifer O'Keefe, George Mason High School, Falls Church, VA. Used with permission.
Literature 1. *Say it in a sentence:* What do you think Marley is trying to get Scrooge to see, understand, and/or do in the part of the story we read for today? 2. How do you know? (Cite specific examples and evidence from the text.)	**Middle School Conventions** **3:** List *three* keys to success when using the semicolon: **2:** Give *two* examples of purposeful and efficient use of the semicolon: **1:** Here is *one* thing I'm hoping you explain better or reteach in a different way:
U.S. History • The *three of the most important* New Deal programs were . . . • But *the most important* New Deal program was _____ because . . .	**Government** A friend says to you at lunch, "I think the president is the most important branch of government." • What *two* misconceptions does your friend have? • What would you say to your friend to help him understand the branches of government and how they work?

Subject-Specific Readiness (*continued*)	
World Language Your friend has left a message on your Facebook wall to let you know what she wants to do this weekend. Use the verb tense we're studying and the target vocabulary from this chapter to write her a three-sentence message on her Facebook wall in [*the target language*].	**World Language** The words *por* and *para* are easily confused. • Write a sentence that shows *por* and *para* being used correctly. • Write a sentence that shows *por* and *para* being used *in*correctly. • How do *you* remember the difference between *por* and *para* and when to use each one? • Optional: Use pictures, shapes, arrows, or some other visual to show or teach someone else how to use each of these words correctly.
Theater Arts Reflect on the production we just watched in terms of set design. Describe your opinion of • The *most powerful* aspect of the set design. • The *least powerful* aspect of the set design. In your answers, be sure to discuss the impact of set design on the quality of the *overall performance*.	**Health** • Think about what you ate *yesterday*. Did your choices reflect the advice of the latest USDA guidelines? Why or why not? (Your response should show that you understand what the guidelines are!) • Think about what you've eaten so far *today*. Specifically, what would you need to eat for the rest of the day to meet USDA guidelines?
Science Lab 1. What was the independent variable in today's experiment? How do you know? 2. What was the dependent variable in today's experiment? How do you know? 3. What did you find out about the relationship between the independent variable and the dependent variable?	**Earth Science** • Draw the Earth's orbit around the Sun. Include any important "labels." • Briefly explain what causes the seasons. • What about today's explanation was "fuzzy"? In other words, what do you hope we'll clear up or talk more about in future classes?
Physical Science • Coach Turner throws a baseball up in the air. As it comes back down, what happens to the velocity of the baseball and *why*? • A 6th grade student claims (and she is serious) that for a force to exist, two objects need to be in direct contact. What would be your expert response to her claim? *Source:* Amy Germundson. Used with permission.	**Chemistry** 1. Given the following reaction, write the law of mass action (equilibrium constant expression): $2A + B \lozenge 3C + 2D$ 2. Given the following concentrations for A, B, C, and D, solve for the equilibrium constant (K) for the above reaction. $[A] = 0.50$ M $[B] = 0.10$ M $[C] = 0.80$ M $[D] = 0.99$ M 3. State whether the above reaction is product favored or reactant favored. Explain your answer. *Source:* Serena Kinsella, J. P. Tucker High School. Used with permission.

Progress Monitoring/Reflecting for All Content Areas	
Today & Tomorrow • Today I learned that . . . • This is important [*to math, to my life*] because . . . • *Tomorrow,* I think/hope we . . .	**How Many Bars?** After today's lesson, I have . . . ____ *Full bars.* I'm getting it! ____ *Some bars.* I'm in and out with this. ____ *No bars.* Lost signal . . . Specifically, here's where I think I need better "coverage":
1-2-3 Summarizer After reading over my draft, • One thing I really like about it is . . . • Two resources I can use to help me improve it are . . . • Three revisions I plan to make are . . .	**Group Work Evaluation** Think back to today's group activity, and answer these questions briefly. 1. How well did your group stay on task/use your time wisely? 2. Which role were you assigned for the group work? 3. Explain your greatest strength/best accomplishment in playing that role today. 4. Describe how you could have done a better job in that role. 5. Did your group encounter any conflicts? If so, how did you work around them?
Where Am I? 1. What did I accomplish today? (Explain and attach evidence.) 2. What do I still have to do? 3. What's my plan of attack for tomorrow? (What are my next steps?)	**Where Were You?** 1. Check the station you visited today. ____Station 1 ____Station 2 ____Station 3 ____Station 4 2. Why did you choose this station? 3. Overall, did you find the task at the station helpful? Why or why not? (Be specific!)

Gauging Interest/Learning Preference	
Rank & Relate 1. Rank the following [*topics, people, events*] that we've studied in order of how interesting they are to you. (5 = most interesting; 1 = least interesting) 2. How do the topics that you ranked #1 and #5 relate or connect to each other?	**This Just In!** 1. Restate the most interesting thing you've learned this week as either a news headline or a tweet. 2. What made this interesting to you? Explain.
Worked for Me! We used the following strategies this week: These strategies seemed to work best for me, and here's why:	**What's Making Things Click?** What happens in this class that *helps* you learn (strategies, the way ideas are presented, your grouping configurations, etc.)? What's one thing I (your teacher) could do to improve [*this class, this unit, this topic*] for you?

Frayer Model/Diagram

What It Is:

A tool for probing and assessing the depth at which a student has mastered a concept (see Frayer, Frederick, & Klausmeier, 1969).

How It Works:

The diagram (see below) asks students to provide the *definition* of a concept, its *characteristics* or *attributes,* some crystallizing *examples,* and some *non-examples* that may be frequently confused with examples.

Concept	
Definition	Characteristics/Attributes
Examples	Non-examples

What It's Good For:

- The Frayer model can be used either as an Entry or Exit Slip or as an in-class processing tool.
- The format of the Frayer model is also conducive to structuring whole- or small-group discussion and synthesis, depending on the concept being studied.
- If used as formative assessment, the Frayer diagram should be completed by *individual* students in the wake of *recent, lesson-level* learning experiences.
- The original Frayer model works particularly well with abstract concepts, overarching concepts in or across disciplines (e.g., *change, systems, perspective, proportion*), and topics or concepts that are often misunderstood or misapplied. It can also work as a vocabulary strategy for expanding or checking students' understanding of the connotations and denotations of a word or term. Events, people, and skills (e.g., acting or reading) are not the intended targets of the Frayer model.

Technology: Search Engines	
Definition	Characteristics/Attributes
Good for	Not good for

Classroom Example:

Mr. Faber used an adapted Frayer model as a quick formative assessment during a series of lessons on the types, purposes, and efficient uses of online search engines (see above). Most of the students in his class had a lot of experience *using* search engines, but most tended to rely on only one kind and had little sense of the actual purpose and function of search engines. Mr. Faber posted the Frayer as a Google Doc for students to complete and submit independently. After reviewing the responses and noting new insights and lingering misconceptions, he launched the next day's lesson by displaying a version of the Frayer, filled in with a range of representative and anonymous responses. Students worked in pairs to discuss, amend, and refine the responses toward a whole-class definition and understanding of search engines.

Tips:

- Before students' first independent use, share a completed or partially completed Frayer model with them and allow them to talk through possible responses with a partner.
- The idea of listing "non-examples" isn't intuitive for many students, so it's important to emphasize that a non-example isn't just anything that is not an example of the concept; the goal is to list those things that may be commonly confused with or misapprehended as examples.
- When adapting Frayer model prompts, no matter what the content is, maintain a focus on the intent of the original model: to gauge whether students have a deeper understanding of the concept that includes but goes beyond explaining what it is.
- Adapt prompts by regarding them as four "lenses" for viewing different layers of the concept.

Frayer Diagram Examples

Math: Proportional Relationships

Definition of proportional relationships	Something that will help you remember what proportional relationships are
Example *Why* is this an example of a proportional relationship?	Non-example *Why* is this *not* an example of a proportional relationship?

The Electoral College

Description	Intentions
List benefits	List drawbacks
On the back, make a case for whether you believe the benefits outweigh the drawbacks or vice versa.	

Writing: Transitional Sentences

Definition	Explain importance
Give two different efficient examples	Give two different inefficient examples

World Language: Verb Tense: _____

English equivalent (of the tense)	When to use it
Regular verb examples (use in sentences)	Irregular verb examples (use in sentences)

Source: Kaitlin Cribb, James Madison University. Used with permission.

Frayer Diagram Examples (*continued*)

Biology: Concept of Dominance

Definition	The three possible genotypes (allele combinations) for a particular trait (give names and genotypes)
When the concept of dominance is most helpful in allowing us to determine phenotype:	When the concept of dominance may not be sufficient to allow us to determine phenotype:

Chemistry: Molarity

Definition	Purpose/role in chemistry
Equation (annotated or explained)	Potential misconceptions

Music: Technique

Definition	Application to your instrument
What good technique looks like and sounds like with your instrument	What poor technique looks like and sounds like with your instrument

Physical Education: Strength Training

Role/purpose in a healthy lifestyle	Types
Dos	Don'ts

7 Differentiating According to Student Readiness

Part 1:

What If Students Are in Different Places?

Fourth period has just ended. Mr. Jacobs sits down with a stack of quizzes and his lunch. In preparation for the next step in his unit on graphing, he had posed four questions for students to answer eight minutes before the bell:

1. Depict the data in the table using the kind of graph you believe is best for showing relationships among the data.
2. What kind of graph is this? Why did you choose this kind of graph?
3. Write two questions that your graph *answers*.
4. Write two questions that your graph *raises*. (These should be questions that can't be answered by your graph but that someone might wonder when looking at the graph or the data it represents.)

After Mr. Jacobs reaches the end of the stack, he looks at the piles of quizzes he has sorted according to like need and thinks, "Well, some kids really grasp this, some are getting closer than they were, and a few are completely lost. I guess my plans for the rest of the week need to change."

An Inescapable Dilemma

Mr. Jacobs is confronted with what school change expert Michael Fullan and colleagues (Fullan, Hill, & Crevola, 2006) call "the inescapable dilemma" of classroom instruction: "One teacher and 30 students, all individuals with different motivations to learn, different starting points, different strengths on which to build, and different areas of weakness that inhibit learning" (p. 30). Mr. Jacobs and other middle and high school teachers face not one classroom like this every day but four, five, or six— one teacher and over 100 students.

As we noted in the Introduction, U.S. education has long struggled to find the best way to "handle" the diversity inherent in public schools, trying everything from separate schools to specialized schools, schools within schools, support programs, and sorting students into tracks and leveled classes. Whether these strategies have "worked"—and for whom—is the subject of much debate, both among researchers and policymakers and in local communities among administrators, parents, and teachers.

Differentiation is distinct from the above approaches in that it *embraces* the diversity inherent in classrooms rather than masking it or regarding it as an inconvenience to be avoided at all costs (Tomlinson, 2014a). Differentiation is *not* a way of talking about *which tracks or classes* students are placed in. It's a framework for *how* the individual classroom teacher approaches making curriculum, assessment, and instruction responsive to all learners—which includes handling significant differences in student readiness.

Critics and skeptics of differentiation argue that by middle and high school, the span of abilities in a typical heterogeneous setting is too great for teachers to reasonably or successfully manage, even with a differentiated approach. For some stakeholders, the extent to which teachers can or should be expected to differentiate for student readiness is at the heart of whether differentiation is a worthwhile or feasible goal at all.

However, differentiation is not an either/or proposition; schools don't need to choose between using one-size-fits-all lessons every day or differentiation. In a class of 30 students—whether it's AP Chemistry or a course for struggling readers—none of them is exactly the same. Differentiating for student readiness is *requisite* to effective teaching and to maximizing each learner's potential (Tomlinson, 2008). The "dilemma" created by academically diverse classrooms is really an *opportunity* for teachers to (1) study how adolescents think about and learn in a discipline, and (2) leverage adjustments they make for *specific* students that improve instruction for *all* students.

Ensuring that each student grows from his or her individual starting point toward and beyond important goals, standards, and expectations *is* a challenge for teachers of *any* class type or student composition. This chapter provides guidance for facing that challenge, including how to think about and discern student readiness and what to do when students seem to be all over the map en route to San Francisco. Our assumption is that *all* students are "ready" for high-quality curriculum, engaging instruction, and rigorous tasks in the context of healthy classroom communities. Sometimes, however, ongoing assessment results reveal that students will need to take different paths to arrive at or make progress toward the same end. When we tailor students' learning routes to make sure they receive the support and challenge they need in pursuit of high-quality goals, we are differentiating for *readiness*.

Readiness Versus Ability

Readiness refers to where a student is in his or her grasp of learning goals at a certain point in time, according to *recently gathered* formative assessment data that are *relevant* to those goals. It is not synonymous with *ability*—a more static label that carries with it fixed notions of who will succeed and who won't.

Readiness can vary from lesson to lesson or from skill to skill. Students may wrestle with certain concepts but grasp others with ease. They may initially struggle to master a skill but catch on after much grappling or practice. Students may initially comprehend content and then hit a roadblock and become stumped. The term *ability* suggests that a student is either a "math person" or not; that he or she either thinks scientifically or doesn't. The term *readiness,* by contrast, reflects the realities of how people learn and the dynamic and fluid nature of intelligence.

Students' *ability* is often inferred from standardized tests designed by companies and is reported relative to other test takers' scores. *Readiness* is best discerned from classroom-level formative assessment designed by classroom teachers and analyzed relative to curricular learning goals. Teachers attending to student readiness avoid making assumptions about students who "get it" and students who "don't get it." Instead, they use formative assessment to discover exactly what each learner needs to propel him or her to the next step toward mastering the learning goals.

For all of these distinctions, does it *really* matter for teachers to think in terms of *readiness* rather than *ability*? Isn't it just semantics? The work of Perry, Steele, and Hilliard (2003) as well as Dweck (2006) has revealed that most students achieve only what they *believe* they are capable of achieving, and teachers significantly—and often unconsciously—influence students' perceptions of what those capabilities are. To be effective, then, teachers must believe that all students can grow *and* communicate that belief, both through the language they use in thinking about and talking about or to students, and in designing tasks. Looking at each student each day through the fresh lens of up-to-the-minute evidence is the only way to truly challenge what labels, past experience, and standardized assessments would otherwise dictate students can and can't do.

Differentiation as Feedback

Chapters 3 and 6 described how effective pre-assessment and formative assessment provide this "fresh lens." Ongoing assessment has the potential to test and revise teachers' hypotheses about students and help both teachers and students maintain a growth mindset. Collecting formative assessment results is powerless, however, unless teachers intentionally analyze and interpret student responses and then use those data, be they qualitative or quantitative, to make better instructional decisions (Wiliam, 2011). In other words, teachers must respond to what formative assessment reveals. The research on student learning maintains that providing effective feedback is the best way to do so (Bransford et al., 2000; Hattie, 2012; Wiliam, 2011).

In Hattie's (2012) meta-analysis of the impact of instructional interventions, *feedback* was named as one of the practices with the most influence on student learning. Wiliam (2011) agrees, but emphasizes the importance of providing *effective* feedback. He explains the proper nature of feedback by likening it to its original conception in engineering: the process by which "information about the current state of a system [is] used to change the future state of the system" (p. 131). Giving instructional feedback, then, is the process by which we use what we know about a student's learning to move that student forward. As Wiliam (2011) and Wiggins (2012) both point out, feedback is not about value judgments or praise; rather, it focuses on providing targeted information that will help students reach established goals.

Feedback does not need to be a conversation, nor does it need to be a didactic list of what students should do next. As Wiliam (2012) points out, "Feedback should require more work from the recipient than from the giver. If feedback highlights everything that is wrong in a piece of work, there's nothing left for the recipient to do" (p. 34). Said differently, information about what students need to grow should reach them through the vehicle of a *task* that students must complete so that they, not their teachers, do the work necessary for learning to happen. In essence, teachers should design differentiated tasks in such a way that these tasks serve *as feedback*.

Finding and Responding to Patterns in Assessment Results

Hattie (2012) emphasizes that the goal of feedback is to give students guidance that is "'just in time,' 'just for me,' 'just for where I am in my learning process,' and 'just what I need to help me move forward'" (p. 122). This makes sense from a research and a learning perspective, but it can be overwhelming from an instructional perspective. How can middle and high school teachers efficiently give such targeted information to 100-plus students?

This is where the use of formative assessment to reveal *patterns* comes in. In all likelihood, not every student in the room will require the same feedback at any given point during the instructional cycle. Teachers can literally sit, as Mr. Jacobs did at the chapter's opening, and sort assessment results into piles of "like need."

Those patterns are sometimes as simple as "got it" and "didn't get it." More often, the patterns revealed are gradations of understanding (some students are ready for the next step; a few have some holes in their understanding that need to be patched before they move on; others need to start again from the beginning). At times, the patterns simply reveal different kinds of errors or misconceptions. In any case, the answer to the question of "How do I sort my Exit Slips?" lies in actually *analyzing the Exit Slips.* Student responses often reveal exactly what they need to move forward.

Discerning patterns in student readiness is a first step that primes teachers for what is perhaps the most challenging aspect of differentiation: deciding how to respond to the differences. Tasks designed to address student readiness should directly address the patterns revealed by formative assessment by (1) providing feedback that is linked to results, (2) helping students recognize and address mistakes or misconceptions, and (3) requiring all students to take a "next step" in their learning.

The following procedure is useful for seeing and addressing patterns in student readiness, as revealed through formative assessment evidence:

1. **Read all the assessment responses** without focusing too long on any one question or student. Get a sense of where each student is relative to the content as well as the general patterns that begin to emerge.

2. Based on the learning goals and the assessment results, **decide what all students could probably benefit from** going forward and devise an introductory activity centered around one or more of those ideas. This could be a demonstration, an illustrative video clip, a well-chosen problem, a discussion for the class, or a clarification from the teacher.

3. **Look for distinguishing patterns** in responses and make piles of those that seem to go together in some way. It's OK to focus on the one or two questions that reveal the most variance among student answers. In other words, say you posed three questions, but student answers to one of those questions provided the most insight into how to move forward. Focus on that question.

4. **Make general notes** about anything that stands out to you about each pile (usually between two and four piles). For example, you may find that certain students share the same misconceptions. Perhaps a small group of students made minor (albeit different) errors but seemed to understand the general process. Still others may demonstrate a sophisticated or fluid understanding of the content.

5. Look more closely at what each pattern reveals and **determine what students will need to move forward.** For example, some students may benefit from a clarifying or annotated example. Others may require step-by-step directions to walk them through a process. Still others may be ready for a challenge that asks them to examine how the concept is used in other situations.

6. **Generate ideas for tasks** that students at each of these different readiness levels can complete and that will provide them with the feedback, scaffolding, or challenge they need to grow toward and beyond the goals.

7. **Develop the most advanced task first.** This helps you avoid the trap of simply giving *more* work to students who already get it and instead ensures that those students will receive "more appropriate work" (Tomlinson, 2014a). In addition, establishing a high-quality advanced task first gives you something to emulate when developing the additional tasks (albeit with more scaffolding or support) so that you don't have to start from scratch with each task.

8. ***Develop clear directions and materials*** for each group: these are your differentiated tasks.
9. Design a way to ***bring everyone together*** for whole-class closure.

The good news for middle and high school teachers is that they are more likely to be experts in their content than are elementary school teachers (Bransford et al., 2000; Sousa & Tomlinson, 2011). When teachers grasp the underlying principles and intricate connections within their discipline, they are better able to discern a variety of ways for approaching and interacting with that content (Hattie, 2012). Constructed properly, such tasks can provide all students with the feedback they need to grow.

Strategies for Creating Tasks Differentiated for Readiness

The following sections discuss several strategies for differentiating tasks for student readiness. Teachers should keep in mind that regardless of the strategy used, four principles must govern implementation:

1. Varying levels of tasks should assess the same core learning goals.
2. Decisions about instructional adjustments should be based on recent information from students' classroom performance—not on labels, assumptions, or even performance in previous classes.
3. All tasks designed in response to evidence of student readiness must be *respectful* (Tomlinson, 2014a) (see pp. 183–185 for more on respectful tasks).
4. All tasks should provide students with the feedback they need to correct misconceptions and take the next step in their learning.

Tiering

Tomlinson (2014a) explains that tiered tasks "are useful when a teacher wants to ensure that students with different degrees of learning proficiency work with the same essential ideas and use the same key knowledge and skills" (p. 133). Tiering can be thought of as either a *process* or a *concept*.

We discuss Tiering as a *process* when we describe designing tasks differentiated for readiness based on pre- or formative assessment data. The steps listed on page 194 describe the process of engineering tiered tasks to meet student readiness needs as revealed from the results of a specific formative assessment.

Tiering is also a *concept* that can be superimposed on other strategies. When we say we are "tiering" strategies, for example, we are describing making different *levels* or *versions* of those existing strategies in response to the varying readiness needs of our students. By this definition, anything can be tiered, including prompts or questions, resources, perspectives, or more complex structures or strategies. We discuss each of these below.

Prompts or questions. Teachers can tier prompts or questions for in-class processing or take-home work or tasks. The examples that follow are ranked from more sophisticated to more accessible:

Art

    A. Which attributes of the painting appeal to your emotions? Which attributes of the painting appeal to your sense of reason or logic? Why do you think that is?

    B. List all the attributes of this painting that you like. Then list all the attributes of this painting that you don't like. Be able to explain why you do or don't like these attributes.

Text Analysis

    A. Where are the most obvious shifts in tone in the poem? How can you tell? Where are the least obvious shifts? How can you tell?

    B. Where do you see shifts in tone in the poem? What purpose do they serve?

    C. Remember that tone is the "feeling" or "impression" that a text (e.g., a poem) gives the reader through the particular words and phrases the author uses. What is the tone of the poem in lines 10–11? What is the tone in lines 12–13? How does the tone change between lines 10–11 and lines 12–13? Why does it change?

Math (Wiliam, 2012)

    Given after teacher has reviewed student work.

    A. You solved all of these equations correctly. Now make up three equations for others to solve: one that's harder than those you just solved, one that's at about the same level, and one that's easier.

    B. [This number] of the equations you solved are incorrect. Find the incorrect solutions and fix them.

Access to resources. When teachers have up-front information—be it from assessments, observations, or performance on previous tasks—that suggests students will need a range of support with literacy, they can pull different levels of resources for students to examine. Students who are proficient readers may excel with a university website examining a scientific phenomenon, whereas other students may need a web-based resource written in language that is more easily understood. Teachers can bookmark or create QR codes for various sites and assign them strategically to give students access to the sources that work best for them.

Another approach is to highlight key material for students with reading difficulties. For example, some students may be ready to tackle a primary source written in 19th century English, while others may need key passages indicated and unfamiliar words defined. These adjustments can benefit students with reading difficulties, language acquisition needs, or attention deficits.

Similarly, teachers may offer different students varying levels of organizers that exercise the same skills. For example, a Y-Chart may support the majority of students as they compare and contrast different elements, while a few others may be more appropriately challenged by a three-ring Venn diagram that asks them to add an additional layer to their comparisons.

Reading journals are another structure that is easily tiered. Teachers can provide some students with definitions, page numbers, and key points to guide them through the text in a supported manner. Other students may receive prompts that ask them to synthesize large chunks of material, consider conceptual connections, and refer to previously read chapters to make unusual connections.

Perspectives. In a novel, a historical account, or even certain textbook chapters, there are often a variety of perspectives represented. Only examining the text through all of these different lenses will produce a full understanding of it. Usually, some of these perspectives are "right there" (e.g., the narrator, the main character, the population of focus in the article), while other perspectives require the reader to make significant inferences. Such diversity in perspectives offers rich opportunities for tiered explorations of content. Students who need the most support in their learning can examine the story, account, or issue through the perspective with the most information available or the most obvious connections. This may be the narrator in a story (e.g., Ponyboy in *The Outsiders*); the voice of the author(s) in an important document (e.g., the signers of the Declaration of Independence); or the population being studied in a scientific journal article (e.g., bluefin tuna). Other students may be ready to examine the text from a perspective without as much access (e.g., Ponyboy's misunderstood older brother, Darry) or information (e.g., British loyalists in the colonies, fishers living and working in regions with fishing restrictions).

Following is an example of one teacher's use of pooled (mixed) perspectives for reading *To Kill a Mockingbird* (Dobbertin & Doubet, 2005):

- Group 1: The Child's perspective (Scout).
- Group 2: The Hero's perspective (Atticus and Mrs. Dubose).
- Group 3: The perspective of the Persecuted (Calpurnia and Tom Robinson).
- Group 4: The Maturing perspective (Jem, Mr. Underwood).
- Group 5: The Outsider's perspective (Boo Radley, Bob and Mayella Ewell, Dolphus Raymond).

The teacher assigned each student to a perspective through which he or she would read the story and examine key characters, places, and events. Students met in both like-perspective groups and pooled-perspective groups to get a "multi-dimensional" picture of what was going on in the story. Together, the class members came to realize how Atticus's words applied to them as readers: "You never really understand a person until you consider things from his point of view—, . . . until you climb into his skin and walk around in it."

Adjustments to sense-making strategies. Chapter 5 presented numerous strategies that teachers can use for whole-class sense making. Many of the descriptions of these strategies also include suggestions for Tiering (e.g., Analytical Role Cards, Debate Team Carousel, Structured Academic Controversy, ThinkDots, Jigsaw). In a Jigsaw, for example, the teacher can tailor expert group materials and tasks to meet the specific readiness needs of students (e.g., strategic choices of reading levels, number of facets addressed, complexity of material).

Contracts and Agendas

Contracts and Agendas function as vehicles for differentiated tasks. Both structures outline a collection of learning activities and organizational measures to ensure student success and grasp of learning goals, but they vary in how they are prepared and implemented.

With Contracts, students do not choose what they will learn—the teacher determines the learning goals—but they do select how they'll demonstrate their mastery of those goals, usually from a list of discrete tasks or problems. Teachers generally use Contracts to assign varying levels of reinforcement or practice to students with varying learning needs. For example, the teacher may create two levels of a Vocabulary Contract if students in the class are operating at two different levels of sophistication with vocabulary. Each version has its requirements, but students receive several choices of how they can meet those requirements.

An Agenda is a teacher-created and -directed schedule of learning experiences and tasks that gives students choices only in terms of the order in which to complete the tasks. Teachers can fill in the appropriate homework, in-class tasks, teacher conference points, and peer partners for students at various readiness levels.

Teachers can pull from textbooks and other instructional resources when compiling a Contract or an Agenda. Because Contracts and Agendas are generally designed to reinforce skills and provide practice (rather than introduce students to content or summatively assess their mastery of learning goals), it is not hard to find varying levels of terms, problems, websites, and so on. Part 2 (pp. 202–205) includes descriptions and examples of both structures.

Respectfully Differentiated Tasks

Respectful tasks are the insurance policy of differentiation. Because students are diverging from a shared route to take slightly different paths for a brief time, it is crucial that the tasks they work on—individually or with others—all but guarantee progress and engagement. Whether teachers are designing tasks in direct response to recent and specific formative assessment patterns or using strategies that anticipate typical or predictable patterns, all students should be working with tasks that honor the content, the goals, and the learner. Tasks are respectfully adjusted for student needs when they meet the following criteria:

1. *The tasks are aligned with the same learning goals (understanding, knowledge, skills), and with one another.* Tasks that are not connected by common goals are not differentiated—they are just different. The same "glue" must hold the tasks together, with understanding as the focus. Likewise, the tasks should be designed so that all student work can be evaluated according to the same criteria.

2. *The tasks are equally interesting, appealing, and engaging from the students' perspective.* If some tasks are the instructional equivalent of limp broccoli while others are veritable ice cream sundaes—that is, if some students are working with tasks that are boring, passive, or a waste of time while others work with tasks that draw them in and keep them hooked—there is little chance that respectful differentiation is occurring.

3. *The tasks ask all students to work at high levels of thought.* When differentiating for readiness, it's tempting to think in terms of "high-level" and "low-level" questions and prompts, but as we noted in Chapter 5, it's important for all students to work with cognitively demanding tasks. Designing the top task first, as we suggested above, is one way to circumvent this potential pothole. Another strategy is to think about how to differentiate within a targeted skill. For example, if a skill goal is to analyze and compare primary sources, adjustments for readiness might include differentiating the sources being analyzed and compared or the process used to do so, but each task should engage every student in the targeted skill.

4. *The tasks mimic what people or professionals in the real world do, or how they think.* All tasks, including differentiated tasks, should approximate or represent in some way authentic ideas, knowledge, processes, or products. It's not respectful to have some students complete a low-level worksheet on simple machines while other students use what they have learned about simple machines to design a multi-age swing set for a local park. This is a stark example, but it vividly illustrates what differentiated tasks must avoid at all costs. All students should work with the authentic task, albeit with different levels of scaffolding and support.

5. *The tasks represent a wise use of students' time.* Tasks created in the name of differentiation should be substantive tasks that make learning more efficient than it might have otherwise been and move students toward or beyond the learning goals. A task that is a fun or interesting diversion but has little to do with curricular outcomes may actually get in the way of progress.

6. *The tasks are comparable in terms of workload or time required to complete the tasks.* When compared side by side, the time and workload implied or required by differentiated tasks should be equal. Do the tasks sound simply like "more work" versus "less work"? Avoid assigning different products that—by their nature—demand different amounts of sweat (e.g., a half-page diary entry versus a video documentary).

7. *The tasks are constructed in such a way that they lead naturally to whole-class closure.* In addition to being aligned with the same learning goals, differentiated tasks should be constructed in such a way that all students—no matter which task they are completing—can engage in the same closing discussion, summarizing prompt, or final problem. This helps the teacher make sure the tasks are not diverging from one another too drastically and solidify the class's sense of community.

Respectfully differentiated tasks are critical to developing in students a growth mindset orientation toward learning and increasing student buy-in to the idea of differentiation in general. Middle and high school students are acutely aware of any implied or actual differences between tasks that they and their peers select or are assigned. Using the above list as a "respect check" in a self- or peer review of differentiated tasks can help ensure that all students are working with motivating tasks that are a good fit for their readiness needs.

Mindset, Student Status, and Readiness Differentiation

Teachers understandably worry that students will label readiness-based tasks or groupings as "dumb" and "smart" and that self-efficacy will be adversely affected by any suggestion that some students are working at a more or less advanced level, even if it is toward common goals. Adolescents' general self-consciousness, desire to fit in, and constant comparison of self with others further fuel teacher concerns about using readiness-based differentiation in the classroom. Indeed, such apprehension prevents some teachers from putting students into groups or using differentiated tasks of any kind.

It is true that when students are put into teacher-created groups or have differentiated tasks, they do a two-part "status check," asking (in their minds or aloud), "Who's in my group versus these other groups?" and "What are we doing versus what they are doing?" Right or wrong, they are interpreting both the compositions of any groupings and the tasks themselves as feedback about how "smart" or capable (or affable or well behaved) the teacher believes they are. Without paying careful attention to key principles of differentiation, attempts to differentiate for readiness can easily create a status hierarchy or discernible "pecking order" in the classroom as well as reinforce a fixed mindset (Dweck, 2006).

Teachers can keep differentiation from becoming a form of in-class tracking by creating respectful tasks, as described above, and by adhering to the principle of flexible grouping. Tomlinson (2003) defines flexible grouping as students consistently working in a variety of grouping configurations over a relatively short period. Groups can vary by

- Configuration (whole-group, half-class, small-group, individual).
- Size of small group (e.g., dyads, trios).
- Element of student learning (readiness, experience, interest, learning profile—more about the latter two in Chapter 8).

- Composition in terms of elements of student learning (homogeneous or heterogeneous).

Students might be working with peers in heterogeneous or homogeneous groups, depending on the curricular goals and task purpose. At times, it makes sense for students to work with peers who share similar readiness in background or prerequisite knowledge or skills, toward intellectual growth. Other times, students should work with peers who share their interests to increase motivation and persistence in the task (see Chapters 4 and 8). At still other times, to increase the efficiency of student learning, teachers will form groups based on students' learning profiles (see Chapter 8). Teachers can also use student-selected groups and groups configured at random (we talk more about this in Chapter 9). Flexible grouping facilitates a belief that intelligence is dynamic and malleable. If students remain too long in any one grouping type or configuration, they may begin or continue to view their intelligence, strengths, and weaknesses as static or immutable. It is therefore crucial that any instructional groupings be flexible.

The way in which teachers make transparent and honor readiness-based tasks also builds student status. When possible, reinforce that you have designed tasks based on students' most recent work—not on a blanket sense of their ability. Tying your task design and grouping decisions directly and explicitly to the latest evidence of what students understand, know, and can do conveys the powerful messages that you have thoughtfully evaluated student work and responses and, most important, that you are keeping a growth mindset about students. Assuming the tasks are respectful, there's no need to keep it a secret that students are working with different tasks. Often the best way to honor what all students have done and to show that everyone has worked with respectful and important tasks is conducting a discussion or synthesis activity that requires students to share, make sense of, or draw from one another's work. The Jigsaw strategy employs this component by design, as do several examples of tiered lessons featured in Part 2 of this chapter (pp. 197–201). In addition, Chapter 9 provides guidance for managing both the assignment and implementation of differentiated tasks.

Frequently Asked Questions

I get that all classes need to differentiate for student readiness, but don't leveled classes make that easier?

Applying this rationale, one would expect to see widespread differentiation in advanced placement courses and special schools for academically advanced students. Research suggests, however, that instruction in these environments is not as student-centered, responsive, personalized, or differentiated as one might hope, given the presumptive "reduced" readiness span (Callahan, 2003; Finn & Hockett, 2012;

Hertberg-Davis, Callahan, & Kyburg, 2006). Despite the prevalence of the assertion that leveled classes make differentiating for readiness more manageable, our experience is that such leveling might actually work against it and prevent teachers from seeking opportunities to study and respond to student differences. The class labels, in effect, tempt the teacher to view and treat the students in that class as one student in terms of readiness, and to differentiate less, not more.

What about labels or designations (e.g., students with IEPs, English language learners, gifted students)? Do those mean anything in the context of readiness?

Labels can be helpful insofar as they convey information that teachers need to consider as they plan instruction to fit their students. Labels do not, however, serve as boxes into which teachers can conveniently group students for every instructional experience. Here are just a few examples illustrating why:

- English language learners do not all speak the same native language, and they are not all at the same stage of language acquisition. They come to the classroom with varying school and life experiences that affect the way they will learn best.
- Students who have been identified as gifted are most likely not gifted in every academic respect, or with regard to specific concepts, topics, or skills in a given unit.
- The autism spectrum is indeed a spectrum: no two students with the diagnosis will require the exact same supports or excel in the exact same areas.
- A student can simultaneously struggle with attention issues and excel in problem solving, or be a talented storyteller who also happens to have dysgraphia or to be learning the English language.

Because students have such a wide array of learning needs that may or may not be communicated by a label, formative assessment is still the best way to determine what a student needs. This is true even if that formative assessment is administered with accommodations (see the next section). It's important to discover where students are with respect to learning goals—not just where they are in terms of their label—and proceed appropriately.

I have students who struggle significantly with reading and writing, which presents big challenges to formative assessment and to providing differentiated tasks.

It is important to ensure that students are progressing in their content-based learning goals as well as in their literacy goals. This may mean administering formative assessment orally rather than in writing, with assistive technology, or by a specialist partner. When we deliver tasks and instruction that target students' content-based needs, we can do so in an avenue that supports their literacy needs (e.g., varied texts and organizers, additional scaffolding in the form of highlighted texts and vocabulary support). We must not assume, however, that a student's literacy profile determines his or her content readiness. Students can excel in their thinking while struggling in their expression of that thinking. We must take care to address our students' actual needs rather than our perceptions of their needs, which may be incorrectly derived from unrelated information.

How do I grade work that has been differentiated for readiness?

In both this chapter and Chapter 6, we have discussed formative assessment as a way of gathering evidence of student learning, and instructional tasks (differentiated and otherwise) as forms of *feedback* to students. Because formative assessment results are collected during the learning cycle, assessment experts advise de-emphasizing them when calculating students' grades. Students should still receive feedback on their work, but it need not include points or grades.

Generally speaking, readiness tasks are not summative assessments: they are instructional interventions. When teachers structure readiness tasks in the manner discussed in this chapter, it is with the goal of growth in mind. We don't measure or record the time of a runner as she is running; rather, we record her time when she reaches the finish line. Likewise, we don't grade students as they grapple with readiness-based differentiation; we grade them summatively at designated, whole-class points in the units (e.g., quizzes, tests, performance assessments). Chapter 8 discusses such tasks in more detail.

Should I let students choose from differentiated tasks? What if they choose the wrong one?

When tasks are differentiated for interest and learning profile (see Chapter 8), you want students to do what seems most motivating and efficient from their per-spective—so go ahead and let them choose, unless there's another reason you want certain students to work with certain tasks.

With readiness differentiation, the goal is to propel students' academic growth. You've designed the tasks with students' particular readiness needs in mind, having interpreted where they are based on evidence. Letting students choose from readiness-based tasks not only leaves their growth to chance but also places the onus for differ-entiation on the students. In general, students understand and accept the idea that sometimes they can choose from tasks and sometimes tasks are assigned to them. Maintaining a balance between the "different kinds" of differentiation can help ensure that differentiated instruction reflects a cooperative and collaborative relationship between teacher and student.

Strategies like Contracts and Agendas (see Part 2 of this chapter) can be used to present students with different readiness-based options while ensuring that students are only choosing from tasks that you can "live with" them doing.

I teach 100-plus students and multiple preps! How can I do this?

As we emphasized in Chapters 3 and 6, the most efficient way of handling volume is to examine formative assessment results from one class section to develop a sense of patterns in the responses before analyzing other class sections. In the case of multiple preps, try experimenting with strategies like Tiering in just one section or course.

Remember that some variance in student responses and thinking during a unit is natural. Slight differences in understanding don't necessarily require differentiating lessons and tasks for readiness. If the assessment results reveal minor questions or bumps in the road that can be addressed with the full class, a brief discussion or clarifying example may suffice. Reserve your higher-prep efforts for instances when the variance will prevent students from moving forward. If there's a chasm between what different students will need before moving on, then that's a sign you probably need to differentiate for readiness.

What's the difference between differentiation for readiness and Universal Design for Learning? They seem similar.

Universal Design for Learning (UDL) is a set of principles or lenses that teachers can apply to unit or lesson design. It emphasizes maximizing the "fit" of the learning environment and instruction for students with certain needs by doing things that will likely benefit many students. UDL is driven less by classroom-level formative assessment than by general research about how the brain works, how people learn, and what groups of students with shared needs (e.g., students with learning disabilities) seem to benefit from. Broadly speaking, UDL suggests providing the entire class with multiple ways to represent, interact with, and show understanding of content. With differentiation, specific avenues are provided to specific students— or groups of students—based on needs emerging from ongoing assessment. In best-case scenarios, classrooms include both UDL and differentiation.

A Case in Point: Mr. Jacobs

When Mr. Jacobs more closely examined the results from his graphing quiz, three patterns emerged:

1. Some students really understood the purpose and nature of graphing. They chose the best possible graph for the data set, they clearly and correctly labeled the graph, and the graph illuminated the data Mr. Jacobs had provided. The questions these students posed forced inferences or comparisons, going beyond what the graph showed on a surface level and digging to what the graph revealed in terms of comparisons of data.

2. The majority of students chose a graph that matched the data. Most parts of the graph were labeled clearly and correctly, but the students posed questions that merely scratched the surface and did not require analysis or interpretation.

3. A small group of students were not able to develop a graph that clearly captured or conveyed the "story" of the data. In addition, the questions they posed were inaccurate, lacked clarity, or did not make sense with the data.

Mr. Jacobs knew he needed to move the first group—those with a solid grasp of the learning goals—further on their journey toward expertise. He located several examples of sophisticated graphs from the business section of the *New York Times* and asked students to examine how the graphs conveyed the complex data in a clear, easily digestible fashion. He then asked students to put their analysis to work for them as they created their own graphs using the complex data set he'd given them: three different graphs to convey different aspects of the data to three different adult audiences (chosen by the students). He also asked that they provide a written explanation for why they chose each graph for the corresponding audience.

The second group had the basics but needed to stretch to achieve more fluency with choosing the appropriate graph for each purpose. Mr. Jacobs asked this group to examine three different graphs (line, bar, and pie) from the Life and Weather sections of *USA Today* to discern why each graph type was chosen for the data it conveyed. He then asked the students to create three different graphs for the three data sets he provided—one for businesspeople, one for their classmates, and one for 4th grade students—and to provide an explanation for their choices.

The final group needed more scaffolding in both analysis and creation of graphs. These students examined the same three graphs as the second group, but in a small-group setting with Mr. Jacobs guiding them in tracking the similarities and differences of each graph type on a chart for them to keep in their notebooks. After they had thoroughly discussed the merits and drawbacks of each graph, students decided together which purposes each kind of graph was best suited for. Then each student created three different graphs (line, bar, and pie) to convey the same set of data for three different audiences: businesspeople, classmates, and elementary students. Students in this group were also asked to explain their graphs, but in terms of why each one was well suited to its designated audience.

At the end of the class period, each group shared one of its graphs, and the class discussed the stories those graphs told about the data. Because all data sets had been related to sales of different kinds of candy in different markets, all students were able to share their findings without drawing attention to differences among the tasks. Mr. Jacobs had ensured that each student had taken the appropriate next step in his or her learning, even though that "next step" was different for different students. Because they all wrestled with the same learning goals—albeit at different levels of complexity—all groups of students could share their graphs and learn from one another. They had reached a place from which they could progress together through the next step in the unit.

Part 2:

Tools and Strategies

Tiering

What It Is:

Tiering, developed by Tomlinson (2014a), is best thought of as a *process* for designing tasks differentiated for readiness based on pre- or formative assessment data. Essentially, teachers use the patterns of student learning revealed in *recent* and *relevant* assessment results to create tasks that will move different groups of students toward the same learning goals. Tiering can also be considered a *concept* to be superimposed on other strategies in response to varying student needs.

How It Works:

1. After articulating learning goals, administering a pre-assessment or formative assessment of students' progress toward those goals, and reviewing the assessment results, decide what *all* students need to do to move forward. Devise introductory elements around those ideas.
2. Look for distinguishing patterns in assessment responses and make piles that seem to "go together" in some way.
3. Make general notes about anything that stands out to you about each pile (e.g., students made minor errors but followed the process).
4. Make specific notes about what students will need to advance in their learning (e.g., a clarifying example, step-by-step directions, a chance to examine the concept in a new context).
5. Generate ideas for tasks students at each readiness level can complete that will provide them with the feedback, scaffolding, or challenge they need to grow toward and beyond the goals.
6. Develop the top task first to avoid the trap of simply giving more work to students who "get it" and to create a model to emulate when developing the additional tasks.
7. Develop clear directions and materials for each group: these are your tiered tasks.
8. Develop a closure step that will bring the class back together and prepare students to move forward.

What It's Good For:

- Tiering is useful when students reveal significant differences in their readiness for a particular concept or skill and need different things to grow toward and beyond the learning goals or grade-level standards.
- Done well, Tiering allows teachers to maintain fidelity to learning goals and grant all students access to important content and ideas. It helps us teach *up* rather than dumb down.

Tips:

- The number of tiers (or whether Tiering is necessary at all) should be determined by the *patterns* that emerge from the formative assessment information. The patterns may reveal the need for one, two, or three tasks.
- If the assessment results lead you to see the need for five or more tasks, then it's likely that the learning goals are too narrow (or too low or too high), the pre- or formative assessment prompts need revision, or your "patterns" need to be broader and more encompassing.
- Often, Tiering involves making minor adjustments to one top-tier task rather than creating multiple parallel tasks.
- Use Tomlinson's (2014a) Equalizer as a visual thinking tool for Tiering or adjusting a task for student readiness.

Tiering Template

Content Area/Topic: _____   **Grade Level:** _____

Learning Goals		
Understanding Goals	**Knowledge Goals**	**Skill Goals**

Pre- or Formative Assessment

Patterns from Assessment		

Tasks to Facilitate Growth		

Whole-Class Closure

Tiering Classroom Examples

Source/Media Analysis

Learning Goals		
Understanding Goals	**Knowledge Goals**	**Skill Goals**
• **U1:** Writers [journalists, media] use words to shape the reader's perspective. • **U2:** Wise readers know that news is reported from a certain perspective and work to discern that perspective as they consume news.	• **K1:** Terms: *bias, perspective, objective, subjective.* • **K2:** Signs of biased perspective in news writing/reporting.	• **S1:** Discern and explain evidence of bias in news stories. • **S2:** Interpret words and phrases as they are used in a text, including determining connotative meanings (CCSS-ELA, Reading Anchor Standard 4). • **S3:** Analyze how specific word choices shape meaning or tone (CCSS-ELA, Reading Anchor Standard 4).

Pre-Assessment
1. Define *bias.* If possible, distinguish between *bias* and *perspective* in your definition. **K1, U1** 2. Review the printed homepage of CNN.com from 7:00 a.m. this morning. Which headline do you believe is the *most* biased, and why? Which headline do you believe is the *least* biased, and why? **S1, S2, S3** 3. How can someone tell if a news story (in print, online, or on radio or TV) is biased? What are the signs or "red flags"? Try to list and explain at least three. **U1, U2, K2**

Patterns from Assessment		
Pattern 1	**Pattern 2**	**Pattern 3**
• Gave accurate and nuanced definition of *bias*; able to make a distinction between *bias* and *perspective*. May have used the terms or concepts of *objectivity/ subjectivity.* • Headline choices and explanations were robust and insightful and showed strong understanding of bias. • Provided clear and accurate explanations of three or more ways of detecting bias; may have referenced sophisticated techniques, such as discerning what journalists choose *not* to include (bias by omission).	• Gave mostly accurate, if incomplete, definition of *bias*; attempted to make a distinction between *bias* and *perspective*. • Headline choices and explanations were reasonable, but may have represented minor misconceptions about bias. • Provided mostly clear and accurate explanations of two or three ways of detecting bias.	• Gave inaccurate or limited definition of *bias*; did not include *perspective* in definition, or made an incorrect distinction. • Headline choices and explanations lacked clear reasoning and/ or revealed significant misconceptions about bias. • Provided no explanation or provided explanation of only one way of detecting bias and/ or provided unclear or inaccurate explanations.

Source/Media Analysis (*continued*)

Introduction/Setup

1. Students discuss (Think-Pair-Share) two captioned photos from different news sources of victims of Hurricane Katrina, noting differences in how each news organization interpreted what was happening in its photo. Guiding questions: *What biases do you see? What are the most obvious clues or signs of these biases? What impact do you think word choice has on a reader?*

2. Students create a T-Chart of their classifications of headlines from the pre-assessment, noting which they perceived as more and less biased and discussing which headlines they would reclassify (if any) and why. Teacher allows time for whole-class debate, questioning, and construction of a definition of *bias*.

3. Teacher provides notes (on a handout or through a brief presentation) on key signs of bias (e.g., use of slang, strong verbs, loaded language). Students use these in their next tasks.

4. Each student is given one of three headline analysis tasks (see below), differentiated for readiness. Students work individually and then form a pair or group with one or two classmates who had the same task. *Note:* all three tasks use the same headlines. Tasks 2 and 3 have the headline source labeled; task 1 does not. (For the daily front-page headlines of major national and international news outlets, go to http://www.newseum.org/todaysfrontpages.)

Tiered Tasks		
Headline Analysis Task 1 (Higher Readiness— Pattern 1)	**Headline Analysis Task 2 (Mid-Readiness— Pattern 2)**	**Headline Analysis Task 3 (Lower Readiness— Pattern 3)**
Review the four headlines from different news sources on the same event/story. [*Students are given headlines, but the source for each is not labeled.*] Follow this process for analysis: a. Characterize the *intent* of each headline. Be prepared to explain your characterizations. b. Rank the headlines from most biased (1) to least biased (4). Explain why you ranked them in that order. c. One of these headlines is from an international news source. Decide which one, and explain your choice. (Show your teacher when finished.)	Review the four headlines from different news sources on the same event/story. [*Sources are labeled.*] Follow this process for analysis: a. Characterize the *tone* of each headline (one word only). Be prepared to explain your characterizations. b. Rank the headlines from most biased (1) to least biased (4). Explain why you ranked them in that order. c. What was each paper's position on what happened, as best you can tell from its headline? What additional information in each story would you need to better decide?	Review the four headlines from different news sources on the same event/story. [*Sources are labeled.*] Follow this process for analysis: a. Circle the words in each headline that you believe most strongly reflect a *biased* point of view. Be prepared to explain why you think those words reflect bias. b. Rank the headlines from most biased (1) to least biased (4). Explain why you ranked them in that order. c. How does each news source feel about what happened? Explain whether and how you were able to tell. Include key words and phrases as well as other clues.

Source/Media Analysis (continued)

Synthesis, Closure, and Next Steps
1. Students share their rankings in mixed-task groups. They can group themselves quickly if their task cards are on different-colored paper. Once groups have assembled, prompt them to share and explain their rankings. Possible prompts to display: *(1) Where do you agree? Where do you disagree? (2) Which signs of bias from our list did you detect? What new signs would you add based on your discussion?* Allow time for reporting and discussing with the whole class. Wrap-up or Exit Slip questions: *Is there such a thing as "bias-free news"? Why do you say so?* 2. For homework or an in-class activity the following day, students read two articles that cover the same national or international news story. These can be tiered for readiness as well. (Newsela [http://www.newsela.com] provides current articles from reputable online news sources, with versions of each article at varied reading levels.) Students rank the stories from most objective to least objective and explain and justify their reasoning. Alternatively, students can use Newsela or other online sources to find their own stories on the same event from three different news outlets that represent different perspectives.

Chemistry: Separation Techniques

Learning Goals		
Understanding Goal	**Knowledge Goals**	**Skill Goals**
• **U1:** *Variation* [in physical and chemical properties] plays a key role in *identification* [of mixture components].	• **K1:** Vocabulary: *pure substance, mixture, homogeneous, heterogeneous.* • **K2:** The mechanics of separation procedures (*evaporation, distillation, fractional crystallization, paper chromatography*).	• **S1:** Evaluate which separation technique(s) should be used for a given mixture. • **S2:** Defend a plan of action for separation with evidence relating to physical properties.

Pre-Assessment or Formative Assessment

Formative Assessment (Exit Card)

1. **K1:** Give examples of the following substances:
     i.   Pure substance _____
     ii. Homogeneous mixture _____
     iii. Heterogeneous mixture _____
2. **K2:** Pick a separation procedure and explain how it is used to separate a mixture.
3. **U1:** Why do mixture components have different physical properties?

Patterns from Assessment		
Pattern 1	**Pattern 2**	**Pattern 3**
• Eight students showed a clear mastery of the essential understanding in separating mixtures. They are able to move on to application of this understanding in more complex forms. • Sample responses included "physical properties let you separate items and see the differences" and "if they were the same substance, they'd both evaporate."	• Six students showed a basic understanding of the role physical properties play in separating mixtures. • They should explore this understanding more, with activities that emphasize how important the role is. • Sample responses included "you can know what's going on" and "you can use them to your advantage."	• Eight students either provided incorrect answers or didn't provide answers to the questions. • They should be guided through the concepts again. • They need scaffolding to (1) pick out patterns of different physical properties among substances and (2) use that pattern to select an appropriate separation technique.

Chemistry: *Separation Techniques* (continued)

Tasks to Facilitate Growth		
Task for Pattern 1	**Task for Pattern 2**	**Task for Pattern 3**
• You and your fellow group members are chemists working for _____ County. One day, it seems that everybody in the county is getting sick, so you go to investigate the water quality. You find that companies have been dumping waste into _____ River, and it's now full of *water, ethanol (isopropanol), acetone, salt,* and *sand*.	• You and your fellow group members are chemists working for _____ County. One day, it seems that everybody in the county is getting sick, so you go to investigate the water quality. You find that companies have been dumping waste into _____ River, but you *don't know what exactly the waste is*. Your supervisor wants you to be prepared for any possible situation!	• You and your fellow group members are chemists working for _____ County. One day, it seems that everybody in the county is getting sick, so you go to investigate the water quality. You find that companies have been dumping waste into North River, and it's now full of *water, hexane, salt,* and *gravel*.
• You must clean up the river water and separate all the chemicals, salt, and sand to have clean drinking water! • Work with your group members to *devise a specific plan of action*.	• To prepare, you and your team will practice example scenarios. • From a container, you will pick two cards labeled with possible substances that could have been dumped into the river. • As a team, *decide which technique would be best to separate a mixture of the two substances*.	• You must clean up the river water and separate all the chemicals, salt, and sand to have clean drinking water! • To clean up the drinking water, (1) research the physical properties of each component; (2) then find which differences would be the easiest to focus on when separating; and (3) *pick the separation technique that would be most appropriate for each component*.

Whole-Class Closure
Once each group has had a chance to complete its activity, the whole class will participate in a "sludge" lab: • Each student is given "sludge" and told its components are water, salt, sand, and rocks. • Students must work in lab groups to plan a way to separate the mixture into its designated components. • After the plan is approved, lab groups may work to actually separate the "sludge" using lab equipment. • A follow-up discussion on the similarities and differences of each group's approach will conclude the lab.

Source: Corey Black, Poquoson High School, Poquoson, VA. Used with permission.

Contracts and Agendas

What They Are:

Contracts and Agendas both function as delivery systems for differentiated tasks.

- A *Contract* is a teacher-initiated framework that has students select tasks to complete to fulfill the expectations of the Contract.
- An *Agenda* is a schedule of learning experiences and tasks created and directed by the teacher that is differentiated for or tailored to student needs. Students have some choices about the order in which they complete the tasks, but not which tasks they will complete.

How They Work:

1. Determine the learning goals and standards you want the Contract or Agenda to address. Include on-grade standards, prerequisite knowledge and skills (for students who need review and practice), and next-step or deeper exploration possibilities for students who need to be stretched.

2. Make a list of learning experiences you would like the whole class to engage in. Ideally, these activities would be at the "proficient" level. Some or all of these activities can appear on all versions of the Contract or Agenda.

3. Decide what students who need extra support should do to fill in the gaps in their learning. Add the appropriate task(s) to the "below-proficient" version of the Contract or Agenda.

4. Figure out how students who are already proficient could take it to the next level. This does not necessarily mean moving to the next skill set (although it can); rather, you may ask high-readiness students to tunnel more deeply into grade-level standards by working with complex levels of the content or skills or by working with the content or skills in ways that mirror what professionals in the working world might do.

5. Devise a task (Agenda) or collection of tasks (Contract) for each version that includes
   — Tasks all groups will complete.
   — Tasks tailored for specific learning needs.
   — Tasks that weave content with literacy or research.
   — A combination of teacher-led, individual, and partner or group tasks.

6. Evaluate each version of the Contract or Agenda to make sure the tasks
   — Appear equally respectful.
   — Will require comparable time for the target groups to complete.
   — Stress the same core learning goals.
   — Use materials that are available or obtainable for classroom use.

What They're Good For:

- Both structures outline a collection of learning activities, along with teacher meeting times and other organizational measures, to ensure student success and grasp of learning goals. They allow for differentiation by providing the teacher with a structure for communicating different levels of resources, tasks, structure, and practice.
- Agendas may require less preparation to create but more preparation to implement.
- Contracts require more time to prepare, but may free up the teacher during implementation.
- Contracts require students to make some kind of choices about what they are or aren't going to do for the Contract to be established and fulfilled; this choice can be motivating to reticent adolescent learners.

Classroom Examples

Contract Example: Show Me the Money!

One example of a Contract is Show Me the Money!, a structure that lends itself well to use with preexisting sets of problems, questions, or tasks. We'll use math homework as an example. Often, mathematics texts and resources organize practice problems by level of complexity, with simpler problems sequenced before multistep problems. With the Show Me the Money! strategy, the teacher reviews the problem sets and selects groups of potential problems, making sure they represent a range of difficulty as well as the necessary concepts and skills. Each group or range is assigned a "money" value (e.g., problems 1–5 are each worth $100, and problems 6–10 are each worth $200). Students can choose which problems to do within parameters that the teacher sets—for example, "Complete $1,500 worth of problems—no more than one $100 problem, at least two $200 problems, and at least one $300 problem." See Figure 7.1 for filled-in versions of these Contracts.

FIGURE 7.1

Show Me the Money! Contract

Show Me the Money! Homework

Assignment: _Problems on textbook pgs. 135–136_

Completion Amount: $_1500_

Problem/Task Values:
- _Problems 1–5_   = **$100** **each**
- _Problems 6–10_   = **$200** **each**
- _Problems 11–15_ = **$300** **each**
- _N/A_   = **$N/A** **each**

Guidelines:
You must complete _no more than one $100 problem,_
at least two $200 problems, and at least one $300 problem.

Show Me the Money! Student Receipt

Assignment: _Problems on textbook pgs. 135–136_

Completion Amount Required: $_1500_

Problems I've Completed:
- _Problem 3_   = **$100** **each** = _$100_
- _Problems 7–10_ = **$200** **each** = _$800_
- _Problems 11–12_ = **$300** **each** = _$600_
- _N/A_   = $---- **each** = $----

                                                        Total: _$1500_

1 Realization and 1 Remaining Question: _____
R = If I don't show my work, I make stupid mistakes.
? = What would happen if the variable were a decimal?

General Agenda Example

Name: _____ Unit: _____ Time frame: _____

Meetings with the Boss

Teacher Meeting and Academic Practice (Homework)	☐ Meet with the teacher for instruction and/or check-in on these days/times: ☐ Complete the following academic practice (to be assigned during the teacher meeting):

Meetings with Colleagues

Small Group/Partners	☐ Complete [this activity/task] with [this peer/these peers]. Here is where/how to access the directions and materials: ☐ Complete [this activity/task] with [this peer/these peers]. Here is where/how to access the directions and materials:

Personal Time

Individual	☐ Complete [this activity/task] alone. Here is where/how to access the directions and materials: ☐ Complete [this activity/task] alone. Here is where/how to access the directions and materials: ☐ Complete [this activity/task] alone. Here is where/how to access the directions and materials:

8 | Designing Differentiated Transfer Tasks for Assessment

Part 1:

Do Students Get It?

Previous chapters have highlighted the need to hook students into content and guide them through the learning process—to engage them in a continual interchange of ideas and feedback as they grapple with content, construct new knowledge, and deconstruct misconceptions. We have focused on the need to support and challenge students as they gain balance and strength in their control of important learning goals. At certain points during and toward the end of the journey, however, the training wheels come off, and students have to show what they can do independently. Are they really getting it? Has everyone made measurable progress on the road to San Francisco? How can teachers know for sure? Most important for differentiation, does everyone need to show what they know, understand, and can do in the same way? In this chapter, we use the entry point of more typical kinds of assessments to consider when and how to differentiate assessments.

Beyond the Test

In many classrooms, quizzes and tests serve as traditional, time-efficient measures to check for understanding during and at the end of a unit. These assessment formats can use a combination of closed- and open-ended items. A carefully constructed quiz or test can yield valuable information about students' grasp of important learning goals. The Questioning Frameworks presented in Chapter 5 can help teachers begin to craft such items for "sampling" students' grasp of key knowledge and skills. But quizzes and tests can capture only so much. Like any single assessment, they provide one snapshot in what should really be a "photo album" approach to verifying what students have learned (Tomlinson & McTighe, 2006).

Perhaps what most middle and high school teachers want to know when it comes to traditional assessments and differentiation is whether they can or should differentiate a test—particularly one that is given at the end of a unit or as a semester exam. As both classroom teachers and professional writers of test items can attest, designing and validating items for quizzes and tests is hard work. It seems unreasonable, then, to devote extra time to create twice the number of items just to differentiate a test—especially because even in the best case, the result would be different forms of the same test, not tests that are differentiated according to student readiness, interest, or learning profile.

Of course, teachers can and should add accommodations such as word banks, essay stems, and additional time, as outlined in students' IEPs or 504 plans. These are perhaps best viewed as ways of differentiating the *process* of taking the test. Any adjustments that change the goals against which the student is being assessed (e.g., removing questions or sections) are better classified as *modifications* and are not differentiation. With constructed-response items, it may make sense to provide several options (e.g., for essay questions) to allow students to demonstrate mastery of the *same learning goals* via different avenues. In other words, it is important to provide students with accommodations on a test, and it is nice to provide them with options, but it is not necessary, desirable, or even feasible to create different "tiers" of a test.

When tests consisting of a variety of selected- and constructed-response items are the optimal, preferred, required, or most efficient means of assessing certain learning goals, teachers are advised to consult high-quality resources for test design and to work to create the best (i.e., most valid and reliable) test possible. Remember that most differentiation occurs *before* a common test, the idea being that a teacher increases the likelihood that students will perform better on the test when he or she has used ongoing assessment to differentiate learning experiences and tasks along the way.

Game Time: Opportunities for Transfer

Even the best-designed quizzes and tests can't yield sufficient information about how deeply students grasp content, or how accurately they understand its nuances. And they are not the best tool for gauging the ultimate mark of "deeper learning" (Pellegrino & Hilton, 2012): whether students can *transfer* what they've learned.

Wiggins and McTighe (2005) have rightly observed that the goal of an education is not to accumulate content knowledge. The true indicator of an effective education is what a person can *do* with that knowledge—how well the person can apply or transfer what he or she has learned from lesson to lesson, from course to course, and from school to real life. In the classroom, tasks that compel such transfer create a situation that is not unlike "game time" for an athlete: students have had time to acquire and make sense of content and skills, and they must now bring their expertise to a set of variables or a circumstance they haven't previously encountered (Tomlinson & Moon, 2013; Wiggins & McTighe, 2005).

At their best, such tasks are performance- or situation-oriented and require students to produce rather than simply regurgitate. Transfer tasks that are true "performance tasks" take students out of the role of "student doing work for the teacher" and into the role of an authentic practitioner who meets a challenge or solves a problem by developing a product or response directed at a real audience (Wiggins & McTighe, 2005).

Transfer tasks are naturally well suited to differentiation. It makes sense to build scaffolding, challenge, and choice into different options of a performance task, in particular, provided that each option aligns with the same learning goals (and can therefore be assessed via the same criteria or rubric). Such tasks can also infuse motivation into the assessment process by providing context for students to demonstrate what they have learned.

Strategies for Designing Differentiated Transfer Tasks

We feature four different strategies designed to help students demonstrate their mastery of learning goals through transfer to new and unique situations: TriMind, The Profiler, RAFT, and Learning Menus. Each of these strategies provides students with a context, asks them to engage in higher-order thinking, and requires them to transfer their learning. These strategies are engaging to students both because of their novelty and because they offer choices. Although each strategy *can* be used to design tiered tasks that are differentiated for readiness (see Chapter 7), they are best used as vehicles for differentiating according to *interest* and *learning profile*.

At its basic level, harnessing student *interest* means giving students access to "those topics or pursuits that evoke curiosity and passion in a learner" (Tomlinson, 2003, p. 3). Although it may be difficult to prepare tasks that appeal to each student's individual and enduring personal interests on a regular basis, it is very possible to routinely design assignment options that harness students' *situational interests*—those that are triggered by novelty, affinity, or choice (Schraw, Flowerday, & Lehman, 2001).

Learning profile is an umbrella term that refers to anything that might influence how students prefer to learn and how they seem to learn best (Tomlinson, 2009, 2014a). This can include research about how the brain takes in and processes information, various thinking-style theories, and ideas about how culture and gender might influence learning preferences.

When differentiating transfer tasks for interest and learning profile, it makes sense to let students choose what appeals to or feels most comfortable for them. The four strategies we discuss appeal to students' interests and learning preferences by presenting choices that may ignite their curiosity, resonate with something important in their world, or simply present something different from the usual school fare.

A RAFT (Buehl, 2009; Santa, 1988) asks students to take on a *role* to address a specified *audience* in an appropriate *format* about a particular *topic*. This novel approach in itself piques students' interest, but the teacher can amplify interest and investment by designing several different options for role, audience, format, and topic—all crafted to address the same learning goals—and allowing each student to select the combination that intrigues him or her most.

Learning Menus (Cummings, 2000) also seek to motivate through offering choices. They function much like specially priced "restaurant week" menus that present customers with just a few dishes to select from for each course. Similarly, a Learning Menu presents students with several options in different categories (main courses, side dishes, desserts) and encourages them to design the "meal" that is most appealing to them and that will help them "digest" the unit's learning goals.

Both TriMind and The Profiler present students with a more specific kind of choice: assignment options designed to appeal to the different ways students prefer to process information. These strategies appeal to students' *learning profiles*. TriMind uses Robert Sternberg's (Sternberg & Grigorenko, 2007) "triarchic" theory of intelligence as a basis for constructing assignment options designed to appeal to analytical, practical, and creative thinking. Likewise, The Profiler features activities geared toward several of the multiple intelligences proposed by Howard Gardner (2006) and situates these tasks in authentic career contexts. Both strategies follow the theorists' recommendations to avoid relegating students to one particular intelligence "box." Instead, they focus on expanding the instructional options offered in the classroom with the goal of harnessing every student's strengths (Gardner, 2006; Sternberg, 2006).

Using the Strategies

RAFT, Learning Menus, TriMind, and The Profiler can be used either at the lesson level to monitor students' grasp of smaller chunks of learning goals, or toward the conclusion of a unit to gauge student understanding of a larger body of principles, content, and skills. In either case, the teacher must take care to craft assignment options with the following "criteria for success" in mind:

- All assignment options should address the same understanding, knowledge, and skill goals.
- All assignment options should involve the same degree of rigor (unless strategic readiness adjustments are made; such adjustments will be discussed within the context of each strategy).
- All assignment options should appear equally respectful to students.
- All assignment options should be accompanied by clear task descriptions as well as transparent expectations and criteria for success.
- Students may be allowed to propose alternative options that the teacher can approve *if* those options adhere to each of the criteria listed above.
- All assignment options should offer a true variety of approaches rather than multiple versions of the same kind of thinking.

- All assignment options should be able to be assessed using the same criteria and rubric. This helps ensure alignment of learning outcomes and streamlines the evaluation process.

This last criterion is vital. Not only is it what enables teachers to differentiate performance tasks that will be used as significant formative and summative assessments, but it also supplies a framework through which teachers can provide different levels of support within those options. Rather than spending copious amounts of time trying to create multiple versions of a test, teachers can instead invest their energy in the development of assessment tasks that both motivate and support students while allowing them to truly demonstrate their learning through *transfer*.

A Case in Point: Ms. Rissa

As Ms. Rissa began to strategize about the year ahead, she made the deliberate decision to review her plan book from the previous year. It didn't take much browsing before she identified several places in her curriculum that could benefit from some "spicing up." She decided her first order of business would be to add some interest differentiation to her Shakespeare unit. Students had enjoyed *Romeo and Juliet* but had been less enthralled with Shakespearean sonnets. She theorized that a RAFT assignment that merged the two (see pp. 237–239) might give students more reason to invest in sonnets while allowing them to explore the play's universal themes in more depth.

The Adventures of Tom Sawyer presented yet another "bland spot" for both Ms. Rissa and her students. The importance of examining Tom's character with a critical eye carried enough weight to warrant concentrated instructional time, but she herself was tired of reading more than 100 essays on that topic each year. Variety was necessary to motivate both students and teacher. When a colleague suggested Gardner's multiple intelligences as a way to think about generating assignment options, Ms. Rissa initially resisted; the model had proved difficult for her when she first began teaching, as she had struggled to create eight meaningful assignment options for each topic. However, her colleague reassured her that targeting only three to four of the intelligences could be more effective (and efficient) than addressing all eight. Ms. Rissa elected to use The Profiler as a way to provide students with Gardner-esque options tied to real-world roles. Once students selected their roles, she would be able to provide an assignment option targeted to each student's readiness for the material (see pp. 230–231), weaving in a chance to address the various skill levels represented in her classroom.

Finally, Ms. Rissa designed a Learning Menu (see p. 262) for students to complete after the class had reviewed figurative language during the first few weeks of school. By structuring the menu in such a way that she could differentiate the readiness level of the techniques each student studied, Ms. Rissa found a way to unite students in their work, support and challenge each student appropriately, and make sure students began the year working in a variety of grouping configurations.

Ms. Rissa realized that these three points of interest differentiation would infuse variety into her classroom for both her students and herself while familiarizing her with the particular logistical requirements of each strategy. As with everything in teaching, she knew that taking the risk and piloting these new strategies was the best way to iron out the wrinkles for the next time she tried them—and to ensure her own growth in the process.

Part 2:

Tools and Strategies

Select forms and templates can be downloaded at http://www.ascd.org/ASCD/pdf/books/Doubet2015forms.pdf.
Use the password "Doubet2015115008" to unlock the PDF.

TriMind

What It Is:

A strategy for designing instructional and assessment task choices that appeal to analytical, practical, and creative thinkers.

How It Works:

According to cognitive psychologist Robert Sternberg (Sternberg & Grigorenko, 2007), the human intellect comprises three sets of abilities—thus, the Triarchic Theory of Intelligence:

- *Analytical:* The ability to analyze, compare/contrast, see the parts and the whole, examine cause and effect, and think in linear and logical-sequential ways. The kinds of abilities measured on most standardized tests. Think: *CSI.*
- *Practical:* The ability to put ideas into action, apply knowledge and skills to the real world, execute tasks efficiently, and engage in on-the-spot problem solving. Think: *MacGyver.*
- *Creative:* The ability to imagine possibilities, think outside the box, innovate, invent, dream, ask insightful questions, propose novel solutions, or intuit. Think: *Willy Wonka.*

School typically emphasizes analytical intelligence, often at the expense of developing or valuing practical and creative intelligence. If teachers used a balance of analytical, practical, and creative tasks and assessments to convey information and monitor understanding, they might find that more students would successfully navigate and master required content.

What It's Good For:

TriMind is great for differentiating the thinking process according to student learning profile. Although the framework can be used to design unit or lesson "hooks," the strategy is best applied to creating individual or group-oriented sense-making tasks or summative assessments.

Tips:

- Use the prompts from the template to generate three tasks—all aligned with the same learning goals—that appeal to creative, practical, and analytical thinkers. Then present those tasks as *options* to students; don't diagnose students' thinking styles and assign the tasks accordingly.
- It's best to avoid labeling the tasks with their associated intelligences; rather, present them as numbered options. That way, students will select the task (rather than the label) that appeals to them most.
- If the analytical task is critical for all students to complete, have them do so, and then use practical and creative tasks as follow-up or transfer task choices.
- If you want students to step outside their typical preference, it's generally better to do so once the content in the unit of study is more familiar to students.
- Even if you're not using TriMind to provide differentiated task choices, it is wise to strive for a balance of analytical, practical, and creative teaching methods and examples in a given unit of study.
- In practice, analytical, practical, and creative are types of *thinking* and do not themselves dictate a particular kind of product. For example, creative tasks should emphasize innovative and fresh thinking but do not require artistic responses. Therefore, begin to design tasks by looking at the *thinking* represented in each Sternberg intelligence preference (see chart below) rather than by selecting a "product."

Sternberg Intelligence	Consider first, "What kinds of thinking can the task emphasize?" . . .	. . . Not "What kind of product?"
Analytical	Comparing, analyzing, critiquing, evaluating, seeing the parts and the whole, using criteria, judging, thinking logically, sequencing, ranking, defending.	~~Make a Venn diagram.~~
Practical	Putting to use, adapting, making practical, applying to real-world situations, translating ideas for an audience, demonstrating, teaching, convincing.	~~Design a how-to booklet.~~
Creative	Making new or unusual connections, inventing, innovating, synthesizing, predicting, transforming, making metaphors or analogies.	~~Draw a picture.~~

TriMind Template

Subject/Grade: _____ **Lesson/Unit Topic:** _____

Learning Goals

Understanding Goals:

Knowledge Goals:

Skill Goals:

Analytical Task Prompts	Practical Task Prompts	Creative Task Prompts
• Show the parts of _____ and how they work together to achieve _____. • Explain why _____ works the way it does. • Diagram how _____ affects _____. • Identify the key parts of _____ and tell why each part is important. • Present a step-by-step approach to _____. • Analyze/evaluate/assess _____. • Compare and contrast _____ for an audience of _____ to show that _____ is better suited for _____. • Justify/defend the position that _____.	• Demonstrate how someone uses _____ in his or her life or work. • Show how we could apply _____ to solve this real-life problem: _____. • Based on your own experience, explain how _____ can be used for _____. • Here's a problem at school: _____. Using your knowledge of _____, develop a plan to address the problem. • Apply this lesson in _____ to your life [or this situation/context].	• Find a new way to show _____. • Use unusual materials to explain _____. • Use humor to show _____. • Invent a new and better way to _____. • Make connections between _____ and _____ to help _____ understand _____. • Become a _____ and use your "new" perspectives to help _____ think about _____. • Create a new _____. • Design an approach to or interpretation of _____. • Imagine what it would feel like to _____.
Analytical Task Idea	Practical Task Idea	Creative Task Idea

TriMind Classroom Examples

Algebra
Understanding Goals: • All forms of equations of lines represent the same line. • Given an equation of a line in one form, any other form can be generated. **Knowledge Goal:** • Forms of the equations of lines: *general, standard, point-slope, vertical,* and *horizontal.* **Skill Goals:** • Find other forms of equations of lines given one form. • Find the strengths, weaknesses, and applications of each form of equation.

Analytical	Practical	Creative
Compare and contrast the various forms of equations and lines. Create a flow chart, a table, or any other product to express your ideas to the class. Label all parts of your chart or table to make relationships clear. Be sure to consider the advantages and disadvantages of each form and represent these in your product.	Decide how and when each form of the equation of a line should be used. When is it best to use which form (discuss data in terms of real-world scenarios)? What are the strengths and weaknesses of each form? Find a clear and authentic way to present your conclusions to the class.	Put each form of the equation of a line on trial. Prosecutors should try to convince the jury that a form is not needed, while the defense should defend its usefulness. Enact your trial with group members playing various forms of the equations, the prosecuting attorneys, and the defense attorneys. The rest of the class will be the jury, and the teacher will be the judge.

Source: From *Differentiation in Practice: A Resource Guide for Differentiating Curriculum (Grades 5–9)* (p. 177), by C. A. Tomlinson & C. C. Eidson (unit developer: N. Smith), 2003, Alexandria, VA: ASCD. Copyright 2003 by ASCD.

ELA: Evaluating an Argument
(CCSS Reading Anchor Standard 7 [RI.9-10.4, 6, 8])

Understanding Goal:
• The power of an argument stems from the author's choices regarding reasoning, evidence, and language.

Knowledge Goals:
• The distinguishing characteristics of sound versus fallacious reasoning.
• Strategic uses of language to appeal to the senses (e.g., imagery); the mind (e.g., logos); or the emotions (e.g., ethos, pathos).

Skill Goals:
• Delineate and evaluate the specific claims in a text.
• Evaluate the strength and validity of an argument's reasoning.
• Assess the relevancy and sufficiency of evidence.
• Assess sound versus fallacious reasoning.
• Evaluate the impact of language and word choice.

Directions:
1. Read one of the editorials bookmarked on your laptop.
2. As you read, record the claim(s) made by the author in a chart or table.
3. For each claim, record quotes that reflect the following: sound reasoning, fallacious reasoning, instances of strong evidence, instances of weak evidence, examples of powerful language.
4. Use your chart/table to help you complete one of the following options:

Analytical	Practical	Creative
As a reader who is interested in the topic the author has addressed, you will evaluate the strengths and weaknesses of his or her argument by composing an extended online comment that the author and other readers will see. Write in the third person, and address whether the author's key claims are warranted, the reasons valid, the evidence relevant and sufficient, and the use of language effective. Use specific examples in your post.	You are the editor of the [media outlet/publisher] to which the author has submitted this piece for publication. Decide whether you will accept the piece and what revisions the author needs to make. Write an e-mail response to the author that indicates your acceptance or rejection and provides feedback on the argument's strengths and weaknesses in terms of whether the author's key claims are warranted, the reasons valid, the evidence relevant and sufficient, and the use of language effective.	Imagine you are a witness to two people on opposite sides of this issue discussing the author's argument. Capture their debate through a dialogue or other means of depiction. Use the voices of the two debaters to address the strengths and weaknesses of the author's key claims. Between the two parties, the discussion should address whether the author's key claims are warranted, the reasons valid, the evidence relevant and sufficient, and the use of language effective.

Science (Projectile Motion)		
Understanding Goals: • Parts of a system can be both related and independent (horizontal and vertical components of vectors). • The gathering of accurate evidence facilitates the generation of accurate predictions. **Knowledge Goals:** • Vocabulary: *x-component, y-component, gravity, kinematic equations.* • Applications of sin and cos. **Skill Goals:** • Solve problems. • Use evidence to make predictions (predict motion of projectile at given times).		
Analytical	**Practical**	**Creative**
Compare and contrast the horizontal and vertical components of velocity at different points of a projectile's path by • Making a video of two spheres (one falling straight down, the other shot horizontally). • Choosing snapshots from the video to overlay in Photoshop to demonstrate that both spheres are always at the same vertical height. • Calculating where the horizontally launched sphere lands. • Creating a narrative, video, or podcast that explains why the horizontal and vertical components of velocity are always at the same height (show calculations).	Study several real-world applications of projectiles (e.g., cannon fire from pirate ships; catapults or artillery in modern military). Choose one real-life application of projectile motion and identify how the projectiles work (for example, an artillery shell needs to get from point A to point B as quickly as possible). • Do you use a high-speed, steep versus shallow angle? • How do you calculate the landing point? Choose a different real-life situation and • Predict the landing point of a projectile. • Complete a lab report template that has written explanations as well as sample calculations.	Compose a short story (written or storyboarded) about the life of projectiles, complete with a backstory and character names. • The story should portray how one life (*x*-component) is similar to and different from another life (*y*-component). • There must be calculations or very detailed explanations for the equations you utilize. • Story elements must include how the two components are both related and different (e.g., gravity affects only the vertical displacement). • The theme of the story should be apparent to the reader and should involve (scientific) relationship and independence.

Source: Devon Collins, Fort Defiance High School, Fort Defiance, VA. Used with permission.

World Religions

Understanding Goal:

Internal beliefs manifest themselves in an external fashion.

Knowledge Goal:

The central tenets of each of the major religions studied.

Skill Goals:
- Analyze the major religions for their core beliefs/tenets.
- Explain how these beliefs/tenets would manifest themselves in everyday life and behavior.

Analytical	Practical	Creative
Examine the core beliefs of [*religion*]. Determine what "evidence" would constitute "proof" of a person being a follower of the religion. Consider concrete and abstract evidence as well as evidence you might find in the person's daily life and through interviews with people who know him or her.	Your best friend has converted to [*religion*]. What changes can you expect in your friend's interactions with you? In his or her choices and daily life? Write an instant messaging conversation in which your friend reveals his or her conversion to you and answers your questions about how his or her life will be different.	Create a metaphor that illustrates through words or visuals how the central tenets of [*religion*] are revealed in the life of a follower of that religion. The metaphor should not be obvious and should provide insight about the religion's essential elements.

The Profiler

What It Is:

- A framework for developing assignment choices geared toward the different intelligence preferences represented in the classroom.
- A means of connecting students to the working world as well as with roles or audiences for their work.

How It Works:

Howard Gardner's theory of multiple intelligences posits that there are a variety of intelligences, or "biological and psychological potentials" that are "capable of being realized to a greater or lesser extent as a consequence of the experiential, cultural, and motivational factors that affect a person" (Gardner, 1995, p. 202). In other words, students have capacities that traditional assignments may or may not tap into; giving students the opportunity to access those capacities may increase their motivation and development.

Although an intelligence is not the same thing as an occupation, "a particular intelligence, like spatial intelligence, can be put to work in a myriad of domains, ranging from sculpture to sailing to neuroanatomical investigations" (Gardner, 1995, p. 202). The Profiler is a strategy that attempts to tap Gardner's intelligences as motivational factors and lend them authenticity by connecting them to associated domains or occupations. In constructing a Profiler assignment, the teacher

1. Selects the understanding, knowledge, and skill goals for students to either begin to explore or synthesize and demonstrate mastery of.
2. Finds three to four intelligence preferences through which students can demonstrate their grasp of the targeted learning goals. (*Note*: the teacher should choose preferences that fit most naturally with the content; it is not necessary or even advisable to use all intelligences at once.)
3. Selects jobs/occupations/domains that would provide students with natural opportunities to exercise those intelligences.

What It's Good For:

Introducing new material or synthesizing previously learned material, whether as a lesson-level check for understanding (see Leadership example, pp. 228–229) or as a more extended assessment (see *Tom Sawyer* example, pp. 230–231).

Tips:

- Every assignment option can cover the same learning goals (see Measures of Central Tendency example, p. 227) *or* can be part of a Jigsaw structure for different products that target different skills and knowledge.
- Other ways to differentiate the Profiler:
  — Group orientation: Students can work individually or in groups or choose which they prefer. Some preferences are more conducive to group work than others; consider alerting students to this when they are selecting their preferences.
  — Readiness level: Make two versions of each "profession" you choose to target: one that is straightforward and one that is more advanced (i.e., complex and multifaceted). Students still choose the option that matches the "profession" in which they are most interested, but the teacher is able to assign the *level* of option that best matches each student's readiness level (see *Tom Sawyer* example, pp. 230–231).

- Begin to design tasks by looking at the *thinking* represented in each Gardner intelligence preference (see chart below) rather than by selecting a "product."
- Once the kind of thinking has been targeted for each task, consider what kind of *occupation* would use that thinking in the workplace and via what kind of *product.*
- Remember that, to some degree, everyone has the capacity for all the intelligences.
- The intelligences are not mutually exclusive but act in concert, so one Profiler task might combine two or more intelligences.

Gardner Intelligence Preference	Consider first, "What kinds of thinking can the task emphasize?" . . .	. . . Not "What kind of product?"
Verbal-Linguistic	Manipulating words or language to explain concepts, relationships, principles, or ideas.	~~Writing a story.~~
Visual-Spatial	Using visuals to depict concepts, relationships, principles, or ideas.	~~Drawing a picture.~~
Logical-Mathematical	Detecting patterns and relationships; handling long chains of reasoning that illustrate concepts, relationships, principles, or ideas.	~~Using numbers to create a graph.~~
Bodily-Kinesthetic	Governing body movements and objects skillfully to demonstrate concepts, relationships, principles, or ideas.	~~Putting on a skit.~~
Musical-Rhythmic	Producing, appreciating, and using rhythm, pitch, tone, and forms of musical expression to depict concepts, relationships, principles, or ideas.	~~Writing song lyrics.~~
Intrapersonal	Reflecting on the impact of concepts, relationships, principles, or ideas on self as well as the impact of self on concepts, relationships, principles, or ideas.	~~Writing journal entries.~~
Interpersonal	Discerning needs of and responding to others to solve problems, clarify ideas, implement principles, and so on.	~~Working on a group project.~~
Naturalistic	Understanding and connecting with the environment; seeing concepts, relationships, principles, or ideas reflected in nature.	~~Creating a nature collage.~~

The Profiler Template

Learning Goals			
Understanding Goals	**Knowledge Goals**		**Skill Goals**

Verbal-Linguistic	**Visual-Spatial**	**Logical-Mathematical**	**Bodily-Kinesthetic**
Writer, commentator, comedian	*Architect, designer, layout editor*	*Analyst, engineer, statistician*	*Actor, builder, choreographer*
Listening, speaking, writing, storytelling, explaining, teaching, using humor, convincing, analyzing, using language, grasp of syntax and semantics.	Understanding charts and graphs, strong sense of direction, sketching, painting, creating visual metaphors, designing objects, interpreting visuals.	Problem solving, classifying and categorizing, finding relationships among abstract concepts, handling long chains of reasoning and data.	Dancing, physical coordination, sports, hands-on experimentation, using body language, crafting, acting, miming, building, moving.
Musical-Rhythmic	**Intrapersonal**	**Interpersonal**	**Naturalistic**
Songwriter, composer, performer	*Poet, songwriter, blogger*	*Counselor, tour guide, talk show host*	*Ranger, botanist, conservationist*
Singing, playing musical instruments, whistling, recognizing and remembering tonal patterns, composing, understanding tonal and rhythmic structure.	Recognizing personal strengths and weaknesses, reasoning, awareness of and ability to evaluate thinking and feelings, understanding role with others.	Seeing things from other perspectives, listening, communicating, empathizing, conflict resolution; understanding others' feelings, motivations, and intentions.	Recognizing, observing, collecting, organizing, sorting, classifying, and caring for elements of nature; noticing changes in environment.

Remember: Develop tasks for only *three to five intelligences* that serve as the *best vehicles* for investigating and communicating mastery of your learning goals.

Task Idea:	**Task Idea:**	**Task Idea:**	**Task Idea:**

Profiler Classroom Examples

Middle School Math: Measures of Central Tendency

Understanding Goals:
- All numerical data sets have a "middle."
- There is more than one way to describe the "middle-ness" of a data set: each measure of "middle-ness" reveals something different about the set.

Knowledge Goals:
- Terms: *mean, median, mode*.
- How to calculate mean, median, and mode.

Skill Goals:
- Analyze and apply the differences among mean, median, and mode.
- Determine when and how to use mean, median, and mode.

Songwriter:	Screenwriter:
An educational website has hired you to (1) choose a popular tune that would appeal to middle schoolers and (2) create accompanying lyrics that would help students remember what mean, median, and mode are, and when it might be best to use each one. (Musical-Rhythmic)	Write a humorous screenplay for a TV learning channel in which the mean, median, and mode of a set of data (as numbers) are discussing how and when they would be most useful. Your "characters" should engage in arguments about which measure of central tendency (MCT) is the best and why. (Verbal-Linguistic)
Newspaper staff:	**Blogger:**
Choose a set of school data (e.g., absenteeism rates, school lunch purchases) and create a series of graphs depicting the mean, median, and mode of the data to better illustrate the issue for students, teachers, administrators, and parents. Your captions should explain what each MCT can and cannot depict. (Visual-Spatial)	Write an entry reflecting on your week, including the decisions you made and the conversations you had. Discuss a situation in which you had to use each MCT (mean, median, and mode) to make decisions or help others do so. Be sure to discuss your thought process—how you knew when to use each mode. (Intrapersonal)

Social Studies: Leadership

Directions:

Choose who you believe is the most influential president from the era we just studied. Select the task that most interests you. In the "Planning Notes" column, outline the steps of how you might go about completing the task. Include ideas for the reference materials and primary sources you might consult for further information. Clear this plan with your teacher before proceeding. You will be responsible for sharing your finished product with classmates who selected a different president. In your mixed groups, you will look for and record similarities and differences among leaders.

Name of President: _____	
Columnist: You've been assigned the "Commemoration Column" this week. Describe your chosen president (leadership style, character traits, and defining accomplishments) in a powerful way that will leave an impression on your readers. (Verbal-Linguistic)	**Planning Notes:**
White House commemoration designer: Design a logo for your chosen president that sums up his leadership style, character traits, and defining accomplishments. Include the text for an accompanying plaque explaining the logo. (Visual-Spatial)	
Documentary soundtrack designer: What three songs best reflect your president? You may refer to songs you know or write your own. Include "credits" that explain how the melodies, rhythms, and lyrics reflect the president's leadership style, character traits, and defining accomplishments. (Musical-Rhythmic)	
Applicant for leadership scholarship: How are you like and unlike your chosen president? In what ways do your strengths and weaknesses vary and overlap? Reference your president's leadership style, character traits, and defining accomplishments, and discuss your own as well. (Intrapersonal)	
Choreographer for presidential play: Choose one of your president's defining accomplishments and be prepared to pantomime it for the class. Be prepared to explain how that accomplishment demonstrates your president's leadership style and character traits. (Bodily-Kinesthetic)	
Talk show host: You are preparing to host your favorite president on a talk show. Whom would you invite to be guests alongside him, and why? Explain how they are good complements or foils to your president's leadership style, character traits, and defining accomplishments. (Interpersonal)	
Associated Press analyst: Prepare notes for an upcoming piece on presidential trends. The story will outline how your chosen president's leadership style, character traits, and defining accomplishments follow a pattern of U.S. presidents throughout history. (Intrapersonal)	
Presidential environmental advisor: Prepare recommendations for the incoming administration outlining how they should (or should not) emulate your chosen president's leadership style, character traits, and defining accomplishments (due to the implications for the environment). (Naturalistic)	

English: **The Adventures of Tom Sawyer**

This culminating product assignment is designed to examine the character of Tom Sawyer in terms of his maturation throughout the course of the novel. Below are multiple approaches to this examination. Students may choose the task that is most appealing to them; the teacher will then determine the level that is best suited for each student.

Occupation	Advanced Readiness Task Options	Grade-Level Readiness Task Options
Artist (Note: you can work alone or with others.)	**Life Is Like a Box of Chocolates** Illustrate Tom's growth through the use of an extended metaphor that compares Tom's growth process to something visual (e.g., the ocean). • Brainstorm ideas that extend this metaphor (e.g., Tom learns lessons and then falls back into old habits like waves roll in and then recede). • Find examples in the novel that support your comparisons. • Illustrate your metaphor, including ideas from your brainstorming list and textual evidence. • You can work quotes into your illustration or include a written portion.	**The Writing's on the Wall** You *are* Tom Sawyer. You will create a "growth mural" of yourself to give to Becky to show her how much you have matured. • Draw a growth chart for Tom (similar to one you'd see on a wall in someone's home). • Choose "benchmark" events from your life that taught you lessons and led to your growth. • Record what you learned from each of those events. • Explain how you're different now from when your story began.
Writer (Note: you can work alone or with others.)	**Investigative Report** You have been assigned "surveillance duty" for this character. Develop a private investigator's report about Tom's emotional and mental growth. • Prepare two surveillance reports on Tom—one for your observations of Tom at the beginning of the story and one for him at the end of the story. • Each of your two surveillance reports should contain specific things the character said, did, and thought, and how other characters responded to him. • End with your professional opinion (supported with evidence) as to whether you believe Tom has grown during your investigation.	**Growth Report Card** You are a psychologist hired by Aunt Polly to examine Tom's behavior and assess his growth. Your report card should include the following: • At least five categories for which Tom will receive "grades." These categories should illustrate important aspects of Tom's character (e.g., treatment of others). • Tom's grade for each category (*A, B, C, D,* or *F*) at the beginning of the story and at the end. • Detailed comments that explain why Tom received the grades he did. These comments should include examples from the text.

Actor (Note: you will need to work with others.)	Live with Dr. Phil!	Lights, Camera, Action!
	Act out an episode of *Dr. Phil* in which characters from the book will discuss Tom's growth (or lack thereof). • Choose the characters who would have the most to say about Tom. • Consider picking several characters who hold differing opinions to give your show a bit of tension. • Write a script that features characters arguing for or against Tom's growth. • Find and use specific evidence from the text that supports each character's opinions.	Choose and perform an important scene that demonstrates Tom's growth of character (or lack thereof). • Choose your key scene and clear your choice with your teacher. • Plan your production thoroughly and rehearse your performance. • Make sure your presentation highlights your group's opinion of Tom's growth. • After your performance is complete, your group will present a "behind-the-scenes" series of interviews in which you defend your scene choice.

Source: Kristina Doubet and Marla Capper. Used with permission.

RAFT

What It Is:

A strategy for creating differentiated performance tasks, originally developed to help teachers think about and plan for teaching different kinds of writing (Buehl, 2009; Santa, 1988). RAFT encourages students to assume a *role* and consider their *audience* while working in a *format* and examining a *topic* from their chosen perspective. RAFT is motivating because it gives students choice, appeals to their interests and learning profiles, and can be adapted to student readiness levels.

How It Works:

The teacher uses the template (see p. 236) to design several horizontal "strips" or role-audience-format-topic combinations that serve as assignment options from which students can select. When using it as an individual assessment, the teacher designs all RAFT combinations to address the same learning goals so that no matter which option students select, they can be evaluated with the same criteria or rubric.

What It's Good For:

RAFT is a flexible strategy that can be used to design introductory unit hooks, sense-making activities, Jigsaws, homework tasks, applications and extensions, or summative assessments. The best RAFTs have clear knowledge, understanding, and skill goals, with all activities leading to those same goals. However, sometimes learning goals are not met in full until students have shared their RAFT tasks in the large group or in mixed small groups. This is most often true if students are not completing the RAFT as an individual assessment.

Tips:

- Decide on your purpose for using the RAFT (e.g., for sense making, as a Jigsaw task, as a summative assessment).
- Craft your learning goals for the assignment in terms of what you want students to understand, know, and be able to do.
- Generate several RAFT assignment choices for students to choose from that will get them to the same learning goals (for a summative assessment) or that, in combination, will address all the content you want to address (for a strategy like a Jigsaw).
- Present RAFT options in an at-a-glance grid format so that students can quickly identify the essence of the task; for substantial RAFTs, provide more specific guidelines for each option.
- To guide students to success as they complete their RAFTs, you can also provide a list of required vocabulary or add a fifth column outlining points of discussion for each RAFT grid. However, the tasks should still "sound" like different options and appeal to a range of student needs and interests.
- You can allow students to mix and match roles, audiences, formats, and topics as long as the mixing and matching generates a task or situation that makes sense and is aligned with the learning goals. You can also allow students to create their own RAFT tasks. A blank row can invite this option.

Important Design Notes

- Although there is no "right" number of options, all tasks must be meaningful and aligned with the learning goals. It's better to have two or three high-quality options than 10 low-quality choices.
- High-quality RAFTs don't need to sound cute or funny. Strive first for authenticity and alignment with clear learning goals. Often, writing out each task as a short paragraph can help ensure that the task is challenging and achievable and makes sense.
- You may want to ask students to include a reflection to accompany their products, as in the "Inside My Mind" RAFT Reflection Sheet and RAFT Self-Evaluation Tool on page 235.

Ideas for Crafting RAFT Prompts

Although the lists on page 234 are not exhaustive and do not necessarily include content-specific examples, they may get the creative juices flowing during the design process. Potential "topics" are not included, as those are most frequently content-dependent.

Possible Roles	Possible Audiences	Possible Formats	
• Accountant	• Ad agency	• Advertisement	• Model
• Advertiser	• Art patrons	• App	• Mural
• Analyst	• Attendees	• Argument	• Museum exhibit
• Anthropologist	• Author	• Article	• Newspaper
• Architect	• Board members	• Award	• Painting
• Art critic	• Boss	• Banner	• Petition
• Artist or illustrator	• Business or	• Biography	• Photographs
• Author (biographer, poet)	corporation	• Blog	• Play
• Botanist	• Celebrities	• Blueprint	• Poem
• Campaign manager	• Committee	• Brochure	• Poster
• Candidate	• Community members	• Calendar	• PowerPoint presentation
• Cartographer	• Concert-goers	• Campaign	• Program
• Cartoon character	• Consumers	• Cartoon/comic strip	• Prototype
• Coach	• Contractor	• Case file	• Public service
• Designer	• Documentarian	• Catalog	announcement
• Detective	• Editor	• Chart	• Puppet show
• Economist	• Experts	• Dance	• Puzzle
• Engineer	• Family members	• Dating profile	• Questionnaire
• Film critic	• Friends	• Debate	• Quiz show
• Filmmaker	• Government agencies	• Demonstration	• Reality show application
• Geographer	• Government or elected	• Deposition	• Recipe
• Historian	leader	• Diagram	• Research project
• Interviewer	• Historical figures	• Dialogue	• Review
• Inventor	• Judge	• Diary	• Scrapbook
• Journalist	• Jury	• Dictionary entries	• Skit
• Lawyer	• Library patrons	• DVD	• Song
• Literary critic	• Museum visitors	• Editorial	• Speech
• Manager	• Neighbors	• E-mail exchange	• Story
• Market researcher	• Packaging company	• Facebook profile/chat	• Survey/data
• Museum director/curator	• Pen pals	• Film	• Television script/show
• Musician (composer/	• Professional	• Flowchart	• Terrarium
lyricist)	organizations	• Game	• Test
• Nutritionist	• Publisher	• Graph	• Testimony
• Panelist	• Radio listeners	• Interview	• Text message
• Photographer	• Readers (newspaper,	• Invention	conversation
• Product designer	magazine)	• Lecture	• Time line
• Researcher	• Relatives	• Machine	• Tour
• Scientist (all fields)	• School board	• Magazine	• Trial
• Statistician	• School staff	• Map	• Tweet (series)
• Strategist	• Students	• Media campaign	• Video
• Travel agent	• Travel agents		• Website
• Zookeeper	• Viewers		
	• Visitors		

"Inside My Mind"
RAFT Reflection Sheet

Directions: Complete and turn in this form with your RAFT assignment.
1. Task choice:
2. Why did you choose this task versus the other options?
3. Explain what your work reveals about the big idea or essential question.
4. The portion of this assignment I am most proud of is _____
   because:
5. Evaluate your work on your copy of the self-evaluation tool, circling the
   rating you believe applies (5 = expert; 1 = novice). Then explain why
   you gave yourself those scores.

RAFT Self-Evaluation Tool

Criteria	Rating	Comments
Accuracy: How correct is your information? Does it accurately reflect the following required content?	5 4 3 2 1	
Support: How thoroughly and soundly do you support your work with resources, including the following requirements?	5 4 3 2 1	
Perspective: Do you stay in role? How effective are you at performing your role and convincing the audience?	5 4 3 2 1	
Focus: Do you stick to the assigned format? Do you fully satisfy the chosen topic with numerous details and examples?	5 4 3 2 1	
Product quality: Is your work of high quality, free from mechanical errors, and ready for publication or sharing with others?	5 4 3 2 1	

RAFT Planning Template			
Learning Goals **Understanding Goals:** **Knowledge Goals:** **Skill Goals:**	**This RAFT is a(n)** ☐ Introductory activity/hook. ☐ Sense-making activity. ☐ Anchor activity. ☐ Jigsaw task. ☐ Assessment.	**Evaluation criteria:**	
	This RAFT is differentiated for student ☐ Readiness. ☐ Interest. ☐ Learning profile. (Check all that apply.) **When and how this RAFT will be used:**		
Role	**Audience**	**Format**	**Topic**

RAFT Classroom Examples

Romeo and Juliet *Sonnet RAFT*			
Learning Goals **Understanding Goal:** • Creativity can thrive within structure. **Knowledge Goals:** • The proper form of a Shakespearean sonnet. • *Iambic pentameter.* • Key characters, relationships, and plot points from *Romeo and Juliet.* **Skill Goals:** • Interpret key conflicts from *Romeo and Juliet.* • Use textual support for interpretations. • Craft chosen meaning around the regulations of sonnet structure and iambic pentameter.		**This RAFT is an** ☑ Assessment. **This RAFT is differentiated for student** ☑ Interest. **When and how this RAFT will be used:** This RAFT will be assigned as we approach the end of *Romeo and Juliet.* In class, as a mini-lesson, we will learn about the structure of Shakespearean sonnets. Students will do a guided search for this sonnet format within *Romeo and Juliet.* Then students will incorporate their interpretations of *Romeo and Juliet* as a sonnet according to their chosen RAFT.	**Evaluation criteria:** See rubric.
Role	**Audience**	**Format**	**Topic**
Romeo (and Juliet)	Each other	Shakespearean sonnet (romantic)	Your first encounter
Juliet	The Capulet family	Shakespearean sonnet (apology)	The murder of cousin Tybalt
Nurse	Your diary (TOP SECRET!)	Shakespearean sonnet (diary entry)	Feelings about Juliet's affairs
Friar Laurence	The prince	Shakespearean sonnet (explanation)	What happened to the star-crossed lovers?

Romeo and Juliet Task Cards

1. **Romeo (and Juliet).**

   The music is blaring, and the food and beverages keep coming. It's a party! Over there . . . look! Isn't s/he beautiful? You've known this person for less than two seconds, but s/he definitely looks like marriage material. Re-create the sonnet from Act 1, Scene 5 that depicts the first encounter with your soul mate.

2. **Juliet.**

   Ugh. The love of your life has just killed your dear cousin Tybalt. What is up with Romeo these days? It seems that his love for you has changed him quite a bit. You're angry with him at first, but as his wife, you decide you have to support him. How do you explain what he has done to your family? Give it a whirl . . .

3. **Nurse.**

   No matter how many times you try to advise her to do the right thing, that girl never listens. You just can't fathom why she would risk her life just for a silly boy! After all, they've only known each other for how long? And she's just a little girl! Tell your diary what you can't say aloud . . .

4. **Friar Laurence.**

   We know. You did your best to stop them, but teenagers are crazy nowadays. It's time for you to pick up the pieces. This might be a teachable moment to preach the power of love. Wait . . . I hope no one thinks it's your fault. Go back and explain to the prince exactly what has happened.

Romeo and Juliet RAFT Evaluation Criteria	Rating
You assume the character's perspective and write consistently (and defensibly) from his or her point of view.	3 2 1
You follow the guidelines of a traditional Shakespearean sonnet: 14 lines (three quatrains and a couplet), ABAB CDCD EFEF GG rhyme scheme, and iambic pentameter.	3 2 1
You bring your own perspective into the assignment without straying too far from the text itself. In other words, what you write might be accepted by Shakespeare as a new addition to his text.	3 2 1
Your RAFT reads smoothly and shows ample evidence of having been read aloud and revised. You include all the steps of your project, including all drafts. Your mechanics are error-free, and the product appears professional.	3 2 1

Source: Tanya Roy, Coppinville Junior High School, Enterprise, AL. Used with permission.

World History RAFT

Learning Goals

Understanding Goals:
- Our societies influence our identity and the choices we make.
- Historical events in one part of the world leave a legacy both in that place and around the globe.

Knowledge Goals:
- What ethnic cleansing is.
- Events and details of ethnic cleansing in Bosnia.

Skill Goals:
- Use primary and secondary sources to support a position.

This RAFT is a
☑ Performance assessment.
☑ Test review.

Evaluation criteria:
See rubric.

This RAFT is differentiated for student
☑ Interest.
☑ Learning profile.

When and how this RAFT will be used:
This RAFT will be used at the end of the lesson on ethnic cleansing in Bosnia during the Yugoslav Wars, which will take place in the middle of a unit on genocide and ethnic cleansing in the 20th century (Rwanda, Bosnia, Cambodia). There will be a lesson on the breakup of Yugoslavia, the events of the Yugoslav Wars, and the failure of the international community to respond. By completing this activity, students should gain a better understanding of what ethnic cleansing is and how it affected Bosniaks in particular. Students will present their completed RAFTs in small groups to classmates who chose options other than their own.

Role	Audience	Format	Topic
Journalist for the *New York Times*	American readers who are unaware of or apathetic about ethnic cleansing in Bosnia	Newspaper column	Ethnic cleansing in Bosnia and why it matters
Banksy (or other guerilla street artist)	Srebrenica Genocide Museum visitors	Mural and explanation	Tribute to Bosnian victims of ethnic cleansing or commentary on the events
Citizen of Sarajevo	United Nations General Assembly	Letter	What day-to-day life is like in Sarajevo during the Yugoslav Wars and why the UN needs to intervene
U.S. Secretary of State	President Clinton	Video	Summary of events in Bosnia and advice on course of action (whether to intervene)

Source: Kirsten Mlodynia. Used with permission.

World History RAFT Task Cards

1. ***New York Times* journalist.** You are writing at the height of the violence; thousands of Bosnians are being killed at Srebrenica, Žepa, and other places. Goražde and Sarajevo are under siege, and the situation is growing increasingly dire every day. Despite this, the world at large seems unaware or uncaring of what is happening. You need to write an article that will catch the world's attention and bring to light the atrocities that are occurring. Make sure that your article describes what is happening in Bosnia so that readers who know absolutely nothing about the situation will understand what is happening and use quotes from interviews you conducted during your recent trip to Bosnia (primary source materials). Explain to your readers what ethnic cleansing is, how and why it is happening in Bosnia, and why they should care. The international community is failing to live up to its promise of "never again," but you have the power to change that. Your story should be about 500 words and contain one primary source picture.

2. **Banksy.** The curator of the Srebrenica Genocide Museum has asked you to create a piece of art to display in the museum as a tribute to the Bosnians who were killed during the war and to serve as commentary on the events of that period. Although the world has moved on from the violence that occurred during the Yugoslav Wars, the events are still very real to the citizens of Bosnia. You need to create a piece of art (e.g., drawing, painting, Photoshop image, graffiti stencil) for the museum to help bring attention back to the tragic events that were allowed to happen. You should also include a 300–500-word description of your art piece explaining its meaning and contextualizing it. To adequately contextualize your artwork, you should describe the ethnic cleansing that occurred in Bosnia and why it is vital that the world remember what happened there. You should use at least one primary source in either your artwork or your description (e.g., photograph, interview excerpt).

3. **Citizen of Sarajevo.** You are living in the besieged city of Sarajevo in March 1994. Every day, snipers take aim and kill people who are trapped in the city. You are running short on the essentials to stay alive, and every day the situation becomes more dangerous. A UN convoy has managed to make its way into the city, and one of the aid workers has asked you to write a letter describing your experiences and living conditions that they can read at a special session of the United Nations General Assembly to persuade members to intervene and help bring an end to the ethnic cleansing. Your letter should explain what your day-to-day life is like living in Sarajevo, why the conflict is occurring, and why what is happening is best characterized as ethnic cleansing. You should include primary source evidence other than your own testimony (e.g., interviews, photographs). The UN is turning a blind eye to the thousands who are being killed, but your letter could drive them to take notice and take action.

4. **U.S. Secretary of State.** You have just returned from a fact-finding mission in Bosnia. The president has asked you to compile the information you gathered into a

brief (three- to five-minute) video that explains what is happening in Bosnia, why it's happening, and how the ethnic cleansing is affecting Bosnian citizens. He is also seeking your advice on whether the United States should intervene in the conflict. His decision has the potential to save thousands and bring peace to a country ravaged by violence. Be sure your video gives him the important facts he needs to understand what is going on and make a good decision. To do that, you need to include at least two primary sources (e.g., photographs, interviews, UN reports).

World History RAFT Evaluation Criteria

	Expert	Developing	Needs Improvement
Required Elements	The final product covers everything asked for: • Definition of ethnic cleansing. • Description of ethnic genocide in Bosnia. • Primary/secondary source support.	All required elements are included, but one is underdeveloped.	One of the required elements is missing, and/or two to three are underdeveloped.
Content	The content of the final product is • Entirely accurate. • Detail-rich. • Relevant to the goal. The primary sources are well chosen and contextualized (relevant to the topic they are used to support) and discussed within their intended context.	The content contains one or two of the following: • Minor errors. • Patchy details. • Some irrelevant information. There are a few minor issues with the contextualization and/or analysis of primary sources.	The content falls short regarding • Accuracy. • Sufficient detail. • Relevance of information. There are substantive problems with the contextualization and/or analysis of primary sources.
Product Quality	• The final product is of professional quality and fit for distribution. • The information is well organized, clearly displayed, and easy to read and understand. • The structure of the product purposefully and clearly communicates the important information.	• The final product is of good quality, but there are one or two elements that need to be improved before it could be distributed. • There are a few organizational problems that make reading and understanding the information difficult. • The structure helped communicate the main points, but some information was confusing.	• The final product is of poor quality or otherwise unfit for distribution. • There are numerous organizational problems that make reading and understanding the information difficult. • The structure is disorganized and shows little regard for communicating the main points.

Government: Electoral College

Choose one of the following tasks to show what you understand about the Electoral College, why we use it, and how or whether you think it should change.

Electoral College RAFT			
Learning Goals **Understanding Goals:** • The Electoral College system for electing U.S. presidents has benefits and drawbacks. • The historical record provides arguments in favor of and against the Electoral College system. **Knowledge Goals:** • Key terms: *electors, electoral vote, popular vote, absolute majority.* • Facts and data specific to relevant U.S. presidential elections (e.g., 1876, 1888, 2000). **Skill Goals:** • Analyze the benefits and drawbacks of the Electoral College system. • Argue for or against the Electoral College with claims supported by logical reasoning and historical evidence.	**This RAFT is a** ☑ Summative assessment. **This RAFT is differentiated for student** ☑ Learning profile. ☑ Interest. **How this RAFT will be used:** Students will choose one RAFT task to show their understanding of what the Electoral College is, why we use it, and how or whether they think it should change.	**Evaluation criteria:** See rubric.	
Role	**Audience**	**Format**	**Topic**
You "online"	A friend	Text-message chat OR series of Facebook wall posts	"Isn't this EC thing outd8ed?"
U.S. senator	Constituents	Speech *or* formal letter defending your position	"In response to your letters and e-mails about abolishing the Electoral College . . ."
Someone who voted for George W. Bush *or* Al Gore in 2000	Congressional representative	Formal letter or e-mail requesting that your representative take action to keep or abolish the Electoral College	"I'm disappointed/ satisfied with the 2000 election results . . ."
Leader of a grassroots organization	Target audience	Ad campaign (pick three: radio, print, television, online)	"Reform the process!"

Directions:

1. **Choice 1:** Imagine that you are having a fast and furious online chat with a friend on the night of the presidential election. The conversation started with your friend saying, "I don't get why the guy with the most votes doesn't win. Seems like that Electoral College thing is outd8ed." Start your transcript with that comment, and compose a conversation between you and your friend in which you explain and either defend or challenge the Electoral College. Be sure to support your claims with reasoning and evidence that draw on past presidential elections.

2. **Choice 2:** Pretend you are a U.S. senator representing our state. Recently, a group of your constituents has been lobbying you to propose changes to the presidential election process that would abolish the Electoral College and rely on the popular vote. Compose a speech that addresses their concerns. Make sure your claims, evidence, and reasoning are based on past presidential elections.

3. **Choice 3:** Put yourself in the shoes of either someone who voted for George W. Bush or someone who voted for Al Gore in the 2000 presidential election. Compose a letter to one of your U.S. congressional representatives that expresses either your disappointment or your satisfaction with the voting process as outlined by the U.S. Constitution and suggests the action your representative take in response to a reform measure on the floor. Your argument should include claims, evidence, and reasoning based on past presidential elections other than the 2000 election.

4. **Choice 4:** Imagine you are the leader of a grassroots organization that advocates for reform in the presidential election process. Design a campaign that includes three different types of media (e.g., radio, print, television, web) that synthesizes and expresses your organization's main arguments for how or whether the U.S. Constitution should be amended to reflect a different process for electing the president. The explicit or implicit claims, evidence, and reasoning in your campaign should include references to past presidential elections.

Electoral College RAFT Evaluation Criteria

Category	Exemplary	Acceptable	Needs Revision
Understanding	Your understanding of the Electoral College and why it is used is sophisticated, nuanced, and thorough.	Your understanding of the Electoral College and why it is used is thoughtful, reflective, and complete.	Your understanding of the Electoral College and why it is used is predictable, flat, or incomplete.
Accuracy	You sought and demonstrated numerous accurate interpretations of the Electoral College's efficacy that go beyond those that an average citizen would deduce.	You sought and demonstrated some accurate interpretations of the Electoral College's efficacy that go beyond those that an average citizen would deduce.	You sought and demonstrated few or no accurate interpretations of the Electoral College's efficacy that go beyond those that an average citizen would deduce.
Voice	You adopted a tone, style, syntax, and language that expand on your role, audience, and/or format.	You adopted a tone, style, syntax, and language appropriate to your role, audience, and/or format.	You adopted a tone, style, syntax, and language that are inappropriate to your role, audience, and/or format.
Support	All of the support you offer for your viewpoint is logically sound and well substantiated with historical facts. You anticipate dissenting opinions and address them soundly. Your representations of history and interpretation of the U.S. Constitution are insightful and creative.	Most of the support you offer for your viewpoint is logically sound and well substantiated with historical facts. You anticipate and address some dissenting opinions. Your representations of history and interpretation of the U.S. Constitution are faithful to often-cited arguments.	Only some of the support you offer for your viewpoint is logically sound and well substantiated with historical facts. You neglect or shallowly address dissenting opinions. Your representations of history and interpretation of the U.S. Constitution are incongruent, contradictory, or illogical.
Craftsmanship	Your work is polished and reflects exceptionally careful attention to editing and revision. This makes your ideas fluid and easy to follow.	Your work is competent and reflects attention to editing and revision. The occasional error does not interfere with the audience's ability to understand your ideas.	Your work contains errors that significantly affect the audience's ability to understand your ideas.

Quadrilaterals			

Learning Goals

Understanding Goal:
- Shapes can be categorized by their properties.

Knowledge Goal:
- The properties of *parallelogram, rectangle, square, rhombus,* and *trapezoid.*

Skill Goals:
- Identify properties of shapes.
- Compare and contrast quadrilaterals.
- Categorize quadrilaterals.

This RAFT is a(n)
- ☑ Sense-making activity.
- ☑ Jigsaw task.
- ☑ Assessment.

Evaluation criteria (reflected in rubric):
1. Properties of the shapes.
2. Subsets on the polygon tree.
3. Explanation of how the shapes of the audience and role relate to each other.

This RAFT is differentiated for student
- ☑ Interest.

How this RAFT will be used:

Students have learned about the properties of quadrilaterals. The RAFT will be given after they have completed a tree diagram showing the relationships among the quadrilaterals. They will be transferring the information into a different format of their choice. The students will have a choice to work with partners or individually. As a closure activity, the students will present their final RAFTs.

Role	Audience	Format	Topic
A square	A rectangle	A love song	What they have in common and why they should be together
A trapezoid	A kite	A letter	Why they feel left out of the parallelogram family
An irregular polygon	A rectangular polygon	A persuasive essay	Convincing the audience to become a rebel in the polygon world
A quadrilateral	A triangle	A how-to guide	How to become a quadrilateral

Quadrilaterals RAFT Task Cards

1. **A square.** You are a square in love with a rectangle. You have a *Romeo and Juliet* romance. You want to convince your love of all the reasons you should be together. To do that, you must tell the rectangle in a love song what you have in common and why your differences don't matter. If you are successful, the rectangle will run away with you, and you two quadrilaterals will live happily ever after.

2. **A trapezoid.** You are a trapezoid with strong feelings about being left out of the parallelogram family. You decide to write a letter to a kite who has also been left out. You must explain why you are both left out of the parallelogram family and explain what qualities they have that you want. Create a plan for how both of you can become parallelograms.

3. **An irregular polygon.** You are an irregular polygon, and nobody messes with you! You must explain to a regular polygon what makes you so cool and convince it to change its ways. To persuade it, you should highlight your differences and explain what changes a regular polygon can make to become more like you.

4. **A quadrilateral.** You are a quadrilateral helping a triangle meet its life goal of becoming a fellow quadrilateral. To succeed, the triangle needs a step-by-step training guide on becoming a quadrilateral. You must highlight the properties of both triangles and quadrilaterals and devise a plan outlining how it can become a four-sided figure.

Quadrilaterals RAFT Evaluation Criteria

Category	3 Points	2 Points	1 Point
Content	The content was correct and complete. All questions raised in the task card were addressed in detail. The finished product was filled with information necessary to get the point across.	The content was correct but was missing some aspects that would have made the finished product a better reflection of the mathematical content.	The content was incorrect and incomplete. There were several errors that took away from the finished product. More detail was needed to reflect the mathematical content.
Accuracy	Explanations and examples were mathematically correct, appropriately illustrative, and error-free.	Explanations and examples were mathematically correct and appropriately illustrative, but there were calculation errors.	Explanations and examples contained errors in principle or appropriateness (and possibly in calculation).
Organization	The final product was laid out well, and the organization contributed to the product's overall success in communicating the mathematical principles outlined in the task.	The organization communicated the product's point for the most part, but portions were confusing and needed to be reread for the mathematical principles to be fully understood.	There was little organization in the final product. The information seemed to be compiled without regard to effectively communicating the point.
Editing and Publishing	The product is virtually error-free and ready to share with others or to post online.	There were few to no grammatical mistakes. Minor editing would be required before sharing the product with others.	There were numerous grammatical mistakes. Major revision would be needed to make the product ready to share with others.

Source: Sarah Hagan and Kelly Freehill, Glasgow Middle School, Alexandria, VA. Used with permission.

Water, Carbon, and Nitrogen Cycles

Learning Goals

Understanding Goals:
- There is a constant balance that exists between all systems on Earth.
- The natural cycles help maintain this balance.

Knowledge Goals:
- The water cycle describes the movement of water without human influence.
- The carbon cycle describes how carbon cycles through our planet and how too much or too little could threaten life.
- The nitrogen cycle goes through many processes under the ground and changes form throughout the cycle.

Skill Goals:
- Describe the processes that occur in a scientific cycle.
- Analyze the interdependence among the steps of each process.
- Synthesize all three processes to represent scientific principles.

This RAFT is a(n)
- ☑ Sense-making activity.
- ☑ Jigsaw task.
- ☑ Assessment.

Evaluation criteria (reflected in rubric):
1. Accuracy.
2. Perspective.
3. Focus.
4. Mechanics.

This RAFT is differentiated for student
- ☑ Interest.
- ☑ Learning profile (Sternberg).

When and how this RAFT will be used:
1. After studying the three different cycles outlined in the learning goals, students may choose the RAFT strip they want to complete. They will submit their top two choices on an index card, and the teacher will use those choices to assign groups (making sure all task options are represented) to begin work the next class period.
2. The next class period, groups of three to four students (working on the same option) will receive task cards and complete the task as outlined in the instructions.
3. Students will form new mixed groups (with all options represented), share products, and compose a list of steps, components, and features the three processes share.

Role	Audience	Format	Topic
Nitrogen molecule	Fellow nitrogen molecule	Facebook chat	"You'll never believe the journey I just took!"
Cloud	The sun	Letter	"You can't always be the favorite."
Atmosphere	All plant and animal life	Public service announcement	"Someone help! I'm suffocating in CO2!"

Cycles RAFT Task Cards

1. **Nitrogen molecule.** You will assume the role of a nitrogen molecule that has just traveled through the entire nitrogen cycle. In your chat with a fellow nitrogen molecule, you must include a detailed description of each stop you made along the journey as well as how you were changed by each process of the cycle. (Analytical)

2. **Cloud.** You will assume the role of a cloud in the water cycle. As a cloud, you are jealous that everyone likes the sun and no one appreciates cloudy days. You're tired of the sun stealing the spotlight. You must write a letter to the sun to explain why you're just as important as it is. In your letter, explain the role that the cloud plays in the water cycle and what would happen to the cycle if you (the cloud) did not exist. Remember to include all the necessary elements of a letter. (Creative)

3. **Atmosphere.** You will assume the role of the atmosphere making a plea to plants and animals to help alleviate the abundance of CO2. In your public service announcement, you must include the causes of the excess CO2 as well as suggestions that could eliminate this problem. Use the processes in the carbon cycle as a basis for your argument. You can choose to write your announcement on a sheet or record a statement using iMovie. (Practical)

Cycles RAFT Evaluation Criteria

Category	4 Points	3 Points	2 Points	1 Point	Comments/ Score
Accuracy	The information and details in the RAFT are all accurate. RAFT properly reflects information, ideas, and themes related to the subject.	The information in the RAFT is accurate but could use more support.	The information in the RAFT has some inaccuracies or omissions.	The information in the RAFT is incomplete and/or inaccurate.	
Perspective	The RAFT maintains clear, consistent point of view, tone, and ideas relevant to the role played; the ideas and information are always tied to role and audience.	The RAFT explains how the character would feel about the topic or situation.	The RAFT shows little insight into how the character would feel about the topic or situation.	The RAFT does not accurately develop the character's feelings about or reactions to the topic or situation.	
Focus	The RAFT stays on topic and never drifts from the required form or type; details and information included are pertinent to the developed purpose.	The RAFT mostly stays on topic but occasionally strays from the focus.	The RAFT discusses some off-topic issues.	The RAFT mostly discusses issues that do not directly relate to the chosen topic.	
Mechanics	The final product contains few to no fragments, run-on sentences, errors, or mechanical mistakes.	The final product contains some fragments, run-on sentences, or other errors and has occasional mechanical mistakes; the writing is generally clear.	The final product contains several sentence errors and mechanical mistakes that may interfere with ideas and clarity.	The final product is marred by numerous errors and contains mechanical mistakes.	
				Total:	

Source: Andrea DeMello and Kelsey Cochran, Rocky Run Middle School, Chantilly, VA. Used with permission.

Learning Menus

What They Are:

Learning Menus outline a variety of instructional options targeted toward important learning goals. Students select and complete the assignment options that most appeal to them.

How They Work:

The teacher articulates learning goals and creates a "menu" of tasks (appetizers, main dishes, side dishes, and desserts) that are designed to help students practice with and display their grasp of identified learning goals. In most cases, students are assigned some or all of the main dishes, but they can typically choose the appetizers, side dishes, and desserts they want to focus on. The menu's design works best when all options in each "course" address the same learning goals. The template (see pp. 255–257) helps the menu designer ensure that all learning objectives are addressed through the task options.

What They're Good For:

- Menus usually encompass what students will be doing during a given period in the classroom—perhaps over the course of a whole curriculum unit—rather than in a single lesson (Jarvis, 2010).
- Menus can serve as sense-making supplements to whole-class instruction (e.g., students move to menu work after a lecture or discussion).
- Menus can also serve as Side Work (e.g., students move to menu work after completing other assigned tasks; see p. 271 for more information).
- Menus can serve as summative performance assessments, if designed as such (e.g., with a rubric that contains assessment criteria for every important learning goal).

Tips:

- Decide on your purpose for using the Learning Menu (sense making, anchor activity, assessment).
- Craft your learning goals for the menu in terms of what you want students to understand, know, and be able to do.
- Begin by designing one or more appetizers, which are opening activities that can serve as hooks for the menu. These could be introductory videos, readings, or tasks (e.g., interviews) that will get students thinking about the ideas they'll "chew on" for the rest of the unit.
- Create your main dishes by identifying core tasks that you want all students to complete.
  - The main-dish section could look the same for every student in the class, *or* there could be more than one version of the menu, each with different main-dish tasks. For example, two menus for different readiness levels could feature four main dishes: two that are common to both menus and two designed for different levels of readiness that look different in each version.

— Regardless of how many menu versions you have, each student will complete all of the main-dish items on the Learning Menu he or she is assigned. Each "dish" should be clearly tied to the learning objectives.

— Choice can be woven into the main-dish section of the menu by asking all students to complete the same *task*, albeit dealing with different *topic areas* (see life science menu, pp. 258–259).

• Design several side dishes to tackle objectives other than those addressed in the main dishes *or* to deepen or expand the investigation of the objectives introduced by the main dishes. Students should select a specified number of side dishes (e.g., two from a list of four), generally according to interest or learning profile preferences.

— Determine the learning goal(s) you want to address or emphasize via the side dishes. All side dishes should address a common concept.

— Incorporate options based on *interest* (e.g., contextualized tasks for math); *learning profile* (e.g., Sternberg's model); or *varied products or modes of expression* (e.g., poems, flowcharts, or podcasts).

— Allow students to select and complete the side dishes that most appeal to them.

• Design several dessert tasks that students will be very motivated to complete (in other words, we should not have to convince students to "eat their dessert"!).

— Desserts should be appealing, engaging tasks that tap into students' interests in relation to the topic.

— It may be useful to think of desserts as enrichment activities, in that they allow students to explore (or become exposed to) an area of interest not usually covered in the core curriculum.

— Desserts can range from short learning tasks to more extensive independent projects.

— Desserts can be included as optional activities that only some students choose to complete, *or* all students may be expected to complete at least one.

— In some cases, it might be appropriate for students to devise their own dessert tasks.

• Don't be afraid to pull appropriate tasks from textbooks or other associated resources.

• For all four "courses," the teacher can tailor choices to different readiness levels.

• Consider—and gather, if necessary—resources (including technology) that might be necessary for students to succeed in each step.

• Create a checklist or rubric to ensure student success on the Learning Menu. If the menu is used as an assessment, create a more formal rubric that attends to the following:

— Criteria should focus on students' grasp of *learning goals* rather than on the *products* they create.

— Descriptors should communicate what "expert," "developing," and "novice" levels of performance would entail.

Source: Tips adapted from guidelines developed by Jane Jarvis, 2010. Used with permission.

Learning Menu Template

Content/Topic:

Unit Learning Goals

As a result of completing the assignments on this menu, students will reach the following goals:	"Course" in which each objective is assessed:
Understanding Goals	
Knowledge Goals	
Skill Goals	

Courses

Appetizers	*Focus/uniting idea*
Main Dishes	*Learning goals and notes about readiness variations, resources, etc.*
Side Dishes	*Learning goals and notes about interest/ learning profile, resources, etc.*
Desserts	*Learning goals and notes about interests, connections, resources, etc.*

Evaluation Criteria

Create a rubric that will assess students' performance on this Learning Menu. When developing your criteria for success, think back to the objectives you developed for the unit. No matter which options students complete, what must they demonstrate that they understand, know, and are able to do? Think about evaluating students' grasp of these learning goals (LGs) rather than the products they create, as well as what "expert," "developing," and "novice" levels of these demonstrations would entail.

	Expert	Developing	Novice
Criterion 1 LG Assessed:			
Criterion 2 LG Assessed:			
Criterion 3 LG Assessed:			
Criterion 4 LG Assessed:			
Criterion 5 LG Assessed:			

Learning Menu Classroom Examples

Life Science: Ecosystems

Understanding Goals for All Courses
- All ecosystems share similar elements, but the specific elements of each ecosystem make it unique.
- Ecosystems are interdependent; each element is affected by the others.

Main-Dish Knowledge Goals:
- Elements common to ecosystems in general.
- Unique elements of and relationships in a particular ecosystem.
- Challenges and changes facing a particular ecosystem.

Main-Dish Skill Goals:
- Analyze an ecosystem for cause-and-effect relationships.
- Predict the effects of changes to ecosystems.

Side-Dish Skill Goal:
- Compare and contrast ecosystems to determine commonalities and distinctions.

Desserts provide extensions of Main-Dish Knows and Dos.

Main Dishes

You must complete the following activities this week:

1. Read Chapter 9 on ecosystems in your textbook.
2. Complete the activity on page 76. Follow all instructions.
3. Choose one ecosystem to study in depth. See your teacher for ecosystem options. To ensure the class studies a variety of ecosystems, different students will receive different options. [*NOTE: This provides an opportunity for readiness differentiation; the teacher may assign ecosystems of various complexities to different students based on their performance on the unit's pre-assessment.*]
4. Complete the Research Graphic Organizer that accompanies your ecosystem. [*NOTE: This provides an additional opportunity for readiness differentiation; the teacher may provide graphic organizers with more structured prompts and guiding questions to students who require more support with research.*]
5. Find someone who has studied the same ecosystem as you and complete the "Checking Our Work" reflection sheet. [*NOTE: Like-readiness partners*]
6. Find someone who has studied a different ecosystem than yours and complete the "Overlap and Opposition" reflection sheet. [*NOTE: Mixed-readiness partners*]

Side Dishes

Choose one option to complete during menu time next week:

1. *Individual reflection on class blog:* What elements do ecosystems share? In what ways do you see them differ? What does this tell you about ecosystems?
2. *Mural for display in children's science museum:* Ecosystems around the world: uniting and dividing. Display and label what ecosystems share and what makes them distinct.
3. *Podcast for next year's students:* What elements do ecosystems share? In what ways do you see them differ? What does this tell you about ecosystems?

Desserts

Complete as many as you have time to do:

1. *Eco-spective:* Create a humorous comic or journal entry from the perspective of one element (e.g., a producer, a consumer) of any ecosystem studied in class. Your pictures and words should depict what that particular element would experience in its unique ecosystem role, as well as the other elements it would encounter.

2. *SpongeBob critique:* What does *SpongeBob SquarePants* get right about SpongeBob's ecosystem? What does it get wrong? Explain or depict what would need to change about the characters, setting, and relationships to make them more accurate. You can suggest new characters and relationships or changes to existing characters and relationships.

3. *SpongeBob spin-off:* Create an idea for a new television cartoon that portrays characters living in any of the ecosystems studied in class. Plan the characters and one situation they'd find themselves in for the pilot episode. The characters and conflict should represent all the roles and at least one relationship from your chosen ecosystem.

High School Math: Parallel Lines

Knowledge Goals
- Definitions of *parallel lines, transversal, corresponding angles, alternate interior angles, alternate exterior angles, vertical angles,* and *same-side (consecutive) interior angles.*
- The parallel postulate and its negations.

Understanding Goals
- Students will understand that *relationships* can help us infer information about a system.

Skill Goals
- Prove whether two lines are parallel.
- Construct two lines that are parallel.

Directions: All of the main dishes and your selected side dishes must be completed by the due date. You are welcome to attempt more than the required number of side dishes and any of the desserts you wish.

Main Dishes

Complete all of the following:

1. See the image of lines cut by a transversal (Image 1). List all pairs of each type of angle relationship: corresponding angles, alternate interior angles, alternate exterior angles, vertical angles, and same-side (consecutive) interior angles.
2. Write the definition of the *parallel postulate* in your own words, clearly enough that someone who does not know what the parallel postulate is would be able to understand. Be sure to underline and explain any terms you use in your definition that your reader may not know.
3. Explain three different ways the angles in Image 1 could tell you that lines *l* and *m* are parallel. You should have three different proofs that each uses different theorems and angles from Image 1 to prove the parallelism of lines *l* and *m*.

Side Dishes

Choose three to complete:

1. Explain why the negation of the parallel postulate gives you two different postulates. Make sure to explain what those two postulates are, and the consequences that come from each of those postulates.
2. With a partner, design a town that has the following attributes: at least two sets of parallel streets (four streets total); at least one set of perpendicular streets (two streets total); at least one street that intersects another street at an obtuse angle; and at least one street that intersects another street at an acute angle. Your town should have at least eight streets. Make sure to name each street and provide a key explaining which streets meet each of the above criteria.
3. Using a compass and a straightedge, construct a pair of parallel lines that both intersect the given line (Image 2) and explain your steps. Label your diagram explicitly to make sure that someone who does not have prior knowledge of parallel lines will be able to understand your explanation.
4. Find two examples in art or architecture that have four or more sets of parallel lines each. Explain how you know they are parallel lines. Provide images of the examples you have found and label or emphasize the parallel lines you identified. Be sure to refer to these images in your explanations.

Desserts

These are optional; you may complete them as anchor activities during menu time or beyond:

1. Explain why some parallel roads in the Midwest must be reshaped so that they do not intersect. Explain how engineers use math to rectify this situation.
2. Using what you know about parallel lines, explain the phenomenon that the Zöllner illusion creates.

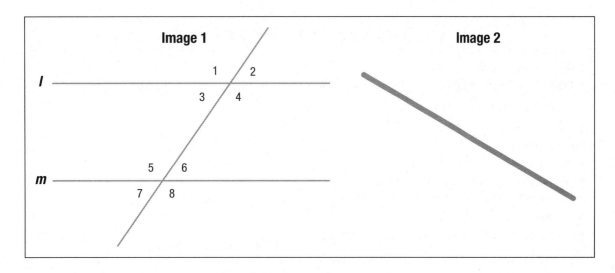

Rubric for Parallel Lines Menu (18 Points Possible)

		3 Points	**2 Points**	**1 Point (Redo)**	**0 Points (Redo)**
Main Dishes	Mathematical Correctness	There are no errors in the math used in the task.	There are one or two errors in the math used in the task.	There are a few errors in the math used in the task.	There are numerous errors in the math used in the task.
	Procedure/ Explanation	The directions for the task are followed correctly with clear explanation.	The directions for the task are followed correctly but with unclear explanation.	The directions for the task are followed incorrectly with clear explanation.	The directions for the task are followed incorrectly with unclear explanation.
Side Dishes and Dessert	Mathematical Correctness	There are no errors in the math used in the task.	There are one or two errors in the math used in the task.	There are a few errors in the math used in the task.	There are numerous errors in the math used in the task.
	Explanation	Explanation is clear and shows full understanding of the material.	Explanation is clear with basic understanding of the material.	Explanation is unclear and shows little understanding of the material.	There is no explanation.

Source: Christopher Devine, Robinson Secondary School, Fairfax County, VA. Used with permission.

Middle School Language Arts: Figurative Language

Understanding for All Courses
- Figurative language allows us to communicate in ways that we cannot using literal language.

Main-Dish Know:
- Definitions of key types of figurative language.

Main-Dish Dos:
- Analyze text to determine use of figurative language.
- Evaluate effect of figurative language on meaning.
- Use figurative language to describe an idea, an object, or a person.

Side-Dish Do:
- Use figurative language to argue a point convincingly.

Desserts: Extensions of Main- and Side-Dish Dos with the purpose of creating humor.

Appetizers

Choose one:

1. Find a song that uses language powerfully to paint a picture in your head. Be ready to share your song, the powerful language, and the picture it creates.
2. Find an advertisement (in any form) that uses a "play on words" to make its point. Be ready to share the ad, the play on words, and its effect on consumers.

Main Dish

Complete the following task:

Review the glossary on figurative language (see Miss Doubet for your assigned terms). For each device,
- Give the definition.
- Find an example of the device in one of the appetizers shared with the class. Explain (1) why it is a good example of that type of figurative language and (2) what it adds to the communication power of the phrase.
- Create an original example of your own to make a point about (1) homework, (2) your favorite item of clothing, or (3) the condition of your room or locker.

Side Dishes

Choose one:

1. Write a song or poem about the merits or downfalls of [*your choice of topic*] using each of your assigned types of figurative language in a meaningful and powerful manner.
2. Write a blog entry praising or critiquing [*your choice of topic*] using each of your assigned types of figurative language in a meaningful and powerful manner.
3. Write a review of [*your choice of book, movie, or musical performance*] using each of your assigned types of figurative language to make your readers take action or believe what you believe.

Desserts

Do as many as you like:

1. Design an ad for your favorite product that plays with words and figurative language in a humorously persuasive way.
2. Design a comic that uses a play on words to evoke a humorous response.
3. Create a series of *Onion*-type headlines that use figurative language and humor to build interest and evoke amusement.

9

Navigating Potential Roadblocks to Implementing Differentiation

Part 1:

How Do I Keep This Sane?

Throughout this book, we have presented differentiation through the analogy of a road trip. Many teachers buy into the value of taking that trip and can envision embarking on the journey and implementing the strategies associated with it—but they can also envision the roadblocks that pop up along the way to make the journey a bumpy one. Often, those roadblocks are related to the challenges associated with management, and the hesitations they induce can deter teachers from even attempting to implement differentiation more fully. In this chapter, we examine such potential roadblocks to differentiation and offer ways to circumvent or address them.

Roadblock #1: Launching Differentiated Tasks

You've designed differentiated tasks, and you're ready to use them with your students. What is the best way to talk about the fact that not everyone is doing the same thing?

Recall from Chapter 1 how crucial it is to help students redefine what *fair* means. Take the time to use activities like Redefining *Fair* (p. 28) and to discuss openly the purpose and benefits of engaging with both common and differentiated tasks and experiences. Keep in mind that all the dialogue about fairness will mean little if the tasks fall short of the criteria for being respectfully differentiated (see Chapter 7, pp. 183–185)—and it goes without saying that adolescents have well-honed radars for detecting disrespectful tasks!

When launching differentiated tasks or experiences, consider whether all students need to see all the tasks. With in-class tasks, consider giving a common set of directions for the process or protocol all students or groups need to use in addition to task-specific directions. You can display and briefly review the common directions before giving students or groups time to digest their own tasks, circling to check in and clarify as needed.

Especially in the case of readiness differentiation, it often makes more sense to briefly reference or preview what the different tasks are without getting into the details. For example, "Based on your Exit Slip responses yesterday, you'll be analyzing one of three sets of primary sources that offer different perspectives on causes of the war. Each of you has a set of questions to help you make sense of the document as well as a specific task to complete. Tomorrow, you'll be sharing your thinking and completing a synthesis task with people from other groups."

If students do need to know more specifically what everyone else is doing, be sure to describe the tasks in an engaging way. There's usually no need to label tasks in a way that draws attention to differences in student readiness (e.g., Level 1, Level 2, and Level 3), but there can be value in giving tasks accurate, invitational titles or framing each task with the question it helps students answer or make sense of. Both the Analytical Role Cards featured in Chapter 5 (pp. 126–129) and the Profiler strategy detailed in Chapter 8 (pp. 223–231) provide examples of using real-world jobs and professions to design and name tasks.

When letting students choose from several options or introducing a summative assessment, it can be tempting to spend an entire class period (or even longer) reviewing and clarifying directions and expectations. It is more efficient, however, to give students time to read through well-described tasks and discuss their understanding of and questions about the tasks with one or two peers before you pull the group together to clarify and answer questions. A major advantage of this approach—even with tasks that aren't differentiated—is that students "work" to make sense of and own the work rather than tuning out or waiting for the teacher to spoon-feed them the tasks.

Finally, as we discussed in Chapter 7, using varied and flexible groupings over the course of a lesson, week, and month can go a long way toward helping students see differentiated tasks as a way of life rather than as an anomaly or a special event. To this end, consider eschewing a single seating chart in favor of whichever arrangement suits your purpose for the day (e.g., a small-group discussion seating chart or a Socratic seminar seating chart). Some teachers have students create "nameplates" on index cards at the beginning of the year and use these to show students where to sit each day or for a set of days. Another quick strategy for mixing it up is to have students quickly line up according to a preference (e.g., how much they like hot dogs, with haters at one end and lovers at the other) or characteristic (e.g., birth month and day). Put students into groups of the desired size with others around them in the line, or "fold" the line (see Figure 9.1) and group students from there.

Roadblock #2: Ensuring Task Completion and Quality

A common concern regarding differentiated group work—or any group work, for that matter—is how to ensure that students stay on task and actually complete what's been assigned to them in a quality manner. The first principle for ensuring task completion is to design the task so that it is *actually a task*. Simply asking middle or high

---

FIGURE 9.1

Fold the Line

Directions:

1. Ask all students in the class to line up across the front of the room in a designated order, according to a factor such as

   - Height (e.g., shortest to tallest).
   - Birthday (month and day only).
   - Favorite color or color students are wearing (in order of ROY G BIV).
   - Distance students travel to get to school (in minutes or miles).
   - Degrees of preference for a given food or TV show.
   - Phone number (e.g., numerical order of last four digits).

2. Allow students to talk to one another as they order themselves, or increase the challenge by asking that they use only nonverbal means of communication.
3. Put a time limit on student movement to communicate a sense of urgency.
4. Once the line is formed, "fold" it in half by bringing the two ends together. Then ask students to pair up with the person across from them. If there is an uneven number, ask the middle three students to work together.

Variations:

- Once the line is formed, students can go in order and state the reason for their placement (e.g., when their birthday is, how much they love or hate the TV show).
- After you've used the strategy once or twice, keep students on their toes by varying whether they "fold" the line or pair with an odd/even partner.

---

school students to form groups and "discuss" something without requiring a record of or reflection on that discussion is an invitation for students to socialize. Instead, teachers should require the group, or even each student in the group, to emerge from their work with a record of progress.

For example, you may require each student to complete a ThinkDots graphic organizer (see p. 138) for use in a future step of instruction (e.g., as fuel for an essay or guidance in solving a problem). Alternatively, you may require each group to emerge with its stance on an issue recorded on poster paper to present to the rest of the class (see Structured Academic Controversy, pp. 135–136). In any case, there should be some measure of accountability required for what happens in groups during task completion.

The second rule of thumb is to make sure all instructions for tasks are crystal clear. The trick when spelling out instructions is to give a full yet easily digestible description of all requirements. A paragraph of detailed instructions may stymie a group of students before they even start, whereas those same instructions formatted in a bulleted or numbered list can lead students clearly through the steps needed for completion.

Finally, it is important to establish and enforce a clear protocol for bringing together a variety of responses during group work. Often, a group task requires students to pool answers they generated during an independent task. A clear procedure must be in place when students are asked to reach consensus in cases like these. It is insufficient to ask students simply to "compare answers"; such a request will most likely lead students to follow the "majority rules" principle or to let one student fill in all the answers. Instead, set up a consensus-seeking *system* for students that requires them to defend responses, honor outliers, and contest passive agreement. The "Check, Please!" Protocol on page 278 is one structure for encouraging this kind of collaborative work. This system works when the whole class has completed the same work (in class or at home) as well as when different groups of students have completed different tasks (in class or at home).

Roadblock #3: Facilitating Group Work

Describing tasks clearly and requiring some measure of accountability are important first steps in helping middle and high school learners become self-sufficient thinkers and workers. Unfortunately, at this stage in their schooling, students may have already developed a certain degree of dependence on adult help. As such, it is even more important to help them develop skills of independence (rather than to eliminate situations that require autonomy). Of course, if we want them to be successful, we must scaffold this process for them.

The first step is to provide instructions both to the whole class (see Roadblock #1) and to small groups (see Roadblock #2) that help students *begin work without your help*. Design tasks in such a way that you can be "off-limits" for the first five minutes; this will free you up to attend to any unanticipated bumps in the road while students use their directions and their resources to begin. Admittedly, your first attempt at this may be difficult; students won't *really* believe that you won't be available. But once they see that you are serious and figure out that they can succeed in your absence, their perseverance will improve.

It's also important to make sure you design tasks in such a way that you will be available to work with every group at some point. This may mean structuring tasks so that you meet with some groups at the beginning of their task, some midway through completion, and others toward the end (see the tiered graphing example tasks on pp. 189–191 for an illustration of this principle). This practice not only improves the flow of group work from a management perspective but also removes the stigma of a teacher-led group. When a teacher works exclusively with any one type of group (e.g., struggling learners), he or she may send status messages that are difficult to undo. All students, regardless of readiness, need teacher guidance and support, especially when the tasks are appropriately differentiated. There will be times when you need to meet first with students who have the most advanced task.

Finally, establish routines to foster independence. *Question Chips* are one structure for encouraging students to determine whether their questions about group tasks are "must-ask" or "could-find-out-myself." You can give each group—or each student, if they are working independently—a limited number of Question Chips (poker chips, card stock, or even paper scraps). These chips represent the number of times students can call on the teacher for help. If students have only three chips, they are less likely to thoughtlessly raise their hands and summon you for easy-to-answer questions. In no way does this mean you should refuse to answer important content-based questions; rather, you can use Question Chips to help students determine whether their queries truly relate to understanding or are simply procedural in nature. If a question is procedural, you can hint, "Do you really want to use a chip on that question?" and even indicate a general area of the directions where students can find the answer.

Colored Cups is another strategy that helps students establish the habit of exhausting their own resources before seeking outside help. In this system, each group receives a stack of three colored cups (usually but not necessarily green, yellow, and red). When the green cup is on top, the group is working fine. When the yellow cup is displayed, students need help, but they can continue working on another step while they wait for assistance. The red cup signals a group's need for immediate attention. As the teacher circulates, he or she monitors the cups and works with groups according to the urgency indicated by the color displayed. On first implementation, you may find that students regard every question as a "red" question; this provides yet another opportunity to foster group independence as you can tell a group that its question is "yellow," point to another step the students can work on in your absence, and wait a few minutes before returning to assist them.

Resource Files and Hint Cards provide additional ways for you to offer assistance to students when you are not immediately available. *Resource Files* include information about routines and problem-solving techniques that are used on a regular basis. Resource Files can be placed in a prominent area of the room and can consist of either physical files (i.e., in file folders) or digital files (e.g., bookmarked websites or computer desktop folders). These files can outline steps for troubleshooting (e.g., what to do when your screen freezes, how to circumvent writer's block) or provide other problem-solving "helps" (e.g., graphic organizers, peer editing protocols, rubrics). *Hint Cards* operate in much the same way, but they are usually lesson-specific resources. If you were teaching a lesson on graphing linear equations, for example, you could probably anticipate the trouble spots and questions that would arise. Create several Hint Cards that contain the probing questions you would ask students when they get stuck. It typically works well to have different Hint Cards for different "sticking points" in the process. Students must first use these resources before consulting the teacher; when they do call you, you can use the prompts on the Hint Cards to continue to talk them through getting "unstuck." Over time, this strategy will reinforce students' own problem-solving skills.

It is important to remember that grouping isn't synonymous with differentiation. Students can complete differentiated tasks individually, too. It doesn't make sense to put students into groups unless you expect them to collaborate. When assigning differentiated tasks, consider your goals and the configuration most conducive to helping students achieve those goals, and group only when it makes sense to do so.

Roadblock #4: Using Time Wisely

Time is our most valuable resource; understandably, we are unwilling to squander it. In a differentiated classroom, as with any other worthwhile venture, we need to *invest* time in order to get it back. In other words, time invested in establishing routines and teaching students how to use resources and move into groups efficiently gains back time in a smoothly running classroom. In general, the following practices require some rehearsal before we can expect them to run self-sufficiently.

- *Moving into groups.* Even middle and high school students need to be taught how to move locations, furniture, and themselves in an efficient fashion. Establishing classroom norms is an important first step, but you will still need to orchestrate movement for students, explain (in words and through visuals) *where* you expect them to move and *how quickly*, and facilitate practice moving into those configurations. It's a good idea to ask students to do a dry run of moving into groups just so they get accustomed to adjusting desks or seats and grouping themselves with different people. You can ask students to move into groups quickly (without anything to "do" in those groups) and time their progress, challenging them to beat their own times or those of other sections. Another option is to use the "mixing it up" strategies discussed in Roadblock #1. Either way, practicing movement in low-stakes situations makes moving into groups in more formal scenarios seem less jarring.

- *Introducing new strategies.* Undoubtedly, some of the strategies discussed throughout this book will be unfamiliar to both you and your students. Just as it's a good idea to have students do dry runs of forming groups, it also makes sense to practice these strategies in a low-stakes or content-free situation before using them to connect students with content. For example, a RAFT can be used to review classroom routines and procedures. Students can engage in a ThinkDots activity to get to know one another or build community (see Figure 9.2). Quartet Quiz (pp. 122–123) is a useful tool to help students generate questions about an upcoming classroom event or project. Introducing strategies in a stress-free manner allows students to relax into the strategies when they are used in conjunction with content.

- *Spacing things out.* Introducing multiple strategies simultaneously can produce overload and confusion, so spread out your introduction of the routines outlined in this chapter slowly, over the course of the first week or two of school. Implement strategies deliberately and purposefully. It is advisable to start with a few and allow your students (and yourself!) time to get comfortable with them before adding more to your repertoire. Remember, too, that it makes sense to use a combination of whole-class and small-group configurations; a differentiated class does not spend the entire time working in small groups!

FIGURE 9.2

Community-Building ThinkDots

If you could have any career in the world, what would it be and why?	What's your favorite place to travel? What new destinations would you like to explore?	If you could invite any three people—living or dead—to dinner, who would they be and why?
You have been banished to a deserted island and can bring only three items. What will you bring? Why?	If you could trade places with a celebrity (for a day), who would it be? Explain.	You won a million dollars! Give a detailed breakdown of what you'll do with the money.

Finally, it's important to acknowledge—and plan ahead for—the reality that kids will most likely complete tasks at different rates. Because of the nature of the authentic tasks students tackle in a differentiated classroom (as well as the different ways students do so), you should expect some degree of ragged finish time. As a rule, it's advisable to have *a bit too much* planned for a task, with the understanding that you will "forgive" the last step or two if students don't get there. Even with preemptive planning, however, students will inevitably finish at somewhat different rates. Accordingly, it's a good idea to have a plan in place.

- *Side Work.* One method for steering students who finish early toward continuing meaningful engagement with content is the establishment of *Side Work* (described by Tomlinson and Imbeau [2010] as *anchor activities*). For servers in a restaurant, "side work" usually consists of tasks that are vital but on the periphery of the primary responsibility of taking care of guests—for example, filling condiment bottles, checking silverware, and stocking service stations. Similarly, Side Work in a classroom engages students in tasks that are important to the discipline but that may not be related to the primary content focus on a particular day. Side Work may involve practice with important skills, extension of vocabulary, or investigation into areas of interest. Agendas (see Chapter 7) and Learning Menus (see Chapter 8) provide efficient structures for delivering such tasks.

- *Deadline extension.* Once in a while, students may become so engrossed in a task or experience such major setbacks that they fall behind in their work. An important principle in a differentiated classroom is that students "getting there" in their learning is more important than when they arrive. Teachers can send this message by asking students to complete an Application for Deadline Extension (see p. 279). This structure ensures that the student applying for the deadline recognizes the importance of the task and takes ownership for its completion. It also sends the message that the teacher is flexible (within reason) and is invested in students' success.

Roadblock #5: Figuring and Reporting Grades for Differentiated Tasks

Evaluating differentiated tasks and incorporating them into grades is less of a challenge than it might initially seem in light of (1) what differentiation is and isn't and (2) consensus among experts in grading and assessment. The biggest obstacle is likely what teachers believe a grade is and should include, which is largely informed by their own experiences with grades as students.

Zooming out to consider how grades are typically figured and reported on a report card illustrates the challenges. When Johnny gets a *B−* in science in trimester 1, there could be many reasons for the grade. Because of the myriad factors teachers tend to include in a grade, it's not clear from the grade itself whether Johnny is mastering the course goals and standards. As Stiggins (2000) puts it, "When we try to pack a wide variety of student characteristics into one grade, that grade is not a valid reflection of any one of them" (p. 441).

Generally speaking, teachers are interested in reporting several categories of information: where the student is relative to content goals or standards (*performance*); how far the student has come with respect to those goals or standards (*progress*); and how the student is doing with certain work habits and dispositions (*process* [Guskey, 2011; Guskey & Bailey, 2010]). Most teachers mix these factors into a single grade so that each category is indiscernible. Although performance, progress, and process are related and likely influence one another, they are not *synonymous,* and lumping them together into one grade adds neither value nor clarity. Figuring and reporting these "3 *P*s" separately—each as a grade or as grades and other ways of reporting—goes a long way to communicate better and more accurate information to stakeholders. It also makes sense for differentiated classrooms, whose teachers are rightfully concerned about seeing success in terms of performance, growth, and behaviors exhibited in pursuit of goals (Tomlinson & Moon, 2013). Optimally, the report card should be structured to provide information in this way (Guskey & Bailey, 2010; O'Connor, 2009).

Even in the absence of a multidimensional reporting system, it's important to make sure that a grade is based on student performance against clear standards. When it comes to figuring this grade, experts advise drawing from and weighting evidence that students have produced *later* in the learning cycle rather than earlier (Brookhart, 2008; Guskey & Bailey, 2010; Marzano, 2000; O'Connor, 2009; Tomlinson & Moon, 2013). The reasoning is simple: work that a student does toward the end of an instructional sequence around given learning goals paints a more accurate picture of what the student has learned. Therefore, summative assessments should be the primary data source for grading. This is one reason why it's important to have more than one kind of summative assessment in and across units. Formative assessment should be weighted less, with students' responses on Entry or Exit Slips, in-class sense-making tasks, and some kinds of practice work excluded from a grade altogether.

Remember that any differentiated formative and summative transfer tasks that you *will* grade (see Chapter 8 for examples) should be aligned with the same learning goals and evaluated using the same criteria or rubric. Most of these will be differentiated for interest or learning profile. The vast majority of tasks that are differentiated for readiness are formative activities that shouldn't be counted in the performance grade.

Roadblock #6: Differentiating in My Subject Area

Many teachers wonder—to themselves or aloud—if differentiation is more difficult or necessary in a certain subject area or course type, or at a particular grade level. In our work in schools, we often hear things like

- "I see how this could work in English, but not in math."
- "This seems easy with high schoolers, but not 6th graders."
- "Differentiation is really more of a remedial/ELL/special education thing than something for AP classes."

As with many endeavors, change often seems easier for other people than it does for us. Although we know of no research that suggests certain disciplines, ages, or levels of a course are inherently optimal for or resistant to differentiation, there is plenty of research (Brighton, Hertberg, Moon, Tomlinson, & Callahan, 2005; Elmore, 2004; Fullan, 2007; Kennedy, 2005; Tyack & Cuban, 1995) that speaks to how difficult it can be to change instructional and assessment practices—including those that are connected to or reflect differentiation, and especially in secondary schools.

In truth, even when teachers believe that different students should be doing different things, they may be unable to envision how it would "play out" in their classroom or subject. Learning Stations (see pp. 280–281) offer a flexible structure for giving students access to materials, tasks, and teacher instruction that are targeted to their specific needs. Whether a teacher decides to tackle two stations—or five—with or without a co-teacher, stations offer a palatable entry point for teachers of all content areas to confront the logistical considerations of the differentiated classroom.

The Bottom Line

Let's face it: all teaching is hard, good teaching is harder, and both good teaching and differentiation call for a range of sophisticated skills that no teacher is ever truly "finished" developing. Often, growing pains related to implementing differentiation are symptomatic of the never-ending, evolutionary process of understanding who, what, and how to teach. Teachers can better "see" how to implement and manage differentiation in a subject or with a given population when they have high-quality examples that they can envision transferring to their own classrooms. Throughout this book, we have tried to include such examples and represent a reasonable range of grade levels and content areas that can inspire and encourage teachers to grow and upgrade their practice. For additional guidance on leading and managing differentiated classrooms, see Tomlinson and Imbeau (2010).

A Case in Point: Ms. Harley

When Ms. Harley examined her Exit Slips at the end of the day, she realized she was going to need to spend the first half of the next block making sure students really "got" the interdependent nature of the factors leading to international—specifically, U.S.—involvement in World War II. On their Exit Slips, a handful of students had presented sound and well-supported arguments about whether U.S. isolationism would have continued had the attack on Pearl Harbor not happened. Many other students had presented logical but less well-supported arguments. Another handful of students had struggled even to articulate a position on the matter. She decided to set up several Learning Stations for the next day's lesson.

Her students were already familiar with the Structured Academic Controversy (SAC) strategy. Ms. Harley had used it during the opening week of class to debate whether history was worth studying, and the class had returned to it previously in this unit to debate the wisdom of the uneasy alliance forged by the United States and Great Britain with Stalin. Therefore, Ms. Harley could direct students with advanced Exit Slip responses to study two additional primary sources and use their new evidence to compose and deliver arguments on both sides of the issue of continued isolationism, SAC-style. She met with this group first to go over the task directions and point the students toward the SAC resources she had bookmarked on the classroom computers. The group received two Question Chips to use for future access to the teacher.

While Ms. Harley met with this group of students, the other students got started on their own assignments, which were outlined thoroughly on their task cards. The majority of students worked in pairs to review their Exit Slip responses from the previous day and add fuel to the fire of their arguments. Key textbook pages and bookmarked websites served as Resource Files for students to find research that would beef up their cases. Ms. Harley checked in with them throughout the process; although every group or pair of students had received two Question Chips, Ms. Harley wanted to ensure the accuracy of the arguments' claims and evidence.

The small group of students who had been unable to formulate arguments began by viewing a video Ms. Harley had bookmarked. At the video's completion, students would select a graphic organizer from the Resource Files and begin working in pairs to formulate a response and support it with evidence from the video and the textbook. Ms. Harley checked in with this group when the video ended to help the students make the transition from viewing to producing and gave them two Question Chips for continued access to her.

At the end of the time allotted, each pair or group presented a position statement to the rest of the class, pulling in key evidence and logic to defend its perspective on the ability of the United States to exist in an isolationist state—both in the past and in the present. Anyone who finished early could move to his or her Side Work (see Figure 9.3).

Ms. Harley emerged from her students' presentations feeling that the whole class could move forward together. Since she liked to group flexibly, she posted a list of some key events the class would be studying next and asked students to choose the two in which they were most interested; she would use their results to form interest groups for an investigative Jigsaw the following week.

FIGURE 9.3

Social Studies Side Work

Directions: Complete Column 1 and research your choice of additional column(s).	Column 1: Era Currently Being Studied	Column 2: Compared with Previous Era (discuss connections)	Column 3: Compared with Present Day (hypothesize reasons for similarities/ differences)	Column 4: Predictions— Future Trends (cite historical patterns to defend predictions)
U.S. Federal Government's Major Policies				
U.S. Economic Health (Description, Causes, and Effects)				
Foreign Policy/ Alliances/Strained Relationships				
U.S. Domestic Culture-Shaping Events or Movements				
U.S. Pop Culture (Entertainment, Sports, etc.)				

Source: From "Teaching High Achievers," by K. J. Doubet, 2013, *AMLE Magazine, 1*(3), p. 13. Copyright 2013 by the Association for Middle Level Education.

Part 2:

Tools and Strategies

"Check, Please!" Protocol

Team Members: _____

Today's Leader: _____

Overview:

- You and your fellow team members will engage in a dialogue around your responses on the task that you each completed independently.
- The goal is to compare your responses and resolve any differences you have by talking through how you went about [*solving the problem, resolving the issue, making sense of the text*], and why.

1. Has everyone in your group *completed* the task?
   - ☐ YES. (Go on to step 2.)
   - ☐ NO. (Ask the person to let the teacher know.)
2. Begin with the first [*question, part, problem*]. Does everyone have the same response?
   - ☐ If YES, go on to the next [*question, part, problem*].
   - ☐ If NO . . .

Do *NOT* assume that one person is wrong and everyone else is right! Challenge one another!

- Talk through your response! Have each person share how he or she arrived at his or her conclusion or solution.
- If you still don't agree, use your resources (e.g., whiteboards, texts, notes, blank paper) to have one person walk through the thinking behind his or her responses for everyone as the group talks it out.
- It's *everyone's* responsibility to make sure that your group arrives at consensus—even if you agree that you don't know, aren't sure, or disagree!

3. Use the same process for each [*question, part, problem*].
4. *Complete this step only if directed to do so by your teacher!* Check your answers with the [*key, model, exemplar*] provided. If your team's response differs from that on the [*key, model, exemplar*], determine why and how you differ. If you believe that your team's response is actually *more* on target than that in the [*key, model, exemplar*], include a defense/explanation of your reasoning.
5. When you're finished, staple all the responses together. *Make sure that the version that represents your group's consensus is on top!*

Consensus Check:

☐ We reached consensus on all [*questions, parts, problems*].

☐ We did not reach consensus on the following:

    Here's why:

Application for Deadline Extension

Guidelines:

Once each marking period, you may choose to apply for a deadline extension on a long-term assignment or project. Your application must be submitted no more than *four* school days prior to the original assignment/project due date. Your *proposed* due date cannot extend beyond two weeks from the *original* due date. Your application must also include (1) an explanation of why you are applying for an extension, (2) a description of the evidence you will share that shows you have started and worked on the assignment, and (3) an outline of your plan/time line for completing the assignment. Applying for an extension does not guarantee you will be granted one.

Name: _____   **Assignment/Project:** _____

Original Due Date: _____   **Today's Date:** _____   **Proposed Due Date:** _____

1. Explain why you are applying for an extension.

2. Describe what evidence of having started and worked on the assignment you will show me.

3. Outline your plan/time line for completing the assignment by your proposed due date.

_____   _____
Student signature   Parent/Guardian signature

___ **Approved**   ___ **Approved with changes**   ___ **Denied**

Teacher Comments:

Learning Stations

What They Are:

Learning Stations are a structure for managing simultaneous instruction, learning activities, and/or tasks. Stations can be used to introduce topics or concepts, provide experience with or review material, or practice or reinforce ideas and skills.

How They Work:

The teacher plans the desired number of Learning Stations around clear learning goals. The plan for using the stations should address the following questions:

- How are the stations related or connected? What is the overall goal or purpose of the stations?
- What will students do at each station (complete a task, use a technological tool, receive peer-to-peer instruction, engage with the teacher)?
- With whom will students do what they need to do (with the teacher, with a peer, by themselves)?
- How will students know what they need to do—what process will they need to use or follow (task cards; an individual menu, guide, or agenda; directions on a screen; spoken directions)?
- Where will the materials for station tasks be located (at the station, with the students)?
- Will all students visit all stations?
- How will students transition between stations? Will students rotate at specific times, or will they "wander" among stations?
- How long will each rotation/visit take? How will students know?

What They're Good For:

- Launching a new topic.
- Providing interest-based activities.
- Addressing a large amount of content in a short amount of time.
- Giving students practice with specific concepts and skills.
- Providing targeted instruction following modeling.
- Providing feedback following formative assessment.
- Reviewing content or practicing skills (e.g., in preparation for a summative assessment).
- Structuring feedback on or facilitating the sharing of student work.
- Providing a structure to give all students access to limited resources, technology, and so on.
- A strategy/model for co-taught classrooms. Both teachers can facilitate instruction in stations, one teacher can "float" while the other instructs at a station, or both teachers can "float."

Tips:

- Strategies for guiding students through station tasks include colored folders with directions inside, bookmarked websites or instructions on electronic devices, station guides for students to carry, and the use of QR codes.
- Establish a signal and a system for moving from station to station.
- Practice rotating among stations in a content-free manner to introduce the strategy; review rotation procedures periodically.

Conclusion: Gauging Success and Making Progress the Goal

That students differ may be inconvenient, but it is inescapable. Adapting to that diversity is the inevitable price of productivity, high standards and fairness to students.
—Theodore Sizer (1992)

Our goal in this book has been to show that differentiation is a feasible, practical, substantive, and worthwhile approach not just to *adapting* to classroom diversity, but also to *honoring and embracing* it.

Differentiation does not require designing eight different assignments, orchestrating convoluted group tasks, becoming a kindergarten teacher, or hosting a veritable three-ring circus. Nor does it involve giving low-level tasks to some students and high-level tasks to others, sorting students by test scores, or decreasing expectations. Such misconceptions can unfortunately and unnecessarily prevent middle and high school teachers from creating more student-centered and responsive classrooms.

At its core, differentiation is about moving *all* students toward and beyond common and important learning goals. Sometimes (but not always), students *share* a route toward those goals. Other times (but not always), ongoing assessment compels teachers to plan two or more routes that vary by readiness, interest, or learning preferences (Tomlinson, 2014a). You've spent a good deal of time examining principles, tools, and examples of how differentiation might look in a middle or high school classroom. The $100,000 question is, *Does it really "work"?*

Does Differentiation Work?

There are several lenses through which to probe whether differentiation yields positive outcomes for middle and high school students. In one sense, it's a question of whether students are more likely to experience academic and personal growth in classrooms where teachers plan with differences in mind than in classrooms where teachers ignore those differences. Both research and common sense say the former environment is probably better for more students than the latter. In other words, intentional and systemic planning and adjustment for varied needs and characteristics are more effective than treating all students as one and the same.

Differentiation is a complex approach to teaching that pulls elements from many disparate educational fields. Accordingly, one way of considering its efficacy is to examine research across the fields from which it pulls, including neuroscience, student motivation and learning, curriculum, assessment, instruction, and so on. Each concept and practice highlighted in this book is informed by theoretical and research bases with regard to these fields. Although it was beyond the scope of this book's purpose to cite the myriad studies that speak to the crucial roles and influence of, for example, taking a concept-oriented approach to curriculum, using ongoing assessment and flexible grouping, or employing rich and respectful tasks, those practices and others we've associated with differentiation are defensibly effective.

Data from one school's implementation of differentiation as part of a detracking initiative provide notable evidence of success. In *The Differentiated School* (2008), Tomlinson, Brimijoin, and Narvaez reported a trend of increased student achievement at Colchester High School in Colchester, Vermont. Colchester was *not* a high-achieving school at the outset of their efforts, yet the school saw growth in several areas over the course of the initiative, including in standardized test scores, the number of students taking advanced placement courses, and the number of students achieving honors designations on the New Standards Reference Examinations within and across testing subjects. Infractions requiring disciplinary action decreased over the same six-year period, as did the student dropout rate. Even more enlightening is what the high school students themselves had to say about differentiation at their school (Doubet, 2007):

> Getting to choose what you want to do and how you want to do it makes it easier to learn because you're doing it in a way that you understand. . . . If you get to choose which way you're doing it, then you're more likely to do it well. (Sasha, 9th grade)

> I think differentiated instruction prevents some kids from burning out and giving up because they were kind of pushed over the limit without as much help or choice in middle school as they've had in these later years. It's fun to be around a group of friends at a bunch of different levels, and to watch them be interested in what they choose to do and not give up. (Dylan, 10th grade)

Now my mom sees me, and she's like, "What is going on? You're doing well! I don't understand what's different." I tell her, "It's not just read-a-book-take-a-test-on-it learning. It's so much more than that; I can actually understand!" (Mallory, 10th grade)

I think a positive is it allows you to amalgamate subjects that aren't normally together, like art and math, or history and art, or English and history —and you can just tell it's more like how it would be in the real world. It's not so centralized like in different subjects. (Serena, 12th grade)

I learned a number of valuable concepts that even connect to material I am learning now [in college]. I now refer to concepts to get the understanding of a particular topic. It's much better than memorizing facts. (Rob, college freshman)

Many teachers avoid differentiation for fear of backlash and pushback from students. These reactions, however, reveal that adolescents respond positively to differentiation "done right"—to the teacher's authentic attempts to make instruction meaningful and accessible to all students and to the active pursuit of student growth in the context of classroom community.

Who's "Doing" Differentiation?

When adopting fresh or upgraded practices, all teachers naturally want to know if they are doing it right. Our own experiences working in and with schools suggests that most good teachers are somewhere along a continuum from novice to expert in practicing and applying some of the principles and strategies associated with differentiation.

Despite many teachers' acceptance of the idea of differentiation and testimony that they "do it," research reveals that differentiation is not commonplace, well understood, or consistently applied in defensible ways, regardless of the characteristics of the students involved (see Tomlinson, 2014b, for a brief review). Why? Is differentiation just too hard? Are students' needs too varied or too difficult to manage?

Let's take a step back to note that there are *numerous* teaching practices that are well supported by empirical research that are neither easy to implement nor pervasive in schools (e.g., formative assessment, timely feedback, cooperative learning). In fact, experts (Cuban, 1993, 2007; Elmore, 2004; Fullan, 2007; Sarason, 1996; Tyack & Cuban, 1995) in the history of U.S. education conclude that classroom instruction in general—particularly at the high school level—has remained decidedly teacher-centered over the past century. The conclusion that because differentiation isn't the norm, it must be impossible or a waste of time belies the challenges and complexities of effective teaching in general. And it ignores other realities about the past and present state of instruction in many U.S. classrooms.

Studies of how teachers understand and practice differentiation reveal that a teacher's conceptions of and skills with it are connected to his or her knowledge of the content area, pedagogy, management, how students learn, the nature of intelligence, and the role and purpose of assessment (Brighton et al., 2005; Hockett, 2010; Moon, Callahan, Tomlinson, & Miller, 2002). In other words, a teacher's facility with differentiation is strongly influenced by the accuracy, depth, and breadth of his or her understanding and application of foundational aspects of teaching. Viewed positively, this means that there are multiple entry points and avenues for teachers to continue their growth.

Ultimately, the goal is less about "doing differentiation" than about continuing to build skill in planning learning experiences—differentiated and otherwise—that bring students closer to meeting or progressing beyond goals and standards.

Final Thought

In Chapter 1 of *The Notebook,* the narrator observes, "It's the possibility that keeps me going, not the guarantee, a sort of wager on my part."

Like all past and present approaches to teaching, differentiation is a sort of wager on the teacher's part—one that risks investing time and energy into studying and knowing students well, and then responding with the best possible curriculum, assessment, and instruction.

Not differentiating is the bigger gamble. Such a wager assumes that both teaching and students can fit into neat and often separate boxes, with few or no consequences for learning or achievement. Schools simply cannot afford to think of students in terms of those who can and those who can't. Practices that judge the potential of adolescents and seem to predestine many to lesser lives rob students of learning, teachers of teaching, and society of innumerable rich and varied contributions.

For our money, we'll bet on differentiation.

References

Anderson, L. W., & Krathwohl, D. R. (Eds.). (2001). *A taxonomy for learning, teaching, and assessing: A revision of Bloom's taxonomy of educational objectives.* New York: Longman.

Aronson, E., & Patnoe, S. (1997). *The jigsaw classroom: Building cooperation in the classroom* (2nd ed.). New York: Longman.

Beers, K. (2002). *When kids can't read: What teachers can do.* Portsmouth, NH: Heinemann.

Bergmann, J., & Sams, A. (2012). *Flip your classroom: Reach every student in every class every day.* Alexandria, VA: ASCD.

Berra, Y. (2001). *When you come to a fork in the road, take it! Inspiration and wisdom from one of baseball's greatest heroes.* New York: Hyperion.

Black, P., & Wiliam, D. (1998). Inside the black box: Raising standards through classroom assessment. *Phi Delta Kappan, 80*(2), 139–148.

Brandt, R. (1993). On teaching for understanding: A conversation with Howard Gardner. *Educational Leadership, 50*(7), 4–7.

Bransford, J., Brown, A., & Cocking, R. (Eds.). (2000). *How people learn: Brain, mind, experience, and school* (Expanded ed.). Washington, DC: National Academy Press.

Brighton, C. M., Hertberg, H. L., Moon, T. R., Tomlinson, C. A., & Callahan, C. M. (2005). *The feasibility of high-end learning in a diverse middle school* (RM05210). Storrs, CT: The National Research Center on the Gifted and Talented.

Brookfield, S. P., & Preskill, S. (1999). *Discussion as a way of teaching: Tools and techniques for democratic classrooms.* San Francisco: Jossey-Bass.

Brookhart, S. M. (2008). *Grading* (2nd ed.). New York: Merrill.

Buehl, D. (2009). *Classroom strategies for interactive learning* (3rd ed.). Newark, DE: International Reading Association.

Bunce, D. M., Flens, E. A., & Neiles, K. Y. (2010). How long can students pay attention in class? A study of student attention decline using clickers. *Journal of Chemical Education, 87*(12), 1438–1443.

Burke, J. (2002). *Tools for thought: Helping all students read, write, speak, and think.* Portsmouth, NH: Heinemann.

Callahan, C. M. (2003). *Advanced Placement and International Baccalaureate programs for talented students in American high schools: A focus on science and mathematics* (RM03176). Storrs, CT: The National Research Center on the Gifted and Talented.

Crabtree, C. A., & Nash, G. B. (1996). *National standards for history.* Los Angeles: National Center for History in the Schools, University of California, Los Angeles.

Cuban, L. (1993). *How teachers taught: Constancy and change in American classrooms, 1880–1990* (2nd ed.). New York: Teachers College Press.

Cuban, L. (2007). Hugging the middle: Teaching in an era of testing and accountability, 1980–2005. *Education Policy Analysis Archives, 15*(1), 1–27.

Cummings, C. (2000). *Winning strategies for classroom management.* Alexandria, VA: ASCD.

Cushman, K. V. (Ed.). (2005). *Fires in the bathroom: Advice for teachers from high school students.* New York: The New Press.

de Bono, E. (1999). *Six thinking hats.* New York: Back Bay Books.

Dean, C. B., Hubbell, E. R., Pitler, H., & Stone, B. (2012). *Classroom instruction that works: Research-based strategies for increasing student achievement* (2nd ed.). Alexandria, VA: ASCD.

Dobbertin, C., & Doubet, K. J. (2005). *HOTTLINX study on differentiated instruction in middle school.* National Research Center on the Gifted and Talented, University of Virginia, Charlottesville.

Doubet, K. J. (2007). *Teacher fidelity and student response to a model of differentiation as implemented by one high school* (Unpublished doctoral dissertation). University of Virginia, Charlottesville, VA.

Doubet, K. J. (2013, October). Teaching high achievers. *AMLE Magazine, 1*(3), 10–13. Retrieved from http://www.amle.org/Portals/0/pdf/magazine/AMLEMag_oct2013.pdf

Dweck, C. (2006). *Mindset: The new psychology of success.* New York: Ballantine Books.

Dweck, C. (2008). Perils and promises of praise. *Educational Leadership, 65,* 34–39.

Earl, L. M. (2003). *Assessment as learning: Using classroom assessment to maximize student learning.* Thousand Oaks, CA: Corwin.

Elmore, R. F. (2004). *School reform from the inside out: Policy, practice, and performance.* Cambridge, MA: Harvard Education Press.

Erickson, H. L. (2002). *Concept-based curriculum and instruction: Teaching beyond the facts.* Thousand Oaks, CA: Corwin.

Finn, C. E., & Hockett, J. A. (2012). *Exam schools: Inside America's most selective public high schools.* Princeton, NJ: Princeton University Press.

Frayer, D., Frederick, W. C., & Klausmeier, H. J. (1969). *A schema for testing the level of cognitive mastery.* Madison, WI: Wisconsin Center for Education Research.

Freeman, S., Eddy, S. L., McDonough, M., Smith, M. K., Okoroafor, N., Jordt, H., et al. (2014, June 10). Active learning increases student performance in science, engineering, and mathematics. *Proceedings of the National Academy of Sciences of the United States of America, 111*(23), 8410–8415. Retrieved from www.pnas.org/cgi/doi/10.1073/pnas.1319030111

Fullan, M. (2007). *The new meaning of educational change* (4th ed.). New York: Teachers College Press.

Fullan, M., Hill, P., & Crevola, C. (2006). *Breakthrough.* Thousand Oaks, CA: Corwin.

Gardner, H. (1995, November). Reflections on multiple intelligences: Myths and messages. *Phi Delta Kappan,* 200–209.

Gardner, H. (2006). *Multiple intelligences: New horizons.* New York: Basic Books.

Guskey, T. R. (2003). How classroom assessments improve learning. *Educational Leadership, 60*(5), 6–11.

Guskey, T. R. (2007/2008). The rest of the story. *Educational Leadership, 65*(4), 28–35.

Guskey, T. R. (2011). Five obstacles to grading reform. *Educational Leadership, 69*(3), 16–21.

Guskey, T. R., & Bailey, J. M. (2010). *Developing standards-based report cards.* Thousand Oaks, CA: Corwin.

Hattie, J. (2009). *Visible learning: A synthesis of over 800 meta-analyses relating to achievement.* New York: Routledge.

Hattie, J. (2012). *Visible learning for teachers: Maximizing impact on learning.* New York: Routledge.

Hertberg-Davis, H., Callahan, C. M., & Kyburg, R. M. (2006). *Advanced Placement and International Baccalaureate programs: A "fit" for gifted learners?* (RM06222). Storrs, CT: The National Research Center on the Gifted and Talented.

Himmele, P., & Himmele, W. (2011). *Total participation techniques: Making every student an active learner.* Alexandria, VA: ASCD.

Hockett, J. A. (2010). *The influence of lesson study on how teachers plan for, implement, and understand differentiated instruction* (Unpublished doctoral dissertation). University of Virginia, Charlottesville, VA.

Jarvis, J. (2010). *Learning Menus.* Unpublished curriculum materials. The Flinders University of South Australia, Adelaide, Australia.

Jensen, E. (2005). *Teaching with the brain in mind* (2nd ed.). Alexandria, VA: ASCD.

Johnson, D. W., & Johnson, R. T. (n.d.). *Structured Academic Controversy (SAC).* Retrieved from http://teachinghistory.org/teaching-materials/teaching-guides/21731

Kagan, S. (2008). *Kagan cooperative learning.* San Clemente, CA: Kagan Publishing.

Kennedy, M. M. (2005). *Inside teaching: How classroom life undermines reform.* Cambridge, MA: Harvard University Press.

Lemov, D. (2012). *Teach like a champion field guide: A practical resource to make the 49 techniques your own.* San Francisco: Jossey-Bass.

Marshall, S. P., McGee, G. W., McLaren, E., & Veal, C. (2011). Discovering and developing diverse STEM talent: Enabling academically talented youth to flourish. *Gifted Child Today, 34*(1), 16–24.

Marzano, R. J. (2000). *Transforming classroom grading.* Alexandria, VA: ASCD.

Marzano, R. J., Pickering, D. J., & Pollock, J. E. (2001). *Classroom instruction that works: Research-based strategies for increasing student achievement.* Alexandria, VA: ASCD.

McTighe, J., & Wiggins, G. (2004). *Understanding by Design professional development workbook.* Alexandria, VA: ASCD.

McTighe, J., & Wiggins, G. (2013). *Essential questions: Opening doors to understanding.* Alexandria, VA: ASCD.

Moon, T. R., Callahan, C. M., Tomlinson, C. A., & Miller, E. M. (2002). *Middle school classrooms: Teachers' reported practices and student perceptions* (RM02164). Storrs, CT: The National Research Center on the Gifted and Talented.

Moore, M. (2008, November 26). Stress of modern life cuts attention spans to five minutes. *The Telegraph.* Retrieved from http://www.telegraph.co.uk/health/healthnews/3522781/Stress-of-modern-life-cuts-attention-spans-to-five-minutes.html

National Association of Secondary School Principals. (2004). *Breaking Ranks II: Strategies for leading high school reform.* Providence, RI: The Educational Alliance.

National Council for the Social Studies. (2013). *The College, Career, and Civic Life (C3) Framework for Social Studies State Standards: Guidance for enhancing the rigor of K–12 civics, economics, geography, and history.* Silver Spring, MD: Author. Available: www.socialstudies.org/c3

National Governors Association Center for Best Practices (NGA Center) & Council of Chief State School Officers (CCSSO). (2010a). *Common Core State Standards for English language arts & literacy in history/social studies, science, and technical subjects.* Washington, DC: Author.

NGA Center & CCSSO. (2010b). *Common Core State Standards for mathematics.* Washington, DC: Author.

National Research Council. (2012). *A framework for K–12 science education: Practices, crosscutting concepts, and core ideas.* Committee on a Conceptual Framework for New K–12 Science Education Standards. Washington, DC: National Academies Press. Available: www.nextgenscience.org

O'Connor, A. (2005, May 3). The claim: Eating carrots improves your eyesight. *The New York Times.* Retrieved from http://www.nytimes.com/2005/05/03/health/03real.html?_r=0#

O'Connor, K. (2009). *How to grade for learning* (3rd ed.). Thousand Oaks, CA: Corwin.

O'Connor, K. (2010). *A repair kit for grading: 15 fixes for broken grades* (2nd ed.). Boston: Pearson.

Pellegrino, J. W., & Hilton, M. L. (Eds.). (2012). *Education for life and work: Developing transferable knowledge and skills in the 21st century.* Washington, DC: National Academies Press.

Perry, B. D. (2000). How the brain learns best. *Instructor, 110*(4), 34–35.

Perry, T., Steele, C., & Hilliard, A. (2003). *Young, gifted and black: Promoting high achievement among African-American students.* Boston: Beacon Press.

Pitler, H., & Stone, B. (2012). *A handbook for classroom instruction that works.* Alexandria, VA: ASCD.

Poincaré, H. (1905). *Science and hypothesis.* London: Walter Scott Publishing.

Popham, J. W. (2006). *Defining and enhancing formative assessment.* Paper presented at the CCSSO State Collaborative on Assessment and State Standards/Formative Assessment for Students and Teachers meeting, Los Angeles.

Ritchhart, R., Church, M., & Morrison, K. (2011). *Making thinking visible: How to promote engagement, understanding, and independence for all learners.* San Francisco: Jossey-Bass.

Santa, C. (1988). *Content reading including study systems: Reading, writing and studying across the curriculum.* Dubuque, IA: Kendall/Hunt Publishing.

Sarason, S. B. (1996). *Revisiting "the culture of the school and the problem of change."* New York: Teachers College Press.

Schraw, G., Flowerday, T., & Lehman, S. (2001). Increasing situational interest in the classroom. *Educational Psychology Review, 13*(3), 211–224.

Shaw, G. B. (1903). *Man and superman.* Cambridge, MA: The University Press.

Silver, H. F., & Perini, M. J. (2010). *The interactive lecture: How to engage students, build memory, and deepen comprehension.* Alexandria, VA: ASCD.

Sizer, T. (1992). *Horace's compromise: The dilemma of the American high school.* Boston: Mariner Books.

Sousa, D. A., & Tomlinson, C. A. (2011). *Differentiation and the brain: How neuroscience supports the learner-friendly classroom.* Bloomington, IN: Solution Tree Press.

Sternberg, R. J. (2006). Recognizing neglected strengths. *Educational Leadership, 64*(1), 30–35.

Sternberg, R. J., & Grigorenko, E. L. (2007). *Teaching for successful intelligence* (2nd ed.). Thousand Oaks, CA: Corwin.

Stiggins, R. (2000). *Student-involved classroom assessment* (3rd ed.). Upper Saddle River, NJ: Prentice Hall.

Stiggins, R. (2005). From formative assessment to assessment FOR learning: A path to success in standards-based schools. *Phi Delta Kappan, 87*(4), 324–328.

Stiggins, R., & Chappuis, J. (2005). Using student-involved classroom assessment to close achievement gaps. *Theory into Practice, 44,* 11–18.

Stiggins, R., & Chappuis, J. (2011). *An introduction to student-involved assessment FOR learning* (6th ed.). Upper Saddle River, NJ: Pearson/Prentice Hall.

Strickland, C. A. (2009). *Professional development for differentiating instruction: An ASCD Action Tool.* Alexandria, VA: ASCD.

Talbert, R. (2012, February 13). Four things lecture is good for [Blog post]. *The Chronicle* Blog Network. Retrieved from http://chronicle.com/blognetwork/castingoutnines/2012/02/13/four-things-lecture-is-good-for/

Tomlinson, C. A. (2003). *Fulfilling the promise of the differentiated classroom: Strategies and tools for responsive teaching.* Alexandria, VA: ASCD.

Tomlinson, C. A. (2005). Presentation at Institutes on Academic Diversity: Summer Institute on Academic Diversity. The University of Virginia, Charlottesville, VA.

Tomlinson, C. A. (2008). The goals of differentiation. *Educational Leadership, 66*(3), 26–30.

Tomlinson, C. A. (2009, February). Learning profile and student achievement. *School Administrator,* 28–34.

Tomlinson, C. A. (2014a). *The differentiated classroom: Responding to the needs of all learners* (2nd ed.). Alexandria, VA: ASCD.

Tomlinson, C. A. (2014b). Differentiated instruction. In J. A. Plucker & C. M. Callahan (Eds.), *Critical issues and practices in gifted education: What the research says* (2nd ed.) (pp. 197–210). Waco, TX: Prufrock Press.

Tomlinson, C. A., Brimijoin, K., & Narvaez, L. (2008). *The differentiated school: Making revolutionary changes in teaching and learning.* Alexandria, VA: ASCD.

Tomlinson, C. A., & Doubet, K. (2005). Reach them to teach them. *Educational Leadership, 62*(7), 8–15.

Tomlinson, C. A., & Doubet, K. J. (2006). *Smart in the middle grades: Classrooms that work for bright middle schoolers.* Westerville, OH: Association of Middle Level Educators.

Tomlinson, C. A., & Eidson, C. C. (2003). *Differentiation in practice: A resource guide for differentiating curriculum (grades 5–9).* N. Smith (Unit Developer). Alexandria, VA: ASCD.

Tomlinson, C. A., & Imbeau, M. B. (2010). *Leading and managing a differentiated classroom.* Alexandria, VA: ASCD.

Tomlinson, C. A., & McTighe, J. (2006). *Integrating differentiated instruction and Understanding by Design: Connecting content and kids.* Alexandria, VA: ASCD.

Tomlinson, C. A., & Moon, T. R. (2013). *Assessment and student success in a differentiated classroom.* Alexandria, VA: ASCD.

Tyack, D., & Cuban, L. (1995). *Tinkering toward Utopia: A century of public school reform*. Cambridge, MA: Harvard University Press.

Webb, N. L., Alt, M., Ely, R., & Vesperman, B. (2005, July 24). *Web Alignment Tool*. Madison: University of Wisconsin, Wisconsin Center for Educational Research. Retrieved from http://wat.wceruw.org/index.aspx

Wiggins, G. (2012). Seven keys to effective feedback. *Educational Leadership, 70*(1), 10–16.

Wiggins, G. (2014a, May 24). The typical HS—student survey, part 2 [Blog post]. *Granted, and . . . Thoughts on Education by Grant Wiggins*. Retrieved from http://grantwiggins.wordpress.com/2014/05/24/the-typical-hs-student-survey-part-2

Wiggins, G. (2014b, February 3). The lecture [Blog post]. *Granted, and . . . Thoughts on Education by Grant Wiggins*. Retrieved from http://grantwiggins.wordpress.com/2014/02/03/the-lecture

Wiggins, G., & McTighe, J. (2005). *Understanding by Design* (Expanded 2nd ed.). Alexandria, VA: ASCD.

Wiggins, G., & McTighe, J. (2011). *The Understanding by Design guide to creating high-quality units*. Alexandria, VA: ASCD.

Wiliam, D. (2011). *Embedded formative assessment*. Bloomington, IN: Solution Tree.

Wiliam, D. (2012). Feedback: Part of a system. *Educational Leadership, 70*(1), 30–34.

Willingham, D. T. (2009, Spring). Why don't students like school? Because the mind is not designed for thinking. *American Educator*, 4–13.

Willis, J. (2006). *Research-based strategies to ignite student learning: Insights from a neurologist and classroom teacher*. Alexandria, VA: ASCD.

Willis, J. (2007, Summer). The neuroscience of joyful education. *Educational Leadership, 64*. Retrieved from http://www.ascd.org/publications/educational-leadership/summer07/vol64/num09/The-Neuroscience-of-Joyful-Education.aspx

Wolfe, P. (2001). *Brain matters: Translating research into classroom practice*. Alexandria, VA: ASCD.

Index

Note: Page locators followed by an italicized *f* indicate information contained in figures.

About the Authors

Dr. Kristina J. Doubet is an associate professor in the Department of Middle, Secondary, and Mathematics Education at James Madison University, where she has received the College of Education's Distinguished Teacher Award and its Madison Scholar Award. As a consultant and ASCD Faculty Member, Kristi has partnered with over 80 schools, districts, and organizations around initiatives related to differentiated instruction, Understanding by Design, and classroom assessment. In addition to numerous journal articles and book chapters, she coauthored the AMLE book *Smart in the Middle Grades: Classrooms That Work for Bright Middle Schoolers* (with Carol Ann Tomlinson) and is coauthoring the forthcoming Corwin book *The Differentiated Flipped Classroom* (with Eric Carbaugh). Kristi taught secondary English and language arts for 10 years and has also served as an instructional coach in elementary and middle school classrooms. She can be reached at kjdoubet@me.com.

Dr. Jessica A. Hockett is an education consultant and ASCD Faculty Member specializing in differentiated instruction, curriculum and performance task design, and gifted education. For the last 10 years, she has worked with teachers and leaders in nearly 70 school districts to improve teacher and student learning. Jessica has published a variety of articles, book chapters, and staff development materials and has coauthored (with Chester E. Finn Jr.) *Exam Schools: Inside America's Most Selective Public High Schools* (Princeton University Press). Prior to completing her doctoral studies at the University of Virginia, she was a secondary teacher in both general and gifted program settings. She can be reached at jessicahockett@me.com.

Related ASCD Resources: Differentiated Instruction

At the time of publication, the following ASCD resources were available (ASCD stock numbers appear in parentheses). For up-to-date information about ASCD resources, go to www.ascd.org. You can search the complete archives of *Educational Leadership* at http://www.ascd.org/el.

Professional Interest Communities

Visit the ASCD website and scroll to the bottom to click on "professional interest communities." Within these communities, find information about professional educators who have formed groups around topics like "Personalized Learning."

ASCD EDge Groups

Exchange ideas and connect with other educators interested in various topics, including Differentiated Instruction, on the social networking site ASCD EDge™.

PD Online

Differentiated Instruction: Creating an Environment That Supports Learning (#PD11OC118M)
Differentiated Instruction: Teaching with Student Differences in Mind (#PD11OC138M)
These and other online courses are available at www.ascd.org/pdonline.

Print Products

Assessment and Student Success in a Differentiated Classroom by Carol Ann Tomlinson and Tonya R. Moon (#108028)

A Differentiated Approach to the Common Core: How do I help a broad range of learners succeed with challenging curriculum? (ASCD Arias) by Carol Ann Tomlinson and Marcia B. Imbeau (#SF114076)

The Differentiated Classroom: Responding to the Needs of All Learners (2nd ed.) by Carol Ann Tomlinson (#108029)

The Differentiated School: Making Revolutionary Changes in Teaching and Learning by Carol Ann Tomlinson, Kay Brimijoin, and Lane Narvaez (#105005)

Leading and Managing a Differentiated Classroom by Carol Ann Tomlinson and Marcia B. Imbeau (#108011)

DVDs

The Differentiated Classroom: Responding to the Needs of All Learners DVD Series (#615049)
Differentiated Instruction in Action DVD Series (#608050)
The Differentiated School: Making Revolutionary Changes in Teaching and Learning (#610008)

The Whole Child Initiative

The Whole Child Initiative helps schools and communities create learning environments that allow students to be healthy, safe, engaged, supported, and challenged. To learn more about other books and resources that relate to the whole child, visit www.wholechildeducation.org.

For more information: send e-mail to member@ascd.org; call 1-800-933-2723 or 703-578-9600, press 2; send a fax to 703-575-5400; or write to Information Services, ASCD, 1703 N. Beauregard St., Alexandria, VA 22311-1714 USA.